OUR WAY

THE LIFE STORY OF SPIKE YOH

The Day & Zimmermann Group, Inc.
1500 Spring Garden Street,
Philadelphia, PA 19130

Book design by:
Arbor Services, Inc.
www.arborservices.co/

Printed in Canada

Our Way - The Life Story of Spike Yoh
Bill Yoh

1. Title 2. Author 3. Biography

Library of Congress Control Number: 2017915840

ISBN 13: 978-0-692-96698-3

OUR WAY

THE LIFE STORY OF SPIKE YOH

BILL YOH

Each age, it is found, must write its own books;
or rather, each generation for the next succeeding.
—Ralph Waldo Emerson

To future generations of the Yoh family.

Contents

The "Captain" and the "Kid" (Spike and Bill) in our younger years

Introduction

We both were growing older then, and wiser with the years
That's when I came to understand the course his heart still steers
—Jimmy Buffett, "The Captain and the Kid"

He was surprised at how relaxed he felt. Yes, he was a little warm given that his suitcoat was buttoned, but he didn't sense any sweat on his brow or clamminess in his hands. After all, this was not the first time he was going to meet Ronald Reagan, the most powerful man in the world. He remembered how much charisma and warmth Reagan had exuded and how literally presidential his presence had been the first time they met when Spike was the United States Savings Bonds Chairman of Pennsylvania. This time, which was during Reagan's second term, Spike Yoh and the other regional fund-raising chairs of the United States Olympic Committee were having a "meet and greet" with the nation's fortieth president. After hellos and handshakes were exchanged, Spike remembers how the president easily moved from talking politics to sports to family. Spike recalls Reagan even asking how his wife Mary and their children were doing.

Reagan wasn't the only president Spike met; he has shaken the hands of eight of them over his lifetime. A few years earlier he had bumped into the thirty-ninth president, Jimmy Carter. Incredibly, the immediate past president was flying on a commercial airplane, he and Spike both heading to Australia. Spike had become accustomed to rubbing shoulders with famous and powerful people. The company he owned and led was on a growth path that would generate more than $1 billion per year in revenue and employ over sixteen thousand people by the time he retired. In addition to presidents, Spike has conducted business and broken bread with governors, world leaders, four-star generals, CEOs of Fortune 100 companies, and presidents of some of the nation's most august universities. As just the second member of his father's family to attend college, Spike Yoh's success and growth have been remarkable.

As is his story . . .

•   •   •   •

The Yoh family is large. We are large in number, in presence, in personality, and in impact. Even many of the people in the family are large. Our patriarch, Spike Yoh, is the embodiment of "larger than life." We are proud Philadelphians, though some of us live elsewhere now. We work hard, and we play hard. We are supportive, and we can be dysfunctional. Family really matters to us, and our bonds of love run deep. Yet we are also diverse in our talents, in our areas of interest, in our beliefs, and in our political views. Finally, we hail from Holland, and the origin of our last name is Dutch. Or at least that's what I had been told—and had believed—for most of my life.

The first Yohs to depart Europe for America set sail from Amsterdam. My grandfather, Harold Yoh Sr., a key player in this story, was inducted into the Netherlands Society of America. Most importantly, in the sixth grade, I did my country report in social studies on the Netherlands. So we were Dutch. Yoh was Dutch. Makes sense, right?

It did. Until my freshman year at Duke when the advisor to whom I was assigned was Professor Yohe. His first name was William, just like mine. During our first (and only) meeting, he informed me that my last name came from his name and that we were both of French Huguenot descent. French Huguenots? Impossible! I had my granddad's Netherlands Society membership and my sixth-grade country report to prove my Dutchness. I was so adamant that I made my way to the registrar's office, filled out the necessary paperwork, and succeeded in dropping William Yohe entirely. In hindsight, I suppose this was a tad impetuous.

Over twenty years later—about six years ago—shades of doubt crept in about this whole Dutch thing. I was attending a work conference in Rotterdam, which happens to be in the Netherlands. The event took place on an old, spartanly appointed cruise ship that had been converted to a permanently docked hotel. The vessel's vintage and décor gave the feeling of a 1960s James Bond movie, only without the model actresses in evening gowns and steel-toothed villains in leisure suits. One of the evening events, for which we boarded another ship (one that actually moved), was a harbor cruise of the major port town. At one point during cocktails, a typical-looking Dutch woman—tall, large-boned, blond hair—held up my business card. *"Yoh,"* she said. *"Dis name ees not Dutch!"*

Okay. *She* was Dutch. Maybe we weren't? On the deck of this ship, with this emphatic declaration against my family heritage, I remembered dismissing my college advisor's contention two decades earlier. Now I wasn't so sure I was in the right.

A few years prior to Rotterdam, a distant cousin had sent around a thorough binder of family genealogy. A couple members of our family, including my dad's sister, Barbara, had put a lot of energy into tracing family roots, visiting libraries, scouring the Internet, speaking with countless relatives, and visiting old homesteads across multiple states. Having pored over much of this research, along with having considered my brief-lasting college advisor and the Dutch business card reader, I have concluded that "Yoh" is French (from Yohe—thank you very much, belatedly, Prof. Wm. Yohe), with its origins in protestant Huguenot reformers in the sixteenth and seventeenth centuries, many of whom left the country due to hostile treatment from Catholic rule. Our ancestors fled to Germany in the 1600s, where the name was changed to "Johe" or "Joh," for there was no "y" in the German language. There is also a possible Hungarian origin, Joö, dating back to the 1200s. This name eventually also made its way to Germany and later became the New World "Yoh." But it's my book, so I'm going with the French, not the Hungarian, descent theory. Recently two of my siblings took advantage of advances in genetics and completed DNA tests. Their results further corroborated that our roots are predominantly Western European.

The "Yoh is Dutch" concept likely took flight given that the last European soil our family touched was Dutch. Adding additional jet fuel to this flight, many of the Yohs in Pennsylvania (not related to us) are considered "Pennsylvania Dutch." While this would seem to indicate roots in Holland, "Dutch" in this case derives from "Deutsch," a reference to the German language and to the many settlers in Pennsylvania who emigrated from Germany for religious freedom. One bit of irony in all of this is that my mother's side of the family actually *does* have some Dutch heritage—heritage they have claimed far less strenuously than my paternal side—along with many other nationalities. Yohs? We are classic New World mutts.

• • • •

And while the origins of our name might have been a mystery, the origins of this book are not.

A kiss. It all started with a simple kiss—a quick peck on the lips from my wife, Kelly. One summer evening in 2015, about a month after my mom had passed away, I was sitting in our family room when Kelly came home from the grocery store. Earlier that day I had had a sudden inspiration: that maybe I should research and write a book about my father's life. The genesis of my idea occurred several months earlier, in February, during a drive from Baptist Hospital in Miami to the Ocean Reef Club, my parents' winter home. My father, Spike, and I were returning from visiting my mother, Mary, who had been hospitalized after falling ill a few days earlier. To provide some respite from the stress of her being sick, I asked Spike a question about his past—something to distract, something about his early career, I think. Our family did not often talk about our parents' pasts. Almost never was the subject initiated by anyone other than them. On this day, to my surprise, Spike poured forth an interesting, detailed response. The specifics are not important. But the exchange illuminated an entirely new room in my brain. My dad had a fascinating story that few people knew much about.

Over the next few days' trips back and forth to Baptist, I asked him other questions and heard equally robust answers. Spike's recall was not as strong on a few topics, and I found those to be even more compelling. Why did he have so much mental visibility around certain aspects of his past and such fog around others? I decided that at some point we should hire a writer to capture Spike's story. The following week I mentioned this to a few family members and began talking to people to learn more about the world of biographers.

Unfortunately, the following months brought further declines in Mom's health, and she passed away in late June. While navigating the rough seas that grief's uncharted waters bring, I started to question: Where was I in my life? Was I happy? What was the status of my career? Was I making enough of a difference? This last question was perhaps the most important. As you'll learn, the Yoh family owns and operates Day & Zimmermann, a long-standing, rather large family business. I had spent twenty years of my twenty-two-year career, plus several summers during high school and college, working at D&Z. At the time of Mom's passing, I had a senior executive role and was a member of the company's ten-person leadership team. Yet at forty-four years old, I was facing a mini midlife crisis.

Then one day on my commute home from work, it hit me. Why don't I write Spike's biography? I possessed some of the requisite skills, like the ability to plan a project, to conduct research, and to make people feel comfortable during a conversation, not to mention decent skill at distilling lots of information into something concise and—hopefully—interesting. I thought I was a pretty good writer. I had written a lot *in* my career. Maybe now I could write *as* my career? Maybe Dad's life story—this book—could be my red sports car.

Which is when "the kiss" occurred. Shortly after I got home from work, I decided I would voice my crazy idea to Kelly. When she later returned from the store, I was sitting on the couch, ready to lay this daunting, life-changing idea on her. I was prepared for a long discussion, full of insightful questions, devil's advocate positioning, and a lot of "Did you think of this?" and "Have you really thought through that?"

As soon as I caught her eye, I said, "You know, I've been thinking. Maybe I should write Dad's biography. Maybe I should transition out of my job and do it myself."

Still holding a shopping bag in each hand, she walked across the room to where I was sitting. She bent down, kissed me on the lips, looked me right in the eyes, and said, "When can you start?"

Really? That's it? It's that simple? That obvious? To her it was. And soon it was to me as well. Over the next few weeks, I spoke to my brothers and then my father. Every time I said out loud what I wanted to do, the idea of actually *doing* it became more real. I will always remember sitting on Dad's deck in Avalon having our first discussion about the biography. It was a warm, breezy summer afternoon, and we sat in tall chairs at a high-top table looking at the wavy green dunes and grey-blue Atlantic Ocean sprawling before us, its breakers' dull, constant roar a ubiquitous drumbeat on the island. As soon as I mentioned what I wanted to do, he immediately switched into brainstorming mode, and I found myself starting the project right then and there. After a few minutes, I had to stop him to ask if his answer to my proposition was, in fact, "yes." It felt like one of those movie scenes where the boyfriend asks the girlfriend to marry him and she gets so excited that she starts crying and hugging him but never actually answers the question. While Spike wasn't crying and hugging me, he nodded, and—looking at me a little like I was crazy—said, "Yes, big guy. That's a yes."

My brothers and I then began a three-month, behind-the-scenes effort to set up a transition for most of my work duties. That fall, the day after Thanksgiving weekend, we announced to our company that I would be writing Spike's story. Spike had been the chairman and CEO of Day & Zimmermann for twenty-two years, so there was a natural connection with the business. Before I knew it, most of my professional duties had been transferred to a few of my capable colleagues. To be honest, I was humbled to see how quickly life at the company continued on. I guess in many ways we are all replaceable. But I digress.

What ensued was an experience unlike any I had had or am likely to have again. During the first three-and-a-half months of 2016, I spent the majority of six different weeks with Spike. We conducted twenty recorded, sit-down interviews. The content spanned his entire life, from ancestry and childhood, through college and early adult years, through his child-raising and leadership years, and on into empty nest, retirement, and the current day. We held the majority of our conversations seated next to each other in two oversized chairs in his bedroom, a small round table between us holding his Diet Coke, my Tervis tumbler of water, and the $67 digital recorder I purchased from Amazon that came to feel like another appendage over the course of that year. His faithful sidekick Duchess—the omnipresent miniature Australian Labradoodle who is treated like the royalty her name implies—always slept on the rug next to him. Directly in our shared field of vision was the only-slept-in-on-one-side sheet configuration of his bed, which served as a daily reminder of my mother's absence. Perhaps even worse were the smatterings of medical supplies still visible in Mom's bathroom to our left, lingering like stubborn drifts of dirty snow in early spring, only uglier.

Spike's health was not good during many of my visits, so he kept the house warm . . . like eighty degrees warm . . . which made for an odd Florida dynamic where I would step *outside* to cool off. I had prepared interview scripts in advance to cover many varied topics. Sometimes Spike read them ahead of time and made notes; when he didn't, it was often because his physical state prevented him. While we weren't conducting interviews, we read newspapers at the kitchen counter over orange juice and scrambled eggs, watched *Fox News*, planned our lunches and dinners, and—when lucky—watched Duke basketball crush their competition on TV. We also got to watch Villanova, Kelly's alma mater twice over, beat Duke's dreaded rival, UNC, to win the national championship. If I couldn't be home to celebrate the win with my own family—we live just over a mile from Villanova's campus—there was no place I would have rather have been than with the man responsible for my rabid love of sports.

Countless hours of meaningful discussion with my father were invaluable. I fully realize how lucky I am to have had that rare opportunity. Knowing, however, where all of those interviews could lead—to the book you now hold in your hands—made me feel even luckier.

To round out Spike's take on, well, Spike, he and I developed a list of people from his life with whom I should speak. Typing all those names onto my laptop screen was like creating a black-and-white slide show of his (then) seventy-nine years on earth. By the time I was done, I was lucky enough to talk to seventy-five different people about my dad, ranging from family members to business colleagues to fellow volunteer leaders to friends from every section of his relationship Rolodex. Most of the interviews were in person, although some occurred over the phone. By the way, states have all sorts of laws about recording phone calls. If you ever want to do so, make sure you get the other person's permission (which I did every time).

Many of the face-to-face interviews took place in office buildings, others in people's homes or hotel lobbies. Not one of them occurred in a Starbucks; I'm not a big fan of their coffee. I got to visit a goat farm where I did some modeling (and not because I'm "model" material), the Peninsula Beverly Hills Hotel where I sipped chamomile out of fine china at "tea time," and Princeton University where I spoke with an icon of American higher education. I had the chance to pore through extensive family archives, finding great meaning in decades-old newspaper articles and legal documents that I would have previously considered trivial. I conducted formal interviews with family I saw almost every day, as well as with people I had never met. The amount of information . . . and opinions . . . and stories . . . and more stories . . . were both humbling and awe inspiring.

For each of the twenty interviews with Spike and the seventy-five with everyone else, I had the daunting but enlightening task of sorting through more than 1,500 pages of transcripts. Yet again I was lucky, in this case to have so much useful material about someone so important to me. But as I have told those people who have pointed out how "lucky" I am for all of these opportunities, it did take my mom's death to spur me to tackle this project. The cliché of being careful what you wish for seems to apply.

The pages before you are the culmination of Spike's memory as told to me, along with the recollections of the major players from each scene of his multi-act life, plus a slew of third-party research, and—covering the last four decades or so—my personal accounts. Throughout the book, I've tried to provide analysis and synthesis to make sense of seemingly disparate events and flesh out the central themes of Spike Yoh's life. One analogy I developed while culling through all of the research is that the project was like having all the pieces of a giant jigsaw puzzle spread on a table, but with no box-top picture to tell me what the finished product was supposed to look like. Once I started the task of writing the manuscript in the summer of 2016, I developed another analogy: that each data point or story was like a bulb in a string of holiday lights, but the way I chose to order them determined how the surrounding space was illuminated. The cord between each bulb served as the transitions between periods of Dad's life, their respective lengths affecting the ultimate vision as well.

Before Spike and I began our interviews, we discussed ground rules. An important one involved how we interpreted the facts of his life. We agreed that he would read along as I produced drafts, and if the events in my story differed from how they actually happened, we would correct them. However—and this was Dad's idea—if his and my interpretations of those events differed, he would acquiesce to my version. To his credit, and as a sign of his total comfort in his own skin, not once did he balk on this commitment. Another equally important ground rule was that this book was not intended to be what I call a "puff piece," but rather something real and relatable. Spike agreed, saying, "I don't want this to be an, 'Oh, isn't he wonderful' type of thing. I want it to be something people can learn from." While the majority of the book is positive—consistent with the way Spike has lived his life—I have not shied away from discussing warts and underbellies. When developing the list of interviewees, Spike made a point to include people who "would be comfortable talking about my shortcomings." From personal to professional to philanthropic, Spike was good—really good, often great—but certainly not perfect. Again to his credit, the only times he pushed back when reviewing some of my less-than-rosy assessments were when I had the *facts* wrong, not when my depiction painted him poorly.

Other than falling in love with Kelly and having our three children, researching and writing this biography has been the most enjoyable and fulfilling period of my life. It was a lot of fun for both Spike and me. It also presented us with unprecedented challenges and provided much-needed catharsis and healing from hardship and tragedy.

More than anything, I hope this book serves as a learning tool for future generations of our family (and perhaps other families as well). I hope our children, grandchildren, and other future relatives use the ensuing pages as a growth opportunity, hopefully an enjoyable one. There is no greater way to inform the future than to study the past. My aspiration is that Spike's past—his story—will help those who read it live more fulfilling and more meaningful lives. Thank you in advance for taking this journey with me.

Chapter 1

American Heritage

If you don't know history, you don't know anything.
You are a leaf that doesn't know it is part of a tree.
—*Michael Crichton*

On his father's side, Spike is a fifth-generation American. The Yohs came to America in the early 1800s, first settling in Berks County, Pennsylvania, northwest of Philadelphia, which up until the year 1800 served as the capital of the new Republic. Other research suggests that the Yohs arrived in the colonies as early as the mid-1700s, some of them fighting for the Continental Army against Britain. Jacob Yoh, born September 1, 1816, is Spike's first known paternal ancestor born in America. Jacob eventually moved to Van Wert, Ohio, an area that remains largely rural even today. So it is no surprise that almost every one of Spike's ancestors was a farmer. One male ancestor did own a grocery store, and another was a barber, but the rest grew crops and raised livestock. Consistent with the times, almost all of the women worked in the home. Some of Spike's relatives had common names by today's standards, such as John, Benjamin, Matthew, James, Virginia, and Sarah, while others went by names such as Elmer, Amos, Wilber, Zelma, Enoch, and Thursa.

Jacob and his wife Sarah had ten children. Two of them, Spike's great-great-uncles, fought for the North in the Civil War. Amos assisted General Sherman in the "scorched earth" destruction of Atlanta before being killed in action at Pickett Mills, Georgia. He was likely one of the few Union casualties during the "March to the Sea," when in five short weeks in late 1864, Sherman's army sped from Atlanta to Savannah, a campaign that contributed greatly to the demise of the Confederate Army's hopes.

Another of their children, Jonas, married Matilda Ann Case. They would become Spike's great-grandparents. Jonas and Matilda had eight children, including Arch Clifford Yoh, born in 1885. Due to the demands of farming, Arch never completed the fourth grade. He married Ruby Hattery in 1905; she was one year older. The Hatterys were of Irish, English, and German descent. As adults, Arch and Ruby managed both of their families' farms. Ruby also proudly found time to teach Sunday school. For fun, the couple attended weekly square dances, where Arch would play the fiddle and Ruby would call the dances.

Arch and Ruby had just one child, Harold Lionel Yoh, born August 22, 1907. He was delivered on their kitchen table by the county doctor, weighing a whopping twelve-and-a-half pounds. Harold would become Spike's father. Full of predawn and after-school chores, Harold's childhood was truly a farmer's upbringing. His formal schooling began in second grade. Eventually he transferred to the brick, one-room Hattery School where his uncle was the schoolmaster. He often rode his horse the two-and-a-half miles to school, carrying his .22 Winchester rifle and checking his animal traps along the way. Given that almost everyone in and around Van Wert farmed instead of attending school regularly, the Hattery School's students ranged in age from young children to adults in their forties. Harold was a strong student. A favorite trick of his was to recite from memory all of the United States presidents, something he would repeat often as an adult.

Yoh Family North American Tree

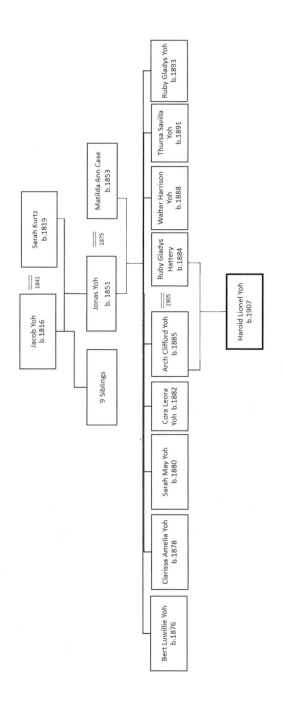

Jacob Yoh b.1816 == 1841 Sarah Kurtz b.1819

Jonas Yoh b.1851 == 1875 Matilda Ann Case b.1853

9 Siblings

Bert Luwillie Yoh b.1876

Clarissa Amelia Yoh b.1878

Sarah May Yoh b.1880

Cora Leora Yoh b.1882

Ruby Gladys Hattery b.1884 == 1905 Arch Clifford Yoh b.1885

Walter Harrison Yoh b.1888

Thursa Savilla Yoh b.1891

Ruby Gladys Yoh b.1893

Harold Lionel Yoh b.1907

From his early years, Harold blazed his own trail. He never felt compelled to honor family traditions or past practices. As a young boy, he displayed an inclination to move away from farming toward more entrepreneurial ventures, experiencing both the successes and failures that business brings. One winter he sold over $600 worth of animal pelts, helping bolster the family's finances through the cold months. Another venture involved breeding rabbits for money, although he sold only two of the two hundred that he bred, his surplus "inventory" decimating the family garden.

Ruby, Harold and Arch on the farm

When Harold was still a preteen, a tornado struck their farm, destroying the barn and hurling him and his father into the air. Together they built a larger barn, only to see it burn to the ground a few years later. These disasters exacerbated what was already a stressful life as a farming family, where so much of one's fortune is at the mercy of Mother Nature, perhaps adding to Harold's conviction that commerce was a more appealing, more rewarding existence.

While attending Van Wert High School in the 1920s, where today a Yoh is on the staff, Harold worked odd jobs to help support his family, one of whom was with the sprawling Pennsylvania Railroad. He continued to develop his strong work ethic, a trait he would pass along to his son Spike. He also exhibited early leadership aptitude, becoming vice president of his senior class and managing various clubs. He played football as well.

What is most relevant to me about Harold's upbringing, however, was that he was an only child. His grandfather was one of ten and his father one of eight. Yet Harold was alone. It is unclear why this was the case, other than the possibility that one twelve-and-a-half pound baby might have been all poor Ruby could handle. Regardless, the fact that Harold was an only child explains so much about who he was and therefore about who Spike would become.

Life has taught me that birth order matters. I'm the youngest of five—the baby—and I have the confidence and the self-esteem, as well as the defensiveness and the stubbornness to prove it. My oldest sibling, Hal, is over ten years older than I. While we were raised by the same parents, in many ways we grew up in different households. As a result, we have fairly different personalities, motivations, and communication styles.

But there was no birth order in Harold's family. Only children are a unique breed. According to psychologists, their social skills tend to develop more quickly since they are with adults the majority of the time. They tend to be highly self-confident and strong minded, and are often quite successful. Based on my own observations in life, however, because no siblings are involved, an only-child's parents are less required to impose consistent standards about house rules, right vs. wrong, and fair vs. unfair. Much of their disciplining depends on their parents' moods or energy levels at the time. Not having to compete for attention can also make "onlies" more self-centered than children with siblings might be (although any child can certainly become self-absorbed under the right conditions). Harold embodied much of what only children can be. The adult he became and the mixed role model he would be for his son had an extraordinary impact on the kind of husband, father, businessman, and leader that Spike Yoh later became.

As Harold progressed through high school, he continued his trailblazing ways, now setting his sights on college, something unprecedented in his family. A confluence of events and factors contributed to this goal. The hardships of farming and natural disaster, along with the constant inability to ever get ahead financially, sparked an entrepreneurial drive in Harold to do more, as exhibited by his various business ventures from a young age. He also had the chance in eighth grade to attend a weeklong program at Ohio State University after winning a local corn-growing competition (I told you he was a true farmer). This early introduction to college stuck with Harold. Finally, while attending college would be difficult financially for him, being an only child meant that tuition funds might be easier to acquire.

During his senior year in high school, Harold saw a magazine ad for the University of Pennsylvania. With his diverse high school experiences and prowess on the football field, he was accepted to the Wharton School of the University of Pennsylvania for the fall of 1925. As the first college that anyone in the family attended, this was not exactly a "safety school." One of the cornerstones of the famed Ivy League, Penn was founded in the 1750s by Philadelphia's number-one son, Benjamin Franklin. Every year it is ranked as one of the top universities in the country. Founded in 1881, Wharton was the first collegiate school of business. Today it is ranked one of the leading business schools in the world.

Despite gaining admission to Penn, only a week before Harold was to leave for college did his parents secure a $500 loan at 10% interest compounded every six months, allowing him to board the train for Philadelphia. Harold left northwestern Ohio for southeastern Pennsylvania, back to the very place where the Yohs had gotten their start in the New World. And so the tradition of farming in our family came to an end.

Harold arrived at the fabled university with little more than a small suitcase of clothes. Immediately he began working various jobs to help his parents fund his education. He joined the rifle team and played football, but certainly the most surprising and stressful incident for Harold during his college years was when he was arrested and jailed for armed robbery. One can only imagine how this news was received by Arch and Ruby back on the farm in Van Wert. Their industrious country boy couldn't possibly have done something illegal, let alone commit such a serious crime, could he have? Fortunately, he was eventually proven innocent, the police having mistaken him for the actual criminal and incarcerated him by accident. While Harold's fraternity, Alpha Tao Omega, provided some financial assistance, the legal fees to get him out of jail and clear his name impacted his family considerably.

In 1929, Harold achieved yet another unprecedented Yoh Family feat by earning his college degree from Wharton. In true entrepreneurial fashion, Harold's early career involved working at various companies in a host of positions. He began his career with the John B. Stetson Company. One of John Stetson's descendants, also named John, would be one of Spike's high school classmates and later have a career that spanned more than twenty years at Day & Zimmermann, the company that Harold and his family would ultimately own. After Stetson, Harold moved into the budding automotive industry, selling and marketing cars for a few different companies. In his mid-twenties, he gave a speech at a car show, where the audience included Henry Ford, Walter Chrysler, and Alfred Sloan.

Harold Yoh, with his Wharton degree in hand, was off and running in his young career. He settled into life in Philadelphia, never again to live on the farm. What he needed next was a bride, perhaps someone who would further cement his belonging in his newfound home.

• • • •

In North America during the seventeenth and eighteenth centuries, towns were often named after the families that founded them. Even so, through today's lens, the fact that both of Spike's maternal grandparents' families gave their names to towns is impressive. Before arriving in the New World, the Hulmes were already a family of some note in England. One of their manors included what is today the city of Manchester. Another ancestor was knighted by King Henry II.

George Hulme arrived in the New World in 1698. He hailed from Cheshire and was mostly English, with a bit of Welsh. On his passage over, George joined none other than William Penn, who, after many years of fighting for his Quaker beliefs, had won the rights in 1681 to the land that would later be named after his father—Pennsylvania. Like Penn, George was a Quaker, and he settled in Bucks County along the Delaware River immediately north of the budding port town of Philadelphia.

George's son, George Jr., became a vast landowner in Bucks County, his estate encompassing 334 acres. He was ultimately disowned from the Quaker Church, however, when he married Ruth Palmer, the sister of his first wife who had died only a year after their marriage. Friends doctrine prohibited a Quaker from marrying a deceased wife's sister. One of George Jr.'s grandsons, John Hulme, purchased land that became the borough of Hulmeville in 1796. Hulmeville still exists today in lower Bucks County, boasting a population of one thousand. John amassed a nice fortune and later started the first farmers' bank in the state of New Jersey.

John had a son also named George who moved to Mt. Holly, New Jersey, and became a farmer. One of his grandsons was Thomas Wilkins Hulme, Spike's maternal grandfather. Thomas earned a civil engineering degree from the University of Pennsylvania in 1889, where he also captained the football team, despite having limited high school experience and a five-foot-eight-inch, 155-pound frame. Thomas started a five-generation (and counting) family streak of Penn graduates, including of course Harold Yoh, Thomas's future son-in-law.

Spike's maternal grandmother's roots are equally impressive. John and Jane Oliphant, members of the Church of England, emigrated from Scotland to the New World in the 1680s. John and Jane's son Duncan purchased land in the colony of New Jersey that became the town of Oliphant Mills in the late 1600s. Oliphant Mills existed for 150 years, eventually becoming part of the town of Medford in 1847. Coincidentally, my in-laws live in Medford today, only two miles from where the original Oliphant mill stood. One of Duncan's grandsons, Jonathan Oliphant, was a captain in the Continental Army during the Revolutionary War. His wartime accomplishments were so great that the Trenton chapter of the Daughters of the American Revolution would later be named the Jonathan Oliphant Post, which remained in existence until 1972. Jonathan's great-great-granddaughter, Mary Augusta Oliphant, born September 10, 1873, was Spike's maternal grandmother.

Thomas Wilkins Hulme and Mary Augusta Oliphant married on October 30, 1900, at St. Andrew's Episcopal Church in Mt. Holly, New Jersey. Mary Augusta's father died when she was young, so she was given away by her uncle, Captain John J. Read (who would retire an admiral) of the United States Navy, with whom she, her sister, and her mother had lived after her father passed. Indicative of the relatively good economic position of both families, Mary Augusta's white satin wedding dress and train were embroidered with gold thread, and she wore a diamond ornament around her neck that Thomas had given her.

Hulme Family North American Tree

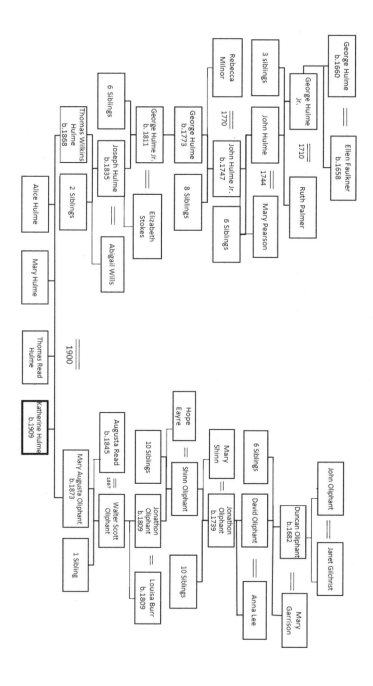

Thomas rose quickly through the ranks in the railroad industry. According to Spike, "My grandfather was a superstar with the railroad." Thomas and Mary Augusta moved four times as he earned promotions, and they had a child after each move. Yes, four children in four different towns. Alice was their firstborn. Spike would have little interaction with his aunt Alice later in life, except that her daughter Carol Herbert would become close with his mother. Mary was born after Alice. Mary and her husband, Courtlandt Schenck, became key and positive figures in Spike's early life. Thomas and Mary Augusta's third child and only son was also named Thomas, but he went by "Tom." He had the middle name Read, after his naval officer great uncle. Tom became an insurance broker and married Dorothy Vare, the two of them both becoming accomplished golfers at Merion Golf Club.

In 1904, Thomas was hired by the Pennsylvania Railroad. He and Mary Augusta moved the family to St. Davids, Pennsylvania, one of a series of small towns that run west from Philadelphia. The Main Line got its name from the "main line" train route laid in the mid-1800s to connect Philadelphia and Harrisburg, part of government plans to link Philadelphia to the Erie Canal and points west. Later in the century, the railroad encouraged suburban development along the route by building stations to serve the smaller communities, most of which are still in use today. The Pennsylvania Railroad and other developers touted this burgeoning area as a place where well-off Philadelphians could conveniently escape city living. This coincided with the massive wealth accumulation that the Industrial Revolution brought to many in the region. Today, the Main Line boasts some of the most affluent municipalities, as well as some of the top public and private schools, in the country. It has also remained home to much of our family since Thomas and Mary Augusta arrived in 1904.

Thomas and Mary Augusta's fourth and final child, Katharine, or Kae, was born on July 14, 1909, at Bryn Mawr Hospital, where her son, Spike, would be born twenty-seven years later . . . and two of my siblings and I decades after that . . . and my kids decades later . . . another family tradition begun. The Hulmes lived a comfortable life, employing multiple servants on their property. The girls attended the Baldwin School, while Tom attended The Haverford School. His graduation in 1925 began a four-generation (and counting) family streak of Haverford graduates.

Katharine Hulme (second from right) with her mother and siblings

When Thomas was named vice president of real estate for the Pennsylvania Railroad in 1924, his promotion garnered congratulatory letters from several prominent business and political leaders. His responsibilities were weighty, the railroad carrying three times as much traffic as any other American rail line, including Union Pacific. The land purchases and real estate development that Thomas oversaw helped grow the Pennsylvania Railroad into the largest publicly traded company in the world, with over 250,000 employees and a greater budget than the United States Government.

Thomas's illustrious career was highlighted by the construction of some of the largest, most beautiful train stations in the country, including 30th Street Station in Philadelphia, the now defunct Penn Station in Manhattan, and several others throughout the Mid-Atlantic and Midwestern United States. Thomas not only thrived in the business world, but he and Mary Augusta heartily enjoyed the Main Line's social scene as well. Thomas was elected president of the exclusive Merion Cricket Club in the late 1930s. His portrait still hangs in the club's main stairwell today.

The Hulmes were a well-known family, with community status matching the professional accomplishments of their patriarch. Unfortunately, when Thomas and Mary Augusta's children were adults, three of them—all but Mary—would become alcoholics. Eventually, each of the three would die from the addiction.

• • • •

Harold Yoh and Katharine Hulme were married on Thursday, June 14, 1934, in the garden of Katharine's parents' home in Haverford, Pennsylvania. The pair had met after college while Harold was honing his car-selling skills. By this courtship and marriage, Harold changed yet another aspect of his family's traditions. He did not marry a farm girl, but rather a "Main Liner" from a well-off, white-collar family. Little did he know when he had that brief job in high school working for the Pennsylvania Railroad that one day he would marry the daughter of one of its most senior executives.

After the wedding, Harold's career yielded mixed results. He was fired from one post for poor performance and lost another when the start of WWII crippled the company for which he worked. However, in 1942, he interviewed for a job as an expeditor for the Budd Company, an automotive metal parts supplier. During the interview, a Budd employee made a passing remark about the attractiveness of the tool design industry. Harold did not know what tool design was. Having grown up in farmland, he had never looked at a blueprint. He was an aspiring businessman, not a technician, with most of his experience to date in sales and marketing. Yet the elegance and importance of tool design stuck with Harold. Shortly after the Budd interview he learned of an available ownership stake in the Duncan Tool Design Company, which had been started in 1940. He came up with the required $3,000, and in February of 1942, the partnership was formed. It is possible that the money came from Katharine's inheritance from her parents, who died in 1939 and 1940. If so, the thought that the success of the Pennsylvania Railroad contributed to our family's first foray into business ownership is compelling.

Harold and "Kae" on their wedding day

Only a year after Harold bought into Duncan, the agreement dissolved, Harold's partner taking ownership of Duncan's Buffalo operations while

Harold commanded the Philadelphia business. Harold Yoh, the one-time farm boy, was now a proud, independent business owner in Philadelphia, with twenty-nine employees on his payroll. One year later, the name was changed to the H. L. Yoh Company.

Equipped with a college degree from Wharton, a marriage to a woman from a well-to-do Main Line family, and sole ownership of his own business, Harold's separation from life on the farm was complete. Unfortunately, while his new life would prove to be fruitful for him, it would be much less favorable to his wife and their children.

Chapter 2

Rough Start

I always picture life as a car. All your selves are in it.
And a new self can get in, but the old selves can't ever get out.
—Bruce Springsteen

At the time of Harold and Katharine's wedding in 1934, the world was in the throes of the Great Depression, which had been crippling the United States—and much of the world—for the previous five years. Amid the economic hardships of the times and Harold's early career starts and stops, he and Katharine started their family. Harold Lionel Yoh Jr. was born at Bryn Mawr Hospital on Saturday, December 12, 1936. The lead news story of the day was King Edward VIII's abdication of the throne of the United Kingdom, less than a year into his reign.

While named "Harold" after his father, the newborn wouldn't make it home from the hospital before acquiring the nickname that would stay with him for the rest of his life. The day after he was born, his mom's brother Tom came to the hospital to meet his nephew. When Katharine told her brother the baby's name, Uncle Tom insisted he be called something else, proposing the name "Spike" after Spike Jones, to whom Tom may have been listening in the car on the way to the hospital. A famous musician and bandleader at the time, Jones's specialty was performing satirical versions of popular

29

songs, using pots and pans as instruments and interjecting sound effects like gunshots and whistles. Perhaps it was Katherine's postpartum daze, coupled with adult Spike's belief that his uncle likely had a few drinks in him when he arrived, that led them to think that this was a good idea. And so began the life of Harold L. "Spike" Yoh Jr.

Two and a half years later, on July 26, 1939, Spike's sister Barbara Leslie was born, also at Bryn Mawr Hospital. Spike and Barbara would be the only two children Harold and Katharine would have. Their marriage lasted only a decade longer.

● ● ● ●

Throughout his entire life, Spike has had an incredible memory. Today, his ability to remember facts and figures about business transactions a half-century old, as well as specifics about sporting events and pranks in high school, rivals modern search engines. But when it comes to his early childhood, the years with his mom, dad, and sister, Spike's recall is less clear, many of the stories becoming spartan, guarded, and largely negative. "My father inspired a huge fear factor in me, and my mother seemed to be drunk most nights." People can build resilience in many ways, perhaps most effectively by facing and overcoming adversity as children. Young Spike's path to grit would wind in and out of his parents' relationships with him and with each other.

But it wasn't all gloom and doom for the toddler. His mother was close with her sister Mary and her husband Courtlandt Schenck, or "Court," as he was known. Spike recalls Uncle Court with much warmth and admiration, saying, "He was my hero." In fact, Uncle Court is the only adult male relative from childhood about whom Spike speaks positively. He liked Uncle Court so much that he gave me the middle name Courtlandt. Spike was also close with Mary and Court's children, his cousins Peter and Joan, who were three and five years older than he was. While the Schencks soon moved to Chicago, depriving Spike and Barbara of some enjoyable family camaraderie, the cousins would remain friendly throughout their lives. Peter attended Lawrenceville, a boarding school near Princeton. During the summers, he and Joan would stay with Spike's family. Spike would also visit the Schencks in Chicago a few times. What really drew Spike to the Schencks was his recognition, even subconsciously at a young age, of what he was missing: a close-knit family that expressed warmth and support for each other.

Spike and his mother, Katharine

For Katharine, the Schencks' move to Chicago was also unfortunate. She was not particularly close with her oldest sister Alice or her brother Tom, but she and Mary had a special bond. Mary provided a listening ear and strong support for her younger sister. Importantly, Mary also seemed to lack the drinking gene that affected her three siblings. When Mary left for Chicago, Katharine lost not just a close friend, but someone from whom she derived strength.

After the Schencks departed, Spike's family moved into their home, which had been owned by Katharine's parents. Given that the Yoh Company had yet to produce meaningful profit, Harold had little money of his own, he and Katharine subsisting largely with the help of the Hulme family. Harold was both practical and savvy, leveraging his in-laws' wealth while he built his business.

Harold focused on his business during the majority of Spike's childhood, as well as on his social calendar and his travels. While much of what Spike recalls about his father is negative, the life Harold led was not entirely unique. Unlike today, when fathers are much more present in the lives of their children, in the mid-twentieth century, this was often not the case. At that time, virtually all husbands worked outside of the home, and almost all wives were homemakers. While today Harold might be labeled an absentee father, men in those days commonly entrusted the majority of the parenting to their spouses. Despite Harold's lack of attention or positive role modeling for his eldest child, the early tenets of his business philosophy would become important parts of Spike's leadership ethos later on.

With the formation of the Yoh Company, Harold finally became the entrepreneur he had wanted to be since his childhood in Ohio. As a business-school-educated dealmaker, he brought adaptability and flexibility to his new company. From his experience in the car business, Harold also recognized the importance of marketing. Combining these influences, Harold quickly evolved his business from a tool design company to a more diversified and lucrative provider of temporary technical personnel, making it one of the first organizations to provide engineering-related resources on a part-time basis. The temporary staffing industry had existed for decades, but it mostly focused on clerical, blue collar, and low-level accounting functions. Not until World War II did a few firms like the Yoh Company start providing temporary engineers and related resources. Today, the technical staffing industry in the United States generates tens of billions of dollars per year.

Harold enjoyed much success building a technical services business during the war and the economic boom years that followed. One of the cornerstones of his growth strategy was geographic diversification. In early 1951, he opened an office in California. The Yoh Company was now doing business on both coasts, as well as several locations in between. Harold could service customers across the United States, while at the same time justifying his love of traveling, a passion he passed along to his son.

Harold's diversification strategy evolved to include not only different geographies, but varied industries as well. The Yoh Company entered many new areas such as power plants, aviation, and food services. In 1952, Harold became the majority shareholder of a start-up food products business in Illinois, which served as a precursor to even greater diversification moves later in his career. Growth and diversification would largely define Harold's professional trajectory. They would also become cornerstones for Spike as well.

• • • •

In his elementary school years, Spike liked to sit by the radio in the afternoons and listen to serials like *Captain Midnight* and *Jack Armstrong*. The former imbued in Spike his lifelong affection for larger-than-life heroes; the latter planted his love of seeing the world, as Jack went on weekly adventures to exotic locations around the globe. Spike recalls being upset one day in April of 1945 when his radio programs didn't air, as the stations chose to instead cover the death of Franklin Delano Roosevelt. Spike also recalls the gas ration stickers affixed to car windshields during World War II, which dictated which days of the week each car could be fueled. Finally, he remembers the end of the war when church bells rang out in the neighborhood and everyone poured from their homes into the streets to celebrate.

During summers, according to Spike's sister Barbara, who helped paint some of the rosier aspects of their childhood canvas, Harold and Katharine would take their young children to Van Wert to visit Harold's parents. The kids had great fun helping Arch and Ruby with their life on the farm. In the mornings, Spike would help Arch milk the cows while Barbara and Ruby collected eggs. Barbara particularly enjoyed the satisfaction of placing the milk and eggs on the front porch for pickup and sale.

While staying in Ohio, the kids would attend the county fair, where Spike first acquired his taste for small-scale gambling by betting on harness races. Van Wert was a far cry from Las Vegas, Atlantic City, or the cruise ships Spike would know as an adult, but the fair whet his appetite for sitting at blackjack tables or playing rounds of golf for a $2.00 "Nassau" wager. Spike never bet big, largely because he never wanted anyone other than himself to control his money. In fact, it wasn't until much later in life that he bought stock in a public company. If he didn't control it, he didn't invest in it.

In addition to their trips to Van Wert, Spike's childhood summers provided his first exposure to the barrier islands of New Jersey, known as the Jersey Shore—not to be confused with or muddied by the 2010s reality television show of the same name. The Yohs would travel to Atlantic City and stay at the Traymore Hotel on the boardwalk. This part of the country has always been a special place for Spike.

With Harold's early business proceeds, he and Katharine purchased a twelve-acre estate on King of Prussia Road in Radnor, Pennsylvania, along the same Main Line that her father's company helped establish a century earlier. Given Spike's overriding impressions of his father, his recollection of why they moved to such a large property is telling. "The old man always wanted to show off." The estate included a manor home, a smaller guest house, and a maintenance building. A man named Harry Waterson lived in the maintenance building and tended the grounds. He constructed a putting green, a greenhouse, and a playhouse for Spike and Barbara. As an aside, I learned much of this information when a man named Jack Ramsey looked me up and visited my office in early 2015—before I considered writing this book. Jack's wife was Harry's only child, and the young couple spent their early years of marriage living in the maintenance building on the Yohs' estate.

Young Spike enjoying his new playhouse at the King of Prussia Road residence

Given Katharine's Main Line upbringing and Harold's desire to fit into that community, they also used the Yoh Company's early profits to join many private clubs, including Merion Golf Club, Merion Cricket Club, several eating clubs in Philadelphia, as well as clubs in Washington, DC and California. The Yohs also employed a full-time housekeeper who cooked their meals.

Spike and Barbara both attended the Booth School, a co-educational elementary school in Devon. Spike went to Booth from prekindergarten through third grade. Over his years at Booth, Spike received strong feedback in both academic and artistic subjects. His report card comments included, "Harold is becoming more of a leader in group activity. He is also becoming very considerate of other members in his group," as well as, "He has a very strong sense of responsibility and is a diligent, perseverant little boy." He was a strong student and a natural leader. Prescient of things to come, he was also described as "gregarious" and "very popular," as well as having "an occasional overly boisterous demeanor."

Hmm. "A leader," "a strong sense of responsibility," "gregarious," and "overly boisterous." Yup. They knew my dad.

Spike was clearly an outgoing person. His sister Barbara, in contrast, was more reserved. Given the big property on which they lived, the kids didn't have many neighbors with whom to play. But Spike would occasionally have friends over, and they would include Barbara in some of their games. She remembers being allowed to hold the football while the boys kicked it, saying, "I was scared to death they'd hit my finger." Although it sounds like a Peanuts cartoon, Barbara wouldn't pull the ball away like Lucy does. Spike and his friends never kicked her finger, at least not intentionally, and Barbara looks back on those times with "great, warm feelings."

During his final year at Booth, Spike had the first of several increasingly traumatic childhood experiences. Because the housekeeper had Thursdays off, the family had dinner on those nights at Merion Golf Club. On one of their drives home from dinner, Spike was sitting—unheard of these days—in the front seat between his mom and dad. Katharine asked Spike to read the license plate of the car in front of them. He could not. The letters and numbers were fuzzy. Apparently, his mother had had an idea that his eyesight was poor. Spike would end up wearing eyeglasses for almost seventy years. Not until after cataract surgery in his mid-seventies did he no longer need them. Anyone who has ever met Spike will recall the black-rimmed, thick-lensed eyewear that were such a defining part of his appearance.

Spike and his "Baby Sis" Barbara

Getting glasses was upsetting for Spike. While he was a good student, he was not a great athlete, so he was worried that adding eyeglasses would only make it harder to fit in. Today he cites his glasses as a turning point of his childhood. After this event, he recalls often feeling lonely and confused. "I was knocked off my secure and stable pedestal." Only several decades later did he realize that it wasn't getting glasses, but rather the dawning of the decline of his parents' marriage, that would rattle his psyche and erode his self-esteem.

In the spring of 1945, Spike was admitted to The Haverford School for the fall semester as a fourth grader. Founded in 1884 by a group of local residents led by—of all people—the wife of the president of the Pennsylvania Railroad, the all-boys Haverford quickly became well known for its academic excellence, a reputation it still enjoys 130 years later. The school's immediate popularity was yet another sign of the railroad's success in establishing the Main Line as a preferred home for successful families with high ambitions for their children. Along with a list of distinguished graduates, Spike's uncle Tom finished Haverford in 1925; Spike's future half-brother Robert would attend, Spike's four sons would graduate from the school, and several of his grandsons would attend, graduate, or are currently enrolled. Today Haverford boasts an enrollment of almost one thousand boys, making it one of the largest boys' schools in the world. Spike and I would become the only father-son duo to serve as chairman of the board of trustees at Haverford.

When he started at Haverford as a nine-year-old, Spike remembers instantly taking to the all-boys environment. "Everything about it made me happy." In his first few years, Spike had some strong young teachers he recalls with fondness, including Rachael Cleaves, Neil Buckley, Charles Boning, Don Boyer, and Charles Dethier. Amazingly, I was fortunate enough to have every one of these teachers as well while at Haverford in the late 1970s and early 1980s. Although when I had them, they had become strong *veteran* teachers.

The leadership prowess Spike exhibited at Booth carried over to Haverford, as he was named president of his section in fourth grade. He continued to perform well academically, making mostly As and Bs over his first three years there. Spike also continued his enjoyment of the arts, participating in both the fall and spring school plays in sixth grade. In "Why the Chimes Rang," in December 1947, Spike was in the chorus. Joe and Jim Hughes, twin brother classmates of Spike's, held the lead roles. Joe would become Spike's best friend at Haverford, while in adulthood, Jim would become one of Spike's dearest friends. In May of 1948, Spike was a "townsman," another chorus-like role. As with his upcoming high school sports career, Spike was never the star, but he relished being part of the team.

Spike and Harold enjoying the outdoors

Religion was a constant part of Spike's upbringing. He attended St. Martin's Episcopal Church in Radnor, PA, where he earned a certificate for perfect attendance at Sunday school and served as an acolyte. Later he was confirmed at All Saints Episcopal Church in Wynnewood. All Saints was his mother's family's church; it is where she is buried. It is also where my brother Mike today serves as senior warden, which is equivalent to chairman of the board. Spike took Bible study at Haverford as well.

Unfortunately, Spike's early years at Haverford paralleled a steady deterioration in his parents' marriage. By seventh grade, his grades suffered, and he no longer earned high-profile leadership positions. Little Spike's world was starting to collapse, and he didn't even know it.

• • • •

Today it is well known that about one of every two marriages in the United States ends in divorce. Historically, the divorce rate has been much lower, but Harold and Katharine were destined to add to the statistics, two flawed people who were not compatible. Harold was an ambitious man with a keen nose for business, but he was also someone who largely prioritized his career and his enjoyment of life over the needs and wants of his spouse, and at times, his children. Katharine was a kind woman raised in a stable home, but she no longer had steady connections to her own family or to many of the close friends from whom she used to draw strength. Her husband's constant traveling and social schedule, combined with the chicken-or-egg dynamics of her increasing drinking and declining marriage, left her feeling isolated in her own home.

During his preteen summers, Spike attended sleepaway camp at the all-male Camp Susquehannock on Tripp Lake in northeastern Pennsylvania. With its idyllic mountainous setting and close proximity to New York and Philadelphia, it was a thriving operation during the postwar boom. Attending summer camp provided Spike with the independence and outdoor experience that summer camp so ably does, as well as much-needed respites from the trials of his home life. Despite the fact that he didn't consider himself overly athletic, he excelled in sports and swimming.

One warm summer afternoon in 1949, during his third and final season at camp, Spike was pulled from his activity and told to go to the main entrance. Pulling into the driveway was a large black Cadillac, its white-walled tires crunching loudly over the long gravel road and creating a trail of dust like a wagon train would in a John Wayne western movie. (He was Spike's favorite actor, by the way.) In the driver's seat, wearing a black jacket and hat, was a fireman from home named John Kirk, whom Spike recognized because

John moonlighted as Harold's chauffeur. The car came to a stop right in front of Spike, and the rear door swung open. Spike saw his father sitting in the backseat. Much to the young camper's surprise, seated next to his father was his secretary, Mimi Jarvis. Spike had no idea what was going on. Why was his dad at camp? Why did he have to have a chauffeur and such a big, fancy car? And why was his secretary with him? Spike remembers feeling "so embarrassed."

This is how Harold chose to tell his twelve-year-old son that he and his mother were getting divorced and that he was now together with Mimi. Among the few vivid memories Spike has from childhood, this one is crystal clear seventy years later. Over time, the embarrassment he felt as the car approached would become the least of his difficulties emerging from this development.

After his father left, Spike finished the camp season in a daze. His initial months of eighth grade were challenging, to say the least. The divorce was finalized six days before Spike's thirteenth birthday, in December 1949. During the proceedings, a judge decreed that Spike would live with his father while Barbara would live with their mother. Both Spike and Barbara recall sitting on a bench outside the courtroom, at twelve and ten years old, while these life-altering decisions were made.

As it would with any person, the divorce had a strong impact on Spike. "Once they split up, I kind of fell apart." The ensuing separation from his sister made Spike feel even more alone. "In many ways I felt like I was an only child. And I'd imagine Barbara felt the same way." Spike was always protective of his little sister. This feeling and behavior increased during the final years of their parents' marriage, during which Harold had become more and more saturated by his financial success and Katharine by her Black & White Scotch. "Baby Sis" was Spike's term of endearment for Barbara, and she never felt more secure than when she was near him. "There were many pictures when we were younger where he's standing behind me with his hands on my shoulders. I just love those pictures."

While Spike was dealing with his own feelings of hurt and isolation, he was also, at the young age of thirteen, forced onto a path of accelerated maturation into a figure who felt the need to care for the females in his life: his "Baby Sis" and his increasingly troubled mother. Unbeknownst to the early teen, resilience was building within Spike, a strength that would buoy him through other challenging times later in life.

• • • •

Harold and Mimi were married just one week after the divorce was finalized. From the start, Spike was unhappy living with his father and Mimi. It got so bad that a few times Spike "ran away" down the hill to the home of some friends where his mother and sister would be visiting. "I would take a little duffel bag and go down there. I would have my railroad tracks. I loved my Lionel trains." Spike's love of trains developed during this difficult time and continued through adulthood, as our family home growing up always housed elaborate train tables.

During one of his runaways, Spike wrote a note to his dad that read: "Dear Daddy, I came to Mommy's on my own accord, because I wanted to. I hear you want me and Barbara to come up there. But we are going to stay down here. I am going to live here. Spike." Heavy stuff for a middle school-aged boy to write to his father. The fact that he still called his parents "Daddy" and "Mommy" and that he implied that the home belonged to Katharine suggest what a young boy he was. The note also demonstrates how he was already assuming the role of protector. He wanted to make sure that Harold directed his anticipated anger at him and not at them. Despite smuggling train tracks to the neighbors' house and writing the note, Spike would be summoned "up the hill" to home. "My old man would get on the phone and he would go, 'Get your ass back here.'"

With his second marriage, Harold became a stepfather for the first, but not last, time to Mimi's young son Don Kriebel. Don lived mostly with his father, however, so he and Spike never developed much of a relationship. Even so, Don was thoughtful enough to attend my mother's funeral in 2015. Mimi had two brothers, and Spike's impressions of each couldn't have been more different. One was a Catholic priest who Spike recalls as "a nice guy." The other, however, had the opposite impact on his stepnephew. Like Mimi had done, this brother also worked for Harold; he was the general manager for the Yoh Company in California. Despite being one of Harold's top managers, Spike recalls, "One day, he left and opened up his own competing business and took much of the Yoh business with him. Real class act." This event helped fuel Spike's discontent for his stepmother.

When remembering this time period, Spike refers to his father as "demanding and a bully." However, he does recall at least one pleasant father-son moment, a weekend getaway to Skytop Lodge, a year-round resort in the Pocono Mountains about one hundred miles north of the Main Line:

> He would try to be a father in some fashion. He and I went to Skytop one time, just the two of us. We had a little cabin to ourselves. We went out fishing and had the usual bets about the most fish and that kind of thing. I remember I caught the most fish, but I brought them back, unbeknownst to him, and put them in the bathtub with some water in it. Of course, after awhile, it started to stink and he found out about it.

In Spike's telling, Harold didn't seem to be upset about the bathtub antic, but rather was enjoying some male bonding with his son. Unfortunately, however, such episodes—from Spike's perspective—were few and far between.

Spike's desire to live with his mother wasn't only about *not* wanting to live with his father and stepmother. He also had a level of admiration for Katharine, recalling, "She had the biggest heart." He remembers that she was the "kindest person and a very thoughtful person" and that "everybody liked her. She was just very kind and giving. She wouldn't forget people. She would give small, little remembrance gifts and send cards to people. She was of the old school, wearing white gloves to church and various social functions."

But Spike also cites the downsides of his mother's addiction. "I hate to say this, but she was weak, and maybe that was caused by her drinking, I don't know." Katharine's circle of support eventually shrank to just a few close friends and one male "drinking buddy," as Spike describes it. Katharine's closest lifelong friend was a classmate from Baldwin named Annie Robinson, with whom she would have lunch weekly throughout adulthood. Every year, according to Barbara, Katharine and Annie "gave each other the same Christmas present, which was a year's subscription to the *Main Line Times*."

While Harold, who lived to seventy-seven years of age and was married four times, amassed a total of five biological children and seven stepchildren, Katharine never again found love or had children.

●   ●   ●   ●

After the divorce, Katharine briefly rented an apartment for Barbara and herself in the now-torn-down Haverford Hotel, on the corner of Montgomery Avenue and Grays Lane in Haverford. It seemed like the kind of place a Hulme would live, even if temporarily. The red brick building had large white columns, a generous porch entrance, and rich décor in the rooms, including Chippendale desks and crystal chandeliers. One of President Eisenhower's granddaughters was married there. It was also across the street from the Merion Cricket Club, where Katharine's father had been president ten years earlier, and less than a mile from The Shipley School, where Barbara was enrolled.

Katharine next rented a home on a street called—ironically—Loves Lane in a quaint English Tudor village a little farther east in Wynnewood, near where Lower Merion High School is located. She would eventually purchase a home across the street from the rental. As was common in divorced families, Spike remembers himself and Barbara having to endure two large meals on major holidays, one with each parent at whichever home or club that parent chose.

While Spike and Barbara were each other's only biological siblings, the two were never as close as during their early childhood football games and "Baby Sis" exchanges. Further exacerbating their separation was Barbara's decision to attend boarding school in eighth grade, largely to escape the unhappy experience of being around her parents. As a result, according to Spike, the siblings "didn't have too much in common. We would relate some way or another back and forth, but we never had the chance to develop a close relationship or have a binding experience after we were split up." The move to boarding school proved to be a good one for Barbara. In particular, she became quite an accomplished athlete, playing varsity field hockey, basketball, and lacrosse. She made the northern New Jersey all-star field hockey team while at the Beard School in South Orange, New Jersey. She had started out at St. Mary's Episcopal School in Burlington, New Jersey, but that school ceased having boarding students after Barbara's first year and she transferred.

Clearly, Spike and Barbara were dealing with the divorce in their own ways. Having a father who was not particularly engaged and a mother who struggled with addiction was a rough one-two punch for the young kids. While Spike dug in, building his grit, Barbara chose to remove herself from the unhealthy environment five years prior to high school graduation.

• • • •

After his parents' marriage ended, Spike's academic performance continued to be middling at best. But back in the 1950s, few student support services or school counseling existed, so according to Spike, "I never understood until somebody told me when I was in college that it was expected when parents get divorced that you suffer academically." As for his drop in grades, Spike recalls, "I had been number one in my section in lower school. But as their marriage fell apart, I went right to the middle of the class rankings." Spike's enjoyment of engineering-related coursework emerged in high school. He recalls liking math the most. Perhaps aiding his study habits, Spike moved in with his mother on Loves Lane, where he would finish high school and live during his college summers and first year after graduation. Unfortunately, Barbara had by then left for boarding school.

While Spike doesn't recall many of his high school teachers at Haverford, Mr. Brownlow still holds a special place in his heart. "Everybody loved Don Brownlow. He was one of a kind and he adopted our class. We would go up to his place on weekends. He was that kind of a teacher." Donald Brownlow, a native of the Germantown section of Philadelphia, was such a popular teacher because, as Joe Cox, one of his headmasters at Haverford, said, "Don taught the history he helped make." During WWII, Brownlow enlisted in the army and on June 6, 1944, found himself aboard a crowded landing craft crossing the English Channel as part of the second wave of Allied troops landing on Utah Beach in the Normandy Invasion. After being one of the lucky soldiers to survive, Brownlow's European Theater experience included fighting in the Battle of the Bulge, which claimed over 100,000 Allied lives. He was then wounded by German tank mortar, for which he received a Purple Heart, before going on to deactivate a mine field, for which he received the Bronze Star. At one point, he was chewed out personally by General George Patton. Those who knew "Brownie" and his loud, uncompromising demeanor will find this *very* easy to imagine. He was later captured by the Germans but escaped by jumping from the back of a moving truck. Mr. Brownlow would go on to write ten different history books. Much to the Yoh family's benefit, during his fifty-five-year tenure at Haverford, he taught not only Spike, but my three brothers and me, as well as one of my nephews—three generations.

Spike's recollection of Mr. Brownlow highlights an important aspect of his upbringing, one that would have a major influence on the rest of his life. Spike has vivid, positive memories about few adults from his' childhood, in fact only two—Uncle Court and Don Brownlow. While mentorship *per se* may not have been used much when Spike was a child, the idea that young people do better as adults when they have role models was as true then as it is now. There were surely more than two men who positively influenced the adult Spike would become, but his lack of acknowledged influencers is striking. Indicative of how he felt about this shortage of adult guidance, Spike remarks, "I never had anyone. I was a pure loner." This lack of mentorship is especially telling as it relates to his father. Throughout his life, Spike learned some beneficial lessons from Harold, including the importance of hard work, risk taking, entrepreneurship, and business diversification, as well as the responsibility that came with power. But when considering templates for a husband, father, and businessman, Spike started with the baseline of doing the opposite of what he observed in his "old man."

Spike now lived with his mother, but his father still wanted to be involved in his schooling, and his style could be blunt. One of Spike's math teachers observed in a report card that, "[Spike] still has trouble restraining his audible remarks on pertinent and impertinent matters. An increase in sincere determination, and a decrease of levity, would improve his understanding of mathematics and the tone of the class without making him a bore." While I interpret this comment to mean that Spike would occasionally blurt things out, verging on acting like the class clown, I wouldn't call the remarks scathing by any means.

Apparently Harold didn't see things that way. In response to the comment, he sent a typed letter to Dr. Severinghaus, the headmaster, stating that he was "most concerned with the remarks made by the math teacher. This statement to me reflects upon either the ability of the teacher to properly teach the subject or his ability to maintain discipline in the classroom, rather than offering a constructive criticism of the student." He went on to demand a meeting with the headmaster and the math teacher. On the one hand, we could commend

Harold for sticking up for his son. On the other hand, it may have been his guilt about the divorce that compelled him to write the letter. Or maybe it was a bruised ego by association or an inability to hear criticism about the son who was his representative in the world. At a minimum, it showed that he was likely more engaged in his son's life than Spike remembers.

At the end of his senior year, Spike ranked thirty-eighth out of the sixty-two graduates in his class. As he recalls, "I was in the middle of the class, which was maybe where I belonged all along." But this mediocre academic performance didn't hold Spike from having a successful life and career. He would become living proof of the old adage that "A" students end up working for "C" students.

● ● ● ●

As a direct reaction to his fraught and lonely childhood, family has always been the most important thing in Spike Yoh's adult life. However, friendship is close to the top of his priorities. His love of camaraderie, especially male bonding, first manifested itself at Haverford. As mentioned earlier, two of his closest friends at school were Joe and Jim Hughes, who were fraternal twins. They would go to each other's houses to play all sorts of sports, tell each other stories, and have sleepovers. After Haverford, Jim attended Yale and became a renowned neurosurgeon in New York City. One of his cases, involving a twenty-two-year-old music student, became the subject of a made-for-television movie in the early 1980s called *Seizure*. Leonard Nimoy of Star Trek's "Spock" fame, played Jim. Spike and Jim would go on to form a special bond, gathering regularly with their wives and families at Spike and Mary's home in Avalon, New Jersey. Along with fellow class-of-1954-graduate Bear Kinkead, they also took their children on some memorable canoeing trips on the Allagash River in northern Maine to a location so remote that it was accessible only by float plane.

Unfortunately, Jim passed away in early 2017 after a tough bout with dementia, a cruelly ironic illness for a brain surgeon. While Jim was not well enough to be interviewed for this book, my final interaction with him was quite special. He and his wife, Janet, visited my father in the summer of 2016, and I joined them for dinner one night. During the meal, I asked the two lifelong friends several questions about their time at Haverford, almost seventy years earlier. Jim perked up incredibly, answering my queries and adding key details to Spike's recollections. Jim's daughter, who had become her parents' caretaker, teared up during the discussion. She commented afterward that the exchange about his Haverford years was the most lucid she had seen her father in a long time.

Despite never being a great athlete, Spike developed a lifelong love of sports during high school. He loved being around jocks and competing as a team. He played football, swam, and played baseball. In his self-deprecating but charming way, Spike referred to himself as "just another player." In baseball, his specialty was bunting. "We scrimmaged early in the season, and I thought I was Coach Prior's secret weapon bunter. But the first time he put me in, I struck out. I barely got to play again."

The sport Spike enjoyed the most was football, despite being only six feet tall and 160 pounds his senior year. His teams were undefeated during his entire nine-year Haverford career. That is, until their last game. As Spike describes it, "In our last game, on Friday the 13th, against our archrival Episcopal Academy, they hurt our best player on the opening kickoff and beat us 7–6." Given that the rivalry has always been intense and continues today, it's all too easy to see why this memory remains indelible. In my own four years of playing varsity football at Haverford, we never beat EA. Although in my senior year we tied 21–21, ending a ten-year losing streak on "EA Day." That game took place almost thirty-five years to the day after Dad's 7–6 loss did, and he was in the stands cheering.

Football wasn't the only pursuit absorbing Spike his senior year. He was the "business manager" of the school play, as well as the founder and president of Haverford's photography club, an activity that foreshadowed things to come. Ask any of my siblings or our friends about Spike's camera. It has been ubiquitous, like another limb. He always took photos. I mean always. And I hated it. We all did. He and my mother were relentless. To this day, when a group that includes members of my family is lining up for a photo, you will inevitably hear one of us repeat my mother's words, using a loud, protracted, more-obnoxious-than-she-said-it tone, "If you can't see the camera, the camera can't see you." But the irony is that today, with smart phones and photography apps, I am a picture-taking, video-shooting junky. I guess this acorn, despite my childhood griping, didn't fall far from the oak.

As a senior, Spike again showed his mischievous side. He loved pranks. And now they involved more than fish in a bathtub. Headmaster Severinghaus (great name for a head of a school, huh? Very Harry Potter-esque) had a corkboard outside of his office with light-up pegs that ranked all of the students academically. One evening early in the spring semester, Spike and a friend decided to reorganize all of the pegs, which would create total chaos for the buttoned-up, order-loving administrator. While this was somewhat innocent, another student later that same night took the corkboard down and destroyed it. For a brief moment, Spike was accused of the second "prank." Although Spike recalls the true facts eventually coming out, "it was a little hairy at the time." Another episode, shortly after, also showed Spike's fun-loving side. Every St. Patrick's Day at Haverford, the senior class would select a "deserving" member of the junior class, cover his eyes, and paint his naked backside green. Spike was also in on those shenanigans. Needless to say, he received a few detentions toward the end of his Haverford career.

● ● ● ●

High school summers were a time when Spike first exhibited his "work hard/play hard" approach to life. He spent the weekdays working at the Yoh Company, now in its second decade. His roles included a stint in the basement lab developing photographs and two summers assisting the senior managers in the accounting department. He refers to these jobs as "a great experience and a great exposure to both the Yoh Company and the world of business. I was hooked." During the weekends, Spike returned to the Jersey Shore, staying with his mother in a ground-floor rental on Sixteenth Street in Longport, just south of Atlantic City. Spike worked as a lifeguard, as well as a bellhop and a grill cook. Coupled with his Yoh Company positions, he was "on the clock" seven days a week.

Barbara spent time in Longport as well, as did their Chicago cousins Peter and Joan Schenck. The Shore provided a chance for Spike and Barbara to reconnect. "Those were great times," Barbara recalls. "We had a lot of friends down there. It was really fun."

Speaking of friends, Longport introduced Spike to Bob Lynch, a boy who went to St. Joseph's Preparatory in Philadelphia. Bob, whose family rented the house next door to Katharine's, would eventually be the best man in Spike and Mary's wedding and work for Spike later in his career. Their first summer together in 1951, Bob remembers Spike being hard to get to know. "I would attempt to make friends with Spike, but he had Peter. He was just a very shy kid when I first met him." One day, however, both Spike and Bob were wearing Phillies hats. The 1950 Phillies had won ninety-one games, finishing first in the National League, before being swept four to zero by the dreaded New York Yankees in the World Series. Phillies fever was rampant, and the two boys connected over their shared love for the team.

Illustrating the "play hard" side of Spike's makeup, Bob recalls how "Spike loved sports, and I loved sports. We would play stickball, but we used our arm as the bat. We also played two-hand touch in an open lot on Eighteenth

Street." Bob remembers Spike being an average athlete, as also evidenced at Haverford, but a very good teammate. "He wasn't a standout. None of us were. But he was very competitive and fun to be with. In fact, I've said this a hundred times, the thing that stands out for me about Spike is how much I enjoyed his company and how much fun he was to be around." It sounds to me like teenager Spike was a lot like adult Spike.

Unfortunately, the following year Bob's father had a stroke. Soon after, his mother passed away and the Lynches stopped renting a house in Longport. But this didn't stop Bob from going to the Shore and spending time with his close summertime friend. "Mrs. Yoh invited me down to spend the summer with them, which enabled me to be a lifeguard with Spike." Bob has warm memories of Spike's mother, which help show the sides of Katharine that Spike does not readily recall. "She was a wonderful woman. I absolutely adored Mrs. Yoh. She was such a sweetheart. Their house was a hangout for all the kids because everybody felt the same way about her." During those early summers, Bob recalls how Katharine navigated the kitchen effectively as well. "Every night at her house, it was like Sunday dinner. She spent hours getting dinner ready. She brought my lunch every day to the beach." Unfortunately, however, even as a young teenager, Bob was aware of Katharine's drinking. "I knew she was in her drinks pretty much every day."

Just as Longport introduced Spike to Bob Lynch, Bob introduced Spike to his first girlfriend, who would become Spike's only serious relationship other than his future wife, Mary. Just like Mary would be, she was a redhead. Bob knew her from back home in Philadelphia where they had dated. Bob took her to his junior prom at St. Joe's, and after they broke up, he took her sister to his senior prom.

Bob recalls the first time Spike met his first love interest in the summer of 1954 after graduation. "One night down in Longport, I ran into her when I was with Spike. There was a restaurant on the corner where we all used to hang out and drink milkshakes. We then went up to Margate and played miniature golf. The next thing I know, he's asking her out." Spike would go on to see her for the rest of that summer, plus date her "long distance" during his first two-and-a-half years of college.

• • • •

As high school progressed, Spike's family life eroded further. He recalls dreading dinners at his father and stepmother's house. "Mimi seemed to have headaches all the time when I went there to eat." Perhaps the headaches were a ploy to avoid spending time with her stepson, or perhaps they were due to the fact that Mimi was pregnant during many of Spike's high school years. She and Harold had three children: Robert in 1952, Ted in 1954, and Marianne in 1955. Ted and Marianne were both born on March 19, exactly one year apart. March 19 is coincidentally my oldest son's birthday as well.

Given the large age gap between him and his half siblings, coupled with his dislike of his stepmother, Spike had little relationship with the three youngsters. As an adult, Robert moved to New York City and became an internationally renowned fashion model, even appearing on the cover of *GQ* magazine. Unfortunately, he died young, succumbing to AIDS in the early 1980s (Spike funded the funeral). Ted would work for the family business at one point, and he visited us occasionally. But due to geography, he and Spike never had a close connection. Spike and Marianne, however, developed a special bond over the years, and she became my godmother. Spike also walked her down the aisle at her wedding. Unfortunately, Marianne contracted ALS in her mid-thirties and passed away after a difficult and drawn-out battle.

Even though Spike's relationship with his father continued to be largely adversarial, the two men did have their bright spots. Harold gave his son the opportunity to work at the Yoh Company, which seeded Spike's passion for the business. Additionally, Harold developed a fondness for Florida, which Spike acquired as well. As his fortune grew, Harold spent more and more time in Palm Beach, where he purchased a fifty-foot yacht called "Venture." There was only one other boat like it in the world, and it was owned by President Herbert Hoover. Belying Spike's limited recollection of fond childhood experiences, there are wonderful pictures on "Venture" of Spike, his father, his grandfather Arch, Barbara, and their friends. Barbara also had her own smaller motorboat, aptly named "Yo Yo."

Harold, Arch and Spike—three generations—aboard "Venture"

Around the time of his divorce from Katharine, Harold took up oil painting. He would go on to create sixty works. One was of Spike and his dog Butch, the two gangsters, which still hangs in Spike's home today. The fact that Spike continues to display his father's artwork shows that underneath the vitriol, Spike does have some pride and nostalgia for his father. Spike's pride stopped well short of displaying some of Harold's other paintings, however, namely those of Mimi in various stages of undress.

The "gangsters" Spike and Butch, as painted by Harold

Meanwhile, as Spike advanced through his teenage years, his mother's decline continued. He would at times prepare their dinners or straighten the house. "I learned to cook to keep her out of the kitchen. I thought that maybe she would drink less that way." In addition to demonstrating his caretaker mentality, Spike's cooking and other chores also showed his budding logic. He knew that these tasks had to be performed, and it was more efficient for him—the energetic, clear-thinking teenager—to do them.

Just as I mimicked my father's love of photography, his ability to cook rubbed off on Spike's sons as well. All three of my brothers and I can cook, and we do so on a regular basis. Do not, however, get us started on who can smoke the best-tasting rack of ribs!

●   ●   ●   ●

One of the most important parts of senior year at a place like The Haverford School is the college admissions process. Like his father, Spike was clearly going to continue his education. But he did not want to attend the University of Pennsylvania. "Dad went to Penn, and I didn't want anything to do with him." He initially had his heart set on Princeton, because his "hero," Uncle Court, had attended. He also applied to a lesser-known at the time but academically strong school in North Carolina, Duke University. He applied to Duke "because of engineering" and because "in those days, Duke was 80% men, so it was easier to get into." Unfortunately, Spike's grades and relative lack of outstanding extracurricular activities conspired against him, and he was rejected from both schools. Yes, that's right. Spike Yoh was rejected from Duke University.

After dealing with this disappointment, Spike recalibrated and applied to Penn State. He submitted his application during the spring of his senior year and was preparing to visit the campus with his father. A senior administrator at Haverford wrote a letter about Spike that the young man was to deliver to the admissions office. When Spike met his father to make the trip, however, Harold had a surprise for his firstborn. They would not be traveling to Penn State but rather to Durham, North Carolina, to Duke. Harold was good friends with George Munger, the recently retired head football coach at Penn. Spike had attended his football camp one summer in high school. Coach Munger was friends with Edward Cameron, Duke's athletic director. Today, Eddie Cameron is best known for the school's basketball arena, which bears his name, Cameron Indoor Stadium. Unbeknownst to Spike, Harold had contacted Munger, who in turn contacted Cameron.

When father and son arrived at Duke, they went immediately to see Cameron in the Athletic Department. After a brief discussion, Cameron picked up the phone, called the Admissions Office, and said he was sending a young man over who should be enrolled for the fall term. Remember, of course, that this occurred *after* Spike had been rejected. Following warm handshakes, Harold and Spike left Cameron's office, walked through Duke's West Campus to Admissions, where Spike, amazingly, was enrolled as a member of the class of 1958. Their next stop was the engineering school, where "I met the administrators, and they met their new student."

Spike later learned that the letter for Penn State given to him by the Haverford official, rather than touting what an asset Spike would be, described his academic difficulties due to his parents' divorce, as well as his involvement in the aforementioned school pranks. As Spike puts it, "not the kind of letter you would want to get into college."

This wasn't exactly your run-of-the-mill college admissions story. But little of what Spike Yoh would do in life could be described as run of the mill. This sequence of events also showed Harold's engagement in his son's college placement, possibly stemming from his own experience and benefit from earning a degree from a high-caliber university. Little did he know that his network enabled his namesake to attend the school that would literally change his life.

• • • •

In August 1954, Spike Yoh packed his bags and headed four hundred miles south to Durham, thus bringing his childhood to an end. Spike's youth was full of both good and bad experiences. He would retain far more of the latter. He saw his parents' marriage fall apart and his father remarry a woman for whom he felt little warmth. He tried to run away from home. His academic performance deteriorated. He had few positive role models. And he often felt alone. But he also developed a strong work ethic, as well as the all-important character trait of resilience. He gained an innate desire to care for members of his family, and he started to discover the value of lasting friendships. He acquired a genuine passion for sports, the Jersey Shore, and redheads.

All of these experiences helped shape the man Spike Yoh would become. He would go on to attain degrees from Duke University and the Wharton School, to be married to his college sweetheart for fifty-six years, and to have five children with her. He would grow his company into one of the largest privately owned businesses in the United States, would oversee transformative change at many reputable educational institutions and other not-for-profit organizations, and would leave an indelible impression on myriad people all over the world. He would do all of this in passionate, yet imperfect ways.

As Spike recalls it, childhood was mostly dark times. Little did he know, however, that happy days were on the horizon.

Chapter 3

Happiness Found

Goodbye grey skies, hello blue
—Norman Gimbel and Charles Fox, "Happy Days"

Starting college at Duke was the greatest turning point in Spike's life. The grey skies of his youth in Pennsylvania were in his rearview mirror, and the blue skies of North Carolina were now above him. Please note that they were "the blue skies of North Carolina," and not "Carolina Blue" skies. Those of you who know my family's zealous affinity for Duke know what I mean.

Duke University's roots trace back to the mid-1800s. Trinity College, Duke's predecessor, used the phrase, *Eruditio et Religio*, "knowledge and religion." This is still Duke's motto today, and it's a phrase that dovetails well with Spike's personal beliefs. In 1924, after several generous financial gifts from the tobacco-producing Duke family, the school was renamed Duke University. With this official founding in the twentieth century, Duke is a relative adolescent compared to other well-known American institutions of higher learning, a fact that will prove important to Spike's experiences there.

When seventeen-year-old Spike entered college in the fall of 1954, tuition and rooming expenses totaled $675 per year. By comparison, total costs for one year at Duke today exceed $60,000, which, after adjusting for inflation, is still a tenfold increase. Dwight D. Eisenhower, former commander of the

Allied armies in Europe, was in his second year as president of the United States. The nation's population was 163 million, half of what it is today. Economically, the country was booming in the post-WWII, Cold War era, and national pride was at an all-time high, although McCarthyism was also in its heyday. *From Here to Eternity* won the Oscar for Best Motion Picture, as well as other awards, including Best Supporting Actor for Frank Sinatra, Spike's favorite crooner, with whom he shared the birthday of December 12. The biggest musical stars at the time also included Perry Como, Doris Day, and Dean Martin. As a television show two decades later would so aptly depict, these were truly *Happy Days*.

Spike as he embarks on his college career

• • • •

In contrast to his few positive memories from childhood, Spike's recollections from Duke demonstrate how much he enjoyed his college years. Because he had considered himself a "loner" in high school, he wanted a room by himself. "For me, it was by request in the room allocation, and I got it." His room was on the Clock Tower Quad, in the middle of West Campus, which is nicknamed "The Gothic Wonderland" due to its beautiful stone architecture. Spike vividly remembers "the room, the location, the whole schmear." The setting might have seemed slightly less idyllic when, one month into freshman year, Durham was hit by Hurricane Hazel. Spike remembers massive damage on campus and the cancelling of that fall's homecoming weekend, but the storm did little to mar Spike's burgeoning appreciation.

The School of Engineering in which Spike enrolled was less than twenty years old. About his decision to study engineering, Spike says, "I liked math. I liked numbers. I liked to figure things out." He also said, "English was a different story. I was never a writer." As to why he chose mechanical engineering, Spike explained, "I didn't know electronics, and the little I looked around, civil engineering paid the least. When I graduated, I didn't know exactly what I wanted to do, but I always figured I was going to work for the Yoh Company. Civil engineers designed buildings and bridges, but mechanical guys were making engines and rockets and all that exciting stuff." In his first semester, Spike did well in math, earning an A in algebra and a B in geometry. Over his four years in Durham, Spike earned mostly Bs and Cs, just as he had at Haverford.

When Spike was at Duke, the engineering program was all male. The absence of women in his core classes eased Spike's transition from Haverford to Duke. Although he had lived with his mother, had somewhat reconnected with his sister in Longport, and had a hometown girlfriend, the bulk of Spike's relationships were with men. Another sign of the times was that there were no African American students at Duke, campus desegregation being a decade away. Coincidentally, one of the first black students to enroll, Wilhelmina Reuben-Cook, would become Spike's friend and colleague on the board of trustees in the 2000s, a fact he notes with much pride.

• • • •

As Spike immersed himself in life at Duke, his tepid connections to his family endured. On Valentine's Day, he sent his mother a card that he signed in what would become his cute-but-sort-of-annoying style, "Guess Who." I mean, the envelope and signature were clearly in his hand, and the postmark, with its stamp for a remarkable three cents, read "Durham, NC" Despite the geographic separation, Spike remained a dutiful son, knowing that his mother was then—more than ever—alone.

Katharine would visit Duke periodically for "Joe College Weekends" during which the school and the students produced various events and performances. Spike's girlfriend would join Katharine on these weekends, staying not with Spike but with his mother in a hotel—another fact that my "traditional" father is proud to note. The truth was that women were then not even allowed to enter the West Campus dorms, but that detail is superfluous as far as Spike is concerned. The hotel where they stayed was usually the Washington Duke, whose Bull Durham Lounge is my favorite hotel bar anywhere. Spike's hometown relationship continued to deepen. As he recalls, "We were talking about getting married and stuff. We were getting pretty serious."

Right after his freshman year ended, Spike's stepmother Mimi passed away suddenly. She died on a train while traveling back from Van Wert with Harold. The circumstances surrounding her passing remain vague. She left three small children, the youngest of which, Marianne, was only two months old. Harold now had Spike and Barbara, eighteen and sixteen, along with three children under the age of three, in addition to a stepson from Mimi's first marriage, although he lived with his father. Given the rapidity with which

Harold married Mimi after he'd left Katharine, it came as little surprise to Spike that his father almost immediately took up with another woman. Esther White, who was older than Harold, had three children of her own from two previous marriages. Her father had been the mayor of Atlantic City. Harold and Esther married just three months after Mimi passed away. By the time Spike was barely old enough to vote, his father was on his third marriage. This proliferation of wives had a profound impact on Spike, compelling him even then to want a life partner to whom he was sure he could stay married and with whom he could provide a stable home life for his own children.

Esther's two older children were grown and already married. Her youngest, Charlotte, lived with her mother and Harold after the wedding. Barbara was a year or two younger than Charlotte but was already off at boarding school and stayed with her mother during school vacations. Barbara remembers feeling that she and Charlotte "had very little in common. Every once in a while we'd talk, but I lived at my mother's so we never developed any sort of relationship." As expected, Spike had only faint relationships with Esther and her children. Over time, however, he says he "came to appreciate who she was and how she loved and cared for her three young stepchildren." Despite the clouded images of his own parents, Spike was centered enough to notice when an adult played an important role in the lives of youngsters.

Among the family dynamics that emerged during Spike's time at Duke, the most important was the evolution of his relationship with his father:

> I'd gotten independent during my time at Duke. It gave me a self-confidence that I'd never had, and I felt very secure in my own skin. I developed the nerve to put my dad in his place. Before he kind of petrified me. Different things happened, including the ongoing frictions relating to Mother, what I was going to do, and what Barbara was going to do. I grew to the

point where I could say to my old man, "No, we're going to
do this, we're going to do that."

These changes were not the result of some big fight or culminating discussion
between the two men. As Spike recalls, "It never got belligerent. It just started
to happen." One of Spike's close friends, Bill Lee, speaks to the impact of
Duke on this father-son relationship:

> I think Spike grew up at Duke. He was a very insecure person
> when he arrived. His mom, whom he seemed to love dearly,
> was an alcoholic and had become unreliable. He was not close
> to his father. My experiences with his dad when we'd go to
> his house and hit golf balls or go in the pool, were positive.
> Then one time years later Spike asked us, "Who is the most
> important person in your life?" I started off by saying my dad.
> We all went around and many said the same thing. Spike was
> the last one to speak, and he said, "I hated that son-of-a-bitch."
> Everybody's mouth dropped open.

Bill's perspective shows not only great pain and animosity Spike felt toward
his father, but also how secretive he was about his feelings, not sharing them
with even his closest friends for several years.

• • • •

In addition to maturing as a son and finding self-confidence in college, Spike
also discovered his zest for social life and, more importantly, his appreciation
for the importance of close friendships. Initially, his peer group was the other
men in his classes. "We were all mechanical engineers, and we'd hang out
at lunch together and talk studies or just BS in general. That was kind of
our social life back in those days." He can still today rattle off the names of
several freshman-year classmates. Until this point Spike didn't drink alcohol.
"I didn't want to drink because of Mother. I also decided I didn't want to

join a fraternity yet, although I had made some acquaintances in Sigma Nu, including Darryl Copeland from my engineering classes, who was a Sigma Nu. I went to some of their parties."

By sophomore year, Spike had grown out of his "loner" status and roomed with another mechanical engineering student named Bo King, who had lived on his hall freshman year. As a sophomore, Spike would join Sigma Nu. He took to Greek life and fraternity parties, in large part due to his emerging passion for fun. His desire for good times surely emanated from the lack of fun he recalls as a child.

While Spike appreciated Bo King as a roommate, Spike's soon-to-become lifelong friends were just emerging. Let me introduce you to the "Ollie Brothers." The Ollies were not brothers by blood, but each of them will tell you that their brotherhood is deeper than their relationships with their own biological siblings. As Zook Mosrie comments, "I had a natural-born brother, but I was never as close to him as I was to these guys."

Spike met Darryl Copeland first, a Midwesterner from Uhrichsville, Ohio. Darryl was an electrical engineering student and an incredibly diligent worker. Spike recalls, "We just had a lot in common. He had a sister and I had a sister, but we became like brothers and shared a lot of things." Darryl's wife Shirley agrees that "they had an incredibly special bond." Darryl would later work for Spike at Yoh and Day & Zimmermann for almost thirty years, helping him grow and diversify the businesses to unprecedented levels. Unfortunately, Darryl passed away in 2013 after a series of heart attacks, the first of the Ollies to move on. Spike delivered his eulogy.

Rob Townsend was a high school quarterback from Delaware with a magnetic personality and a unique sense of humor. He would go on to have successful careers in both the public and private sectors in his home state. He and his wife Sally now spend big chunks of every year in the Caribbean. Nice.

Azett "Zook" Mosrie was a country boy from West Virginia who transferred
to Duke his sophomore year. In the same way few people refer to Spike as
"Harold" (growing up, it was usually solicitors who did so when calling the
house on our banana-yellow rotary phone on the wall of the kitchen, and we
knew enough not to get Dad), no one calls Zook anything other than "Zook."
A first-generation American, Zook says, "My parents were from Lebanon.
They had no college education and really couldn't read or write." He is a
living testament to the American Dream, having become an ophthalmologist
in Tennessee where he ran his own practice for almost forty years. He and his
wife Caroline's lake house, which we have visited numerous times, contains
one of the finest wine collections south of the Mason-Dixon Line.

Spike, Darryl, Rob, and Zook were all Sigma Nus, and they lived together
in the same dorm, or fraternity "section." Another Sigma Nu, Bill Lee, hailed
from Delaware like Rob. Bill went on to be a successful lawyer and State
Supreme Court Judge, twice running for governor. While Bill was not officially
part of the Ollie Brothers at Duke, he remained close with them and some
years later was formally "inducted." To this day, Bill can out-charm and
out-dance anyone half his age.

The bond shared by these men is unique, one that spawned three generations
of friendship, camaraderie, and love. Rob says, "We came together initially
and we stayed together. I think we were attracted to one another because of
our basic values and our approach toward life. But we were also ready to raise
hell and do cartwheels and survive whatever schemes Spike would cook up."
From the beginning, Spike was their leader. As Caroline concludes, having
heard the Ollies' college stories over and over and over, "Spike was always,
I guess, dominant, and he always had a sense of direction for whatever was
going on. His opinion has always been revered, starting way back." Rob agrees.
"He was our leader. Not a question."

Jack Winters, Duke's Assistant Director of Athletics, speaks of being impressed by "the history of the Ollie Brothers and their families, how close the first generation was, and how solid and close the second generation was. It just kept rolling. I thought, how special and how neat, that you've got these five guys at the core, and then the spouses, and then the children and the grandchildren. It's such a unique story." After more than sixty years of friendship, Bill Lee might best sum up the Ollies: "It's a tapestry. There aren't all of these major things that happened. Our lives just kind of got woven together. We enjoy each other. It is always fun and meaningful whenever we see each other."

During college, one of the things that ingratiated Bill with the original Ollies was a yearly event his family hosted in Rehoboth, Delaware. As Zook recalls, "We all liked Bill because he had an unbelievable New Year's Eve party. It was a big deal to be invited. The party was to die for." Bill noted that "it was a black-tie party with shrimp and champagne."

Zook, Rob, Darryl and Spike pictured at Bill Lee's New Year's Eve party

It was during one of the fraternity brothers' trips to Rehoboth that the "Ollie" name was born. Rob, with his creative sense of humor, would give nearly everyone he met a nickname. Eventually Darryl became "Ivory Jim." Bill was "Molars." Zook was "The Great Zook." Okay, maybe that one wasn't the most original, but with a first name like "Zook," how much of a nickname did he need? Rob himself was "Sunset." But Rob's biggest moniker-manufacturing involved Spike and the whole group. "We went out for dinner and there was a bowl of olives on the table. Spike was picking up the olives and trying to land them in people's drinks. I started calling him 'Ollie,' and that derived to 'The Great Ollie,' and then to 'The Great Ol.'" Never one to want things to be just about him, Spike recounts that, "Rob, in his typical fashion giving everybody a name, called me 'The Great Ol.' So then I said, 'If I'm 'The Great Ol,' then you are my 'Ollie Brothers.'" The irony is that Spike hates olives. He detests them. I guess that's why the young prankster started lobbing them in everyone's drinks. The men eventually also made up a song called, "Put a Bar in the Ollie Car." It wasn't until researching this book that I learned that the song wasn't real, but something else these clowns invented.

Though there was plenty of clowning, some of them also dedicated themselves academically. According to Zook, "Spike and Darryl worked the hardest. They were studying for their engineering classes all the time." Yet Zook and Rob, who roomed together, were "always finding something to do." Often this something was going to Meola's Chili House, a Durham restaurant that had a jukebox and served beer. Spike soon started joining them on their outings, noting that even Darryl would "once in a while break loose and go." Spike recalls, "There was always something going on. We did some crazy things, but they were fun. Oh God, they were fun." Speaking of fun, Spike eventually started partying with his fellow Sigma Nus, becoming the primary planner for many of their events. "I was the fraternity's social chairman, for two years in fact. [That] was unusual. Yeah, I became the party guy." The Sigma Nu events, with Spike often concocting the theme or deciding the destination, were very popular. Indicative of the times, one event he planned was "American Bandstand, Duke Edition." He, of course, cast himself as Dick Clark.

Throughout his college exploits—and beyond—Spike's late-night antics never slowed him down the next day. As anyone who has spent time with Spike Yoh knows, no one could burn the wick at both ends like he could. Spike's closest friend Darryl, however, was a close second in this regard, much to the dismay of their wives later in life. The Ollies also regularly attended Duke sporting events, particularly basketball games. They would pile into a car and travel to see Duke play at other schools. Such trips became a hallowed tradition over years and decades, particularly when it came to the basketball team's many Final Four appearances.

One of the Ollies' more memorable exploits during college was Darryl's wedding. His fiancé Shirley wasn't just his high school sweetheart, but his "Sunday school sweetheart," the two having met in church as children back in Ohio. They were married in December 1957, during winter break of the Ollies' senior year. Shirley and her sleepy little hometown were shocked by the invasion from Durham. "All the Sigma Nus came to Uhrichsville for our wedding. Our town had never seen anything like them. They ate more, drank more, and stayed up later than any group we'd ever seen. A few of them [excluding Spike] stayed an extra week when the wedding was over, and they kept right on going."

Spike learned how to have fun while also tending to his studies. He found an enjoyment that he had not experienced as a child. The freedoms of college life, the closeness of his friendships, and the pride he developed as a "Dukie" transformed Spike into the upbeat, positive person that he remains today. This experience, largely highlighted by his meeting the Ollie Brothers, made an indelible imprint on Spike's makeup and priorities later in life.

During college summers, Spike continued to work both at his father's company during the week and as a lifeguard in Longport on the weekends. One summer, Spike worked as a draftsman at Yoh, earning $1.35 per hour. He commuted each day into the city from Loves Lane via train, which of course ran on the tracks originally laid by the Pennsylvania Railroad. For lunch, he would "go out and get a sandwich and a Coke and eat at my drafting board." Showing his innovative side, but also his lack of future as a draftsman, Spike describes—with a knowing chuckle—how he was never one to be constrained by convention. "One time I was drafting for an American Viscose job, and I couldn't get the drawing to fit on the paper, so I did it in quarter-inch scale one way and half-inch scale the other way. I thought it made a lot of sense, but they are supposed to be of the same scale." He also played on the company softball team. "That was fun. We'd finish up work, play our game, and go out together afterwards." His work ethic had now taken roots, and his work hard/play hard mantra was blooming.

● ● ● ●

Spike continued to date his girlfriend through the first semester of junior year, but the first sign of trouble appeared that December. A friend reported having seen her at the Army/Navy game in Philadelphia, where she appeared to be on a date with a midshipman, a student at the United States Naval Academy. Spike then remembered that he had tried calling her house several times that same day, but she was not home.

But he was still contemplating marriage, to the point where he had "pinned" her, meaning he had given her his fraternity pin as a gesture signifying that they were "engaged to be engaged." Given that she was a devout Catholic and he was Episcopalian, Spike went to see a Catholic priest. "I told him how passionate her family was about the church." The priest informed him that he was essentially wasting his time because the marriage would not be recognized in the Catholic Church unless he converted. Given Spike's

Duke-inspired self-confidence and his own religious conviction, he concluded that "nobody was going to tell me what to do. I was not going to convert, so the relationship had to end." A few weeks later, in February of 1957, Spike broke off the courtship. He was now single for the first time in two-and-a-half years.

Enter Mary Michael Milus. She would be Spike's only other girlfriend, but much more importantly, his wife of fifty-six years until her passing in 2015. They would have five children together and create what many people consider to be the closest, most loving partnership they ever knew.

In the late 1800s, a couple named Mary and Joseph Milus left Poland to start their family in America. Yes, their names really were Mary and Joseph, and yes they really took a trip together to have a baby. They settled in New Hampshire, not Bethlehem, and had a son named Paul, not . . . (you get the idea), in 1901. His middle name was Robert. The surname Milus was likely anglicized upon their arrival, possibly from the name Milewski, an older Polish name of some nobility affiliated with the town of Milewo. The Miluses were quite poor and could only afford to provide for Paul's education through eighth grade. But a benefactor stepped in and allowed Paul to finish high school and attend college. He graduated from Presbyterian College in South Carolina, earned a degree in chemistry, and went to work as a chemist at the DuPont Company in Wilmington, Delaware, in the mid-1920s. There he met a local girl named Marjorie Bogart, also born in 1901. She had one half-sister and was of English and Dutch descent. (For those of you paying attention, this is the *actual* Dutch heritage I referenced at the start of the book.)

Paul and Marjorie were married a short time later and then had a daughter, Mary Michael, born in Wilmington on February 2, 1937, eight weeks after and thirty miles southwest of where her future husband, Spike, was born. Four years later, the Miluses had a son, Paul Robert Jr. As Paul Sr.'s career progressed, the family moved every six to twelve months to various DuPont plants throughout the country, including Oklahoma and Tennessee.

In 1945, during the family's time in Tennessee, Paul was away on business and had a cerebral hemorrhage. He died in his hotel room. I remember my mom once saying something about getting off the bus after school and seeing a police car in her driveway the day the news arrived in Tennessee. Their world immediately turned upside down, as Marjorie was made a widow with an eight-year-old and a four-year-old. She would never remarry or again find love—like Spike's mother Katharine. Spike and Mary would each grow up in households without both of their parents together. These dynamics later shaped Mary and Spike's shared philosophy and approach toward marriage and raising a family.

After Paul's death, the young family of three returned home to Wilmington and moved in with family friends. They eventually purchased a home on Thirty-Fourth Street. Marjorie got a job across town as a secretary at the prestigious Tower Hill School, which allowed her to send both of her children there tuition-free. I have to believe this was the primary reason she chose to work where she did. Furthermore, both of Marjorie's kids' college expenses—Mary's at Duke and Paul's at Trinity College in Hartford, Connecticut—were also paid for. Although it is unclear if Tower Hill, DuPont, or another benefactor funded college, both kids received full educations from childhood through college at reputable institutions. Marjorie is to be greatly commended for making this happen. Educational philanthropy played a key role in our relatives' lives, another factor influencing Spike and Mary's future priorities.

Mary and Paul were four years apart and therefore never in the same division of school at the same time. Paul recalls that his sister had one particularly close high school friend, Charlotte Rode, who would be in her wedding and remain a strong acquaintance for some years after. He also remembers his sister as being somewhat serious, at times like a second mother. "She was kind of straight-faced and proper." The family took a few vacations over the years, including Washington, DC and New York City. Paul recalls the latter as "the first propeller plane ride we took." Paul himself spent a few summers at

Lone Pine Camp in the Adirondack Mountains, just a few miles from where Mary and Spike would take their family on vacation several decades later.

Because she was working full time, Marjorie had a maid named Mini. As Paul remembers, "She lived in the poor part of Wilmington. She would cook dinner for us because my mother didn't get home until late in the day." Paul remembers Marjorie taking Mary and him to visit Mini's family at their home, bringing gifts on Thanksgiving and Christmas. He pointed out the parallel with the woman who worked for Mary and Spike later in life, Jean Bright. Jean was also from an underserved neighborhood. Paul recalls how Mary was so good to Jean and Jean's family, something she modeled after her mother. Spike notes that "Jean was like family to us." I can corroborate. Jean was wonderful. In addition to undergirding my parents' household for forty years, she taught me how to play gin rummy and drink hot tea, with milk and sugar. When she passed away, our family was seated in the first row at her standing-room-only, emotional—and at times high-energy—Baptist funeral.

After graduating from Tower Hill in 1955, Mary headed to Duke—quite an outcome given the difficult circumstances of her childhood. She majored in psychology and sociology and had a part-time job to help pay for living expenses. Showing signs of her own leadership prowess, she was voted president of her sorority. Mary was five-foot-ten, tall for a woman even today, but especially so in the 1950s. She had auburn red hair. And she was Episcopalian. With the middle name "Michael," her friends at Duke took to calling her "Mary Mike," which was shortened to "M&M," and then understandably to "Candy." I guess Rob Townsend wasn't the only giver of nicknames in Durham. He would eventually employ his skill with "Candy" as well, however, dubbing her "Candarenie," the end of which is pronounced "ree-nee." This pet name would stand the test of time, eventually showing up on T-shirts, glassware, and even a few boat transoms.

Mary Michael "M&M" Milus as a young college student

In her sophomore year, Mary had a class with Zook, who recalls that "she was just wonderful." It turns out that Bill Lee knew her from high school back in Delaware as well. After Spike broke up with his hometown girlfriend, Bill recalls, "I knew he liked redheads, and I knew Mary from home." As it turns out, neither Zook nor Bill actually introduced Spike to Mary, but as the saying popularized by John F. Kennedy goes, "Success has a thousand fathers."

The story of how Spike actually did meet Mary is solidly entrenched in Yoh family lore. The crucial moment took place on a warm Saturday in February in 1957, around lunchtime. One of the many great things about going to Duke after growing up in Pennsylvania is that there are such things as "warm February Saturdays." Spike was driving his used 1954 two-tone-blue, four-door Oldsmobile with Jim Nash, a fraternity brother, riding shotgun. On their way to town, they drove through East Campus, which was the women's campus.

Given Spike's recent breakup, I'm guessing they were literally "cruising for chicks." Spike recalls:

> We came up to the famous [for the Yoh family] bus stop bench. It was ten cents to take the bus downtown. If you were driving through East Campus, you would often pick up anyone waiting there and save them the money. That was basically what we did. I was with Jim, and he knew Mary from class. She was waiting there with three other girls, and the three got in the back of my car, and Mary got in the front between Jim and me. She seemed very pleasant and smart. And she had red hair.

Spike was clearly on the rebound, and this redhead from Delaware was about to catch him.

Spike summoned the courage to call her dorm room three days later. At that point, his unique first name got jumbled. "I called her room, and her roommate answered. I then heard her say that there was some guy on the phone with a funny-sounding name like Clyde." Mary got on the phone with "Clyde," who turned out to be Spike, and Spike asked her out. Their first date was the following Saturday at the Saddle Club, a red-and-white-checkered-tablecloth kind of place with live music. Spike wore a tie. Although he never smoked cigarettes, he possesses a Saddle Club ashtray to this day.

Was it love at first sight? According to Spike, "No, no, no. It might have been with me, but number one, she didn't want to get serious. Number two, she didn't exactly approve of my *active* social life. I wanted more out of the relationship initially than she did." As their relationship started to grow, Zook, who still had his class with Mary, found himself stuck in the middle of some early relationship missteps. "Spike would come to my room and say, 'You know what she told me today? You know what she said?'" Mary would corner him after class about "some petty thing he may have done that she didn't like." Doing his best cupid impression, Zook would explain to each that they both really liked each other. In particular, he defended his fraternity brother to Mary. "I would say, 'Listen, he really likes you. You're lucky. He's really a great guy.' She decided that the stuff she thought at first was so awful actually wasn't that bad. She realized that it was mostly just good, clean fun."

For her part, Mary made a great first impression on everyone in Spike's world. Darryl's future wife Shirley clearly remembers getting to know her:

> I got to spend some time with Mary during a Joe College Weekend. They were big deals in those days. We had a candlelight ceremony where the Sigma Nus serenaded all the ladies. It was a lot of fun. Mary was always very congenial and always a good sport, going along with whatever outings Darryl and Spike dreamed up.

Shirley then deadpans in a deserving self-congratulatory tone, "Every once in a while, she and I would congratulate ourselves for putting up with them."

The gaze says it all; Spike and Mary falling in love

Spike and Mary started to become serious, showing a lot of affection for one another—particularly after their initial Zook-paved-over speed bumps. However, as many couples do, they got angry with one another on occasion. Spike's fits of ire were likely an outgrowth of his unhappy childhood, while Mary seemed to have the proverbial redheaded temper. Rob Townsend remembers one night in particular: "I was in my car in front of the dorm where Mary lived. Spike was walking her up the steps to the front door. I don't know what he said, but she hauled off and walloped him, one of those 'kappow' slaps! His glasses went flying off his head. I've been kidding him about that ever since." When asked about the episode, Spike says, "I don't remember what I said, but I'm sure I deserved it."

The young couple during summer break from Duke

Spike and Mary continued to date through the spring and summer. Spike recalls of that summer of 1957, "We lived only thirty miles apart, so it wasn't far. Mary worked at DuPont in Wilmington. We would spend a lot of time together after work." He remembers meeting her mother and brother. "It wasn't anything dramatic. I liked them from the start." He sometimes spent the night at the Milus residence in Wilmington, sharing Mary's brother Paul's room. "He had a cuckoo clock and the darn thing would go 'cuckoo!' every hour, all night. I finally had to take it down off the wall. From then on, they were nice enough to move the clock out of his room when I stayed over."

Somewhat to Spike's surprise, when they got back to Duke that fall, Mary wanted to slow things down. "Going back for my senior year and her junior year, she announced that she did not want to go steady. She didn't want to get too connected and wanted to see other people. So I recalibrated and said okay. It was my senior year, and I had a great time with my friends and went on a few dates with other women here and there." Continuing to see Mary while they dated other people created an awkward moment or two. "I went over there one time to see her, and one of my professors was there to pick her up for a date." But true love eventually ruled the day. Spike recounts the pivotal moment:

> Mary was coming down the steps into the Duke Union Dope
> Shop, and I was going up with this attractive transfer student
> from the University of Miami who was the head baton twirler.
> Mary and I stopped on the stairs with people going in both
> directions, blocking traffic, and had a quick but really nice
> chat. After that exchange, she made a comment to Zook about
> wanting to get serious again. I guess that was it.

In December of 1957, six months before his graduation, Spike pinned a girl for the second time. Weeks later, at Darryl and Shirley's wedding in Ohio, which Spike attended alone, he publically professed his love. As Bill Lee remembers, "Everybody had had too much to drink and Spike had gone upstairs, but apparently he woke up and came back down in his boxer shorts. Many of our dates were still there, so I whipped off my coat and wrapped it around him. All he was saying was, 'I'm in love with Mary. I am so much in love with Mary.'" Apparently, she was in love with him too.

• • • •

A few months later, in June of 1958, Spike graduated from Duke with a degree in mechanical engineering. His sister Barbara and mother Katharine attended, as did his father Harold and his third wife, Esther. Of course, Mary was there, having just completed her junior year, as were the Ollie Brothers, though a few of them should have graduated a year earlier, either prior military service or too many trips to Meola's Chile House requiring them to take the extra time.

College had been a time of profound personal transformation for Spike. It was a time when he began to understand who he really was, which meant taking some responsibility for imperfections and shortcomings. What he discovered was multifaceted and life setting. He realized he could be someone who did what he wanted, at times regardless of what others thought or desired. He began to say what was on his mind, even when he might not have thought things all the way through. He entered adulthood still without any mentors or role models. He discovered that he enjoyed having an active social life but one that was at times more active than his course load may have warranted.

But Spike's growth in college had more to do with the development of his positive traits, ones that would largely define who he would be for the rest of his life. At Duke, Spike found the voice that allowed him to better handle his father. The two would work together for eighteen more years. While there would be hard times for the son during that stretch, never again would he feel bullied by the old man.

Perhaps because he had found his voice and more self-confidence, Spike experienced deep happiness in his college years. As he departed Durham, he vowed to always be optimistic, to always see the glass as more-than-half-full, and never to let negative events or thoughts keep him down. This is a major, defining trait of who he would become and how he is known. It's also a characteristic, I'm proud to say, that I have tried to embody through much of my life as well. Thank you, Pop.

Spike found lifelong friendships at Duke. He had friends from Haverford and from Longport, some of whom would remain close for decades to come. But the Ollie Brothers transcend friendship. There is a love among these men that is rare, that is cherished, and that is indelible. His peer group also allowed his natural leadership prowess, which had lain fallow since his elementary school years, to reemerge. It would never go unsown again.

Along with friends, Spike found his bride, his life partner, his soul mate. While they were not yet engaged when he graduated, Spike was certain that he and Mary would marry. Given both of their difficult, nontraditional upbringings, he was fueled with hope and conviction that theirs would become a life full of love, happiness, and understanding.

At Duke, Spike also found his love, well, for Duke. "Duke showed me that I liked to adopt with passion any entity that I'm associated with, whether it was a school, or the country, or the church, or my family. I don't just take things for granted; I feel passionately connected. Duke was the first time I felt that way about a place. I grew up with nothing of passion or connection, but I fell in love with Duke." Ever since his days in Durham, Spike has not wanted to be alone, but instead to be part of a group . . . or an organization . . . or a community. "Our" became his possessive pronoun of choice.

Finally, in Duke Spike found an institution that paralleled key facets of his own ethos, namely around tradition and ambition. Relative to other institutions such as Ivy League schools, Duke was less steeped in tradition. It did not have wheel ruts carved by generations of graduates like those other schools. There was no thick plaster mold of what being a "Dukie" meant. Like Duke, Spike did not have time-tested traditions to steward. His upbringing was, by his account, mostly forgettable. As he left Duke, he was committed to carving his own path and to creating his own set of traditions. Duke was also ambitious. It sought to achieve greatness, and to do so in its own collaborative, driven way. Spike has always been ambitious. From his marriage, to his family, to his business, to his volunteer leadership, Spike has been the embodiment of everything the word ambition means.

Spike is, as a result, "Duke Blue" to his core. He and the university have spent a lifetime giving mutually to one other, enriching one another's experiences along the way.

Chapter 4

Go West, Young Man

Only the beginning of what I want to feel forever
Only just the start
—*Robert Lamm, "Beginnings"*

While Spike's departure from Duke in the spring of 1958 was unremarkable as an event, it was symbolic as a course heading for his future. The ensuing years encompassed some of the most important personal and professional milestones of his life. Furthermore, Spike's newfound approach to and philosophy about life were taking hold:

> There was this phrase. These were "Happy Days." That was the one thing that was predominant. Everything was hunky-dory. Everything we did was with a smile. I don't remember worrying about the economy. Everything was good. I got to go to college where I wanted to, and I got a car. I never wanted much, so I didn't need much. And I had job security. Life was great.

These words are all the more telling given the mixed experiences of his upbringing.

The summer after college, while Spike worked full time at the Yoh Company, he and Mary saw each other almost every night, with Spike driving down to the Miluses' home in Wilmington and either bringing Mary up to Pennsylvania or staying over in Paul's room, minus the cuckoo clock. Of Mary's summer job at DuPont, Spike says, "They offered her a full-time job, which was an interesting thing. She even considered dropping out of school." This showed Mary's high level of competence, particularly given how few women had professional roles compared to men in those days. Not one to squander an opportunity to push herself, however, she opted to work at DuPont only during the summers and would go on to finish her degree.

One August weekend, boyfriend and girlfriend caravanned with their newlywed friends Darryl and Shirley to Hershey, Pennsylvania, to see an Eagles preseason game. Afterward, Spike and Mary traveled to Van Wert, the first time Mary would see where Spike's father was raised. According to Spike, "That was fun. I enjoyed showing her our roots and some of the unique things about life on the farm." To again highlight his traditional, pious makeup, he then offers, "We were still virgins at the end of the trip." Later he clarifies, ". . . and until we were married."

Earlier that year, Spike had applied and been accepted to Wharton's Master's in Business Administration program, continuing the family tradition at Penn. Starting in the fall, he took courses in the mornings and worked at the Yoh Company headquarters across town in the afternoons. "I started at Wharton, and then I had a half-time job with Yoh in marketing. I needed the money, and it allowed me to do some real work on how we handled customer information. I felt like I was being useful because I was studying marketing and could apply some of what I was learning right away." Spike's desire to always be adding value was showing itself. He was living with his mother in Wynnewood but also rented an air-conditioning-less apartment near Penn for the month leading up to exams. Given his coursework, his work schedule, and Mary being down in Durham, Spike didn't do much other than go to school, go to work, and study. His work ethic was again shining through.

But he was also ready to commit his life to Mary, so he purchased an engagement ring early in the fall. He picked an October weekend to drive to Duke to propose, and asked Bill Lee, who was attending Law School at Penn, to join him. Bill remembers the occasion well:

> Spike asked me to drive down with him. He said, "I've written a poem." He handed me the poem to read it, and it was beautiful. It never occurred to me that he could write anything quite so sentimental and emotional. It ended with "Will you marry me?" My first reaction was, "What if she says no?" It absolutely stunned him. That never occurred to him. He actually had nothing to say for a couple of seconds, and then he said, "I think she's going to say yes."

The poem and his reaction showed two important, now constant aspects of Spike's makeup: how much self-confidence he had developed and how sentimental he was becoming. Later in life, many of us, particularly his daughters-in-law, will talk about what a sap he can be.

Spike picked Saturday, October 10, 1958, as the day to ask Mary to marry him. He has always had a thing for number combinations, and "10/10" felt right. He was born on "12/12" and Mary on "2/2." So to him, "10" was the missing ingredient. As Spike remembers, "Bill and I got down there Friday afternoon and we all went out. The next morning before the football game, Mary and I went out to the Eno River." The Eno River is a short drive northwest from campus and was a popular location for both group parties and romantic sneakaways. The weather was ideal—bright sunshine, 75 degrees, light breeze—a perfect fall day in North Carolina. "Mary wore a long skirt," Spike says. "She always wore a long skirt." He spread out a blanket, asked Mary to sit down, and with his heart pounding, read the poem. He produced the ring from his pocket and she said yes. After some time for hugging and kissing (*only* hugging and kissing), Spike reports, "We all went to the football game and that night went to Johnny's to celebrate." Johnny's was a supper club in Raleigh. He remembers returning Mary to her dorm long after curfew. "We had to call in and say that she'd gotten engaged. Of course they forgave her."

Spike points to that moment as a time when "her life turned around and mine turned around. Stability-wise, it's all we could care about, each other and going forward and what we wanted to do. It was decided."

• • • •

Spike returned to Philadelphia after the weekend to continue his graduate studies and work duties. He remembers that even as a recent college graduate, "I wanted to be head of the Yoh Company. I guess I had wanted to do that since I was a little kid." It's interesting to note that he wanted this role, given his at-best ambivalence toward his father. He wouldn't consider Penn as a college because of him but was interested in following in his footsteps after school. Perhaps it was to show that he could do it better than his old man, or that he was a natural-born leader and running his namesake company was his preferred way of flexing this muscle. Spike understood that working at Yoh would mean working with and for his father, but he was buoyed by no longer having the "fear factor" he had felt as a boy. He also took solace in the fact that his father wasn't around all the time. "Dad and Esther took these long, three-month trips all over the world." So even though he worked in his father's company, the two weren't interacting on a routine basis.

Spike and Mary planned their wedding for June 20, 1959, just a week after Mary was to graduate from Duke. Spike recalls his father's one contribution to the whole process. "Six months before the wedding, he had a party, and the pretense was to introduce Mary and me. But it was really for him. It wasn't a party for us." Whether or not this account is true, it shows Spike's suspicion and ill will where his father was concerned. Spike's sense of the gesture as self-serving, however, seems more reasonable when one considers that

Harold did not fund the rehearsal dinner, a customary parents-of-the-groom responsibility.

At Mary's graduation, Spike joined her mother Marjorie and her brother Paul for the ceremony. Spike remembers, "Her mother was very proud of her." Fittingly, the main memory of the weekend for teenaged Paul was Spike's new car. "I just remember that black Chevy with the ragtop and the red seats. It was hot!"

Spike's bachelor party, on the heels of the mother-of-the-bride-funded rehearsal dinner the night before the wedding, started at Katharine's house on Loves Lane. In attendance were friends from Haverford, Longport, and Duke. Harold and Uncle Court both stopped by for a drink before the boys headed into Philadelphia for the evening. Spike recalls that the pre-party led to "one guy in the bathtub who never made it out." The group visited a few bars in town, and other than a brief run-in with the police when the gang was being a bit overly boisterous between destinations, the event was relatively innocent. They all made it back to Katharine's, where the bathtub sleeper was still asleep.

Mary's mother planned and funded the entire wedding—yet another tremendous accomplishment for the single-mother secretary who was, undoubtedly, a role model of fortitude for young Mary. The ceremony was at Trinity Episcopal Church in Wilmington, Delaware, followed by a reception at DuPont Country Club. This is the same venue where Spike's oldest grandson Ryan would celebrate his marriage to his wife Ashley fifty-two years later. Spike describes the wedding as "not over the top, but better than standard." Mary's maid of honor was Susie Thomas, her roommate throughout Duke and the woman responsible for the "Clyde is on the phone" comment two years earlier. Also in her wedding party were Charlotte Rode, her best friend from Tower Hill, and Brooke Bryan, also from Tower Hill. While Mary and Charlotte remained close into early adulthood, Mary had few lasting high school or college friendships, much in juxtaposition to Spike's meaningful group of buddies. Not until a few years into their marriage when the couple settled outside Philadelphia did Mary start to forge close friendships of her own.

Spike's sister Barbara was a bridesmaid as well. Barbara recalls that Mary "seemed very nice. She was a redhead. She was a Dukie." That's a pretty accurate and succinct description of her future sister-in-law. After graduating from boarding school in 1957, Barbara attended Endicott Junior College, north of Boston. She received her associate's degree shortly before her brother's wedding. In 1988, Endicott dropped its "junior college" designation and began awarding bachelor's degrees. After Endicott, Barbara recalls that "Spike wanted me to go to Duke. But because I had gone to boarding school for five years and then to Endicott for two, I wasn't going to live my life by school bells anymore." Barbara would, however, later see two of her daughters earn degrees from Duke. This memory of the sibling exchange concerning Barbara's future shows that even though the siblings may not have valued the same pursuits, Spike was still focusing on what he thought was best for "Baby Sis."

As his best man, Spike chose Bob Lynch, his summer buddy from Longport. Bob says, "I really liked Mary very much from the beginning. She was outgoing and very friendly." It may have seemed a bit odd that Spike would choose Bob as his best man, rather than an Ollie Brother. As Bob recalls, "I was very flattered, quite honestly. I sometimes think that he was very close to Darryl [Copeland], but Darryl was one of the Ollie Brothers, and if he asked Darryl to be his best man, then the other ones would be hurt." Barbara agreed. "I don't know about that decision, except if you choose one Ollie, you have to choose them all." Joining Bob in Spike's wedding party were Darryl as well as fellow Ollie Brothers Zook Mosrie and Bill Lee, cousin Peter Schenck from Chicago, and Haverford classmate Jim Hughes. Ollie Brother Rob Townsend was in basic training with the army at Fort Knox and unable to attend. Spike's half siblings, Robert, Teddy, and Marianne, were still young and did not have roles in the ceremony.

On the morning of the wedding, Bob was responsible for driving to Katharine's house to collect the groom. Unfortunately, he was late. As Spike recalls, "It was a two o'clock wedding, and all the ushers left and I was waiting for Bob. I was in the house by myself. He was supposed to pick me up at like eleven. It was a little after noon, maybe twelve fifteen, before he showed up. Of course, I'm panicked. There is nobody in the house but me, and there were no cell phones." Bob admits to being tardy but that the timing was a bit different. "I wasn't *that* late, but I was late, and he was mad as hell. To him, two minutes is late." Anyone who knows Spike knows how important—seemingly life-or-death important—it is to be on time. Regardless of how late Bob was, the reason was that he had gone to see his priest. It had not occurred to Bob until then that there might be an issue with him, a practicing Catholic, being the best man in an Episcopal wedding. As one may expect, particularly in the 1950s, Bob's priest had real problems with Bob's playing that role. Fortunately for everyone, Bob was undaunted by his priest's foreboding remarks and soldiered on.

Once they arrived in Wilmington, Spike happily recalls, "The wedding went off perfectly. It was just really pretty. Mary looked beautiful. Her brother brought her down the aisle." Mary's dress covered her shoulders and blossomed at her thin waistline into a satin bow in the back and a beautiful train. Her long arms dove into short, white gloves that held a bouquet of white roses and baby's breath. At the reception, Bob delivered the best man speech. "All I remember saying was that I've known Spike a long time and that he's the greatest guy in the world. I think he deserves the best, and since I met Mary, I realized that he got the best." Well done, Mr. Lynch.

For the first time, Mr. & Mrs. H. L. "Spike" Yoh, Jr.

Spike and Mary honeymooned at the Elbow Beach Club in Bermuda, a popular destination. They had a wonderful time socializing with more than one hundred other newlywed couples and remained friendly with a few of them afterward. On the night of their return, Spike and Mary stopped by her mother's to collect their wedding gifts and then drove to his father's house. Unfortunately, Spike stepped in a pothole in the driveway and broke his ankle. After a late-night trip to the emergency room, Spike's right leg was casted. The injury would not have been much more than a nuisance except that the happy couple was departing the next day for California where Spike would work in the Yoh Company's Los Angeles office between Wharton semesters. Yet even with a cast on his right leg, Spike was at the wheel for most of the trip to California. His insistence on doing so much driving may have been "Exhibit A" of the stubbornness and control-freak-ness to which we children are accustomed.

That summer, the newlyweds rented a one-room apartment in Hollywood, complete with a Murphy bed in the wall. Spike recalls the eye-opening impression he got of his father's West Coast operation. "Here I am out there trying to get some kind of semblance of the place and learn what's going on, and the guy in charge was ripping off everything. It was terrible [and this was after Mimi's brother had previously usurped much of Yoh's California business]. The office was a complete mess and in shambles. They were just having one hell of a party." Spike soaked all of this in and informed Harold, but his report evoked surprisingly little reaction in the president and owner of the company.

Upon their return from California, Spike and Mary moved into the first floor of a duplex on City Line Avenue in Philadelphia, the building owned by two sisters who lived on the second floor. Spike continued commuting to Wharton and to the Yoh Company, while Mary worked in a child guidance clinic at Lankenau Hospital just down the road from where they lived. Pivoting from a promising career at DuPont to one in healthcare again showed her high aptitude and capabilities. Spike remembers the blissful nature of their first year together. "We never had a problem. We never argued, never. I cannot even think of one thing. Mary was so tolerant." Perhaps this "Mary was so tolerant" line is most telling as to why they never fought early on. He recalls that they "didn't have any money, but we ended up having a great Christmas present to give to our parents. Mary was pregnant." This was December of 1959. Unfortunately, Mary had a miscarriage a few days later.

Spike recalls how his mother and his new bride interacted that first year. "Mother loved advising Mary on how to be a lady. Mother often wore white gloves and explained to Mary when and where to do so. With Mary's mom down in Wilmington working so much, I think Katharine liked the chance to mentor her." Mary took to her mother-in-law's tutelage and started to acclimate to the nuanced characteristics of her husband's Main Line upbringing, as well as to enjoy her new social milieu.

• • • •

After their first year of marriage, Spike completed his Wharton MBA with a major in marketing, and the couple headed back to California. This time, it was not a summer trip but a relocation. Spike had a sense he didn't want to settle down in Philadelphia just yet. "I had grown up there and it was too close. I wouldn't be on my own." He recalls his father saying, "Why don't you go out to California and work in the office out there?" Although his motive is unclear, the suggestion could indicate that Harold had faith that his son could clean up the mess in Los Angeles he had uncovered the summer before.

Unbeknownst to Spike, when he reported for work in Los Angeles, Harold had big plans for his firstborn. "I got there in the middle of the week as a member of the corporate staff. I said hello and all that stuff. On the following Monday morning at six o'clock California time, nine o'clock Philadelphia time, the old man calls me at home right before I left for the office and tells me that my education is over and it's time to go to work. He said to go in, fire the manager, and take over." So in the summer of 1960, at twenty-three years old and less than a week into his post-schooling career, Spike was vice president and Western Region manager of Yoh, his first time as the leader of an operation.

After a quick assessment of the soon-to-be-former office manager, Spike decided it was best not to fire him, but to move him back into the sales role he previously held and in which he had done well. Even at his young age, Spike's keen intuition led him to the conclusion—frequently seen in business—that the best salespeople don't always translate into the best managers. But as often happens in such situations, the manager could not navigate the demotion and soon left the company. As I've observed in my own career, it can be hard to "put the toothpaste back in the tube."

Consistent with his observations from the previous summer, Spike found the Los Angeles operation to be inefficient, with only seven billable contract employees (those who work at customer locations and account for Yoh's revenue) and seven staff members (those who work in a Yoh office and are responsible for selling our services and recruiting the contract employees. They are not billable). Typical ratios for successful offices in the staffing industry are ten-to-one, yet the West Coast branch amounted to one-to-one. Spike recalls his first major conclusion. "Sales were what we needed. We had people in the office that really weren't the best. Everybody had been there a while and they'd gotten used to it. We were not digging in and not feeling part of what needed to be done in the field. Furthermore, personnel files were not properly coded. We were not doing things well." In addition to spending most of his weekdays drumming up new business, Spike "would go in on evenings and weekends to help find candidates to fill our openings." Just six weeks into his tenure as manager, Spike got an important boost:

> I thought some of my training [in marketing] was paying off. I started to tell the folks in the office that they had to make more sales calls. Instead of just making one-for-one replacements of our contractors when their assignments ended, we had to go on a lot of new sales visits to grow the business. One quick result was that we discovered a big project at Raytheon up in Santa Barbara, which we won. That gave us forty or fifty more people and provided some instant stability.

Adding that many billable employees to the paltry seven contractors that were in place gave the office immediate solvency, as well as Spike some instant credibility.

After one year in California and despite additional customer wins and Spike's tireless efforts to turn the office around, Harold sent directions from headquarters to "close it down." While Spike's father was traveling extensively, he rarely came to Los Angeles. Although he lacked a firsthand impression, he concluded they should close the office based on its lack of profitability, which was determined not solely by its revenue and local costs, but also by the overhead allocation methodology the company used. Yoh had three regions: Eastern, Central, and Western. As Spike and his team grew the West, they were charged with more and more corporate costs—allocated to the regions based on revenue—without benefiting from any additional home office support. "As our volume increased, we became the biggest of the three regions, so our profit and loss statement absorbed a much higher percentage of the overhead. When you looked at the bottom line, almost all of the new business we brought in was offset by higher charges from Philadelphia."

Spike again employed his marketing degree and analytical mindset. "I put some information together that showed client-wise and numbers-wise what we were doing, which we had never done before. Anyhow, once the old man saw it, he said, 'Okay, keep going.'" Spike learned a valuable lesson from this sequence of events, one that he adopted and ultimately passed on to us children: To fully understand an operation, you have to visit the office and interact with the staff and the customers. Using only financial analysis, which can be biased or flawed, as in this case, does not tell a complete story. This combination of analysis and direct observation became a cornerstone of Spike's management style from then on.

Shortly before Spike and Mary had moved to Los Angeles, another Yoh Company employee was transferred there from Philadelphia as well. Armed with only a fourth-grade education, Bill Shand had shown a prowess for hard work and connecting with customers. Bill was older than Spike and quickly became a mentor (finally, a mentor!). In addition to showing Spike the ropes of selling staffing services, Bill was also the first person to demonstrate the importance of being values driven. Core values or beliefs, both professional and personal, would become the guiding light for just about everything Spike went on to do in his life. His interaction with Bill was a key part of the germination of this ethos.

Spike has commented on the lack of consistent business ethics in the industry at the time, a reputation that led to many competitors being referred to derogatively as "job shops":

> In the staffing business, you hear so many crooked things. I mean, the business is essentially buying and selling people — who we call contractors — so it was maybe understandable that reputations could get clouded. Also, there was a lot of cash going back and forth. Sometimes it was fuzzy what was legitimate business practice and what was sneaky. I learned early on that some of our competitors — and customers — could be rather slick.

Spike recognized something different and admirable about Bill:

> He had savvy. He had good morals. He always stood up for what was right. Even when we could get some work doing something one way, Bill would say, "No, we can't do that." He always stuck by the basics. Mary and I would have dinner at his house about once a week. He sort of adopted me during that time and looked after me. I don't know if he and my dad had been in conversation back and forth or not about looking after me. I'll never know, I guess.

We can now add Bill Shand to the short list of mentors in Spike's life — maybe at the top of the list. Some years later, Spike asked Bill to be my godfather. I had several memorable visits with him and his family, most notably during the Los Angeles Olympics in 1984. I also remember his wife Kay's poodle that she named Pita, which stood for "pain in the ass."

As the Western Region grew, Spike and Bill took more and longer sales trips together. Spike recounts one in particular:

> Salt Lake City. We heard that a government agency in Utah was putting out a bid. Shand got on the phone, and it was due the next day, so we get on an airplane, a propeller plane, to fly to Salt Lake and then drive up to the town where it was. We're driving in Utah, almost to where we needed to be, and this car of kids comes racing right in front of us and goes right into a tree. Bill goes over to the kids, and I go to a neighbor's house. This was about one o'clock in the morning, and the police came.

Several hours later, Spike learned that the kids had been badly injured, but they all survived. While they didn't win the job, this trip was an example of how business travel bonds people together, in this case connecting Spike and Bill through their witnessing of a traumatic event. Business trips are rarely as exciting or glamourous as nontravelers suspect them to be, but far more than glamour can be had on the road. Furthermore, this project also showed how Spike and the Los Angeles office expanded their territory well beyond Southern California.

Staying with his belief that growth was the most important thing for the Western Region, Spike and his team continued to win new contracts. Of the aviation business, Spike says, "The B-70 was a big, big program in Los Angeles. North American Aviation was the prime contractor. The big hangars that they had built for airplanes were all filled with drafting boards. The design was unbelievable. You'd walk into this hangar, and you'd see like 1,500 engineers drafting. We had sixty or seventy people in there." But they also fell victim to the perils of being a commercial supplier in an up-and-down business. Spike remembers the contract coming to a screeching halt. "On Friday the 13th the government cancelled it. They sent us a telegram to come get our people and drafting boards out of the hangar on Monday. It was amazing. On Friday the entire hangar was full, and on Monday it was empty." In fact, another contract was also cancelled on that same unlucky day. The office "got hit hard, really set back." The grit and resilience Spike had developed in childhood were being put to the test. And just like it did during his last high school football game, Friday the 13th again showed Spike its ominous effect.

Around the same time, however, a contract from McDonnell Aircraft established the Western Region once and for all as the most formidable of the three divisions of Yoh (despite the recent project cancellations). As Spike explains:

> McDonnell Aircraft was starting a project in St. Louis. We had heard about it through one of our guys in the office who had a strong customer relationship. I called my dad and said, "Potentially we're looking at this big job." He says, "Oh. We're looking at that too back here in Philadelphia, and you're up against the big competition that we know how to deal with." I said, "Well, you haven't been doing very well lately, and I've been doing pretty good. Let me have this one because our guy is inside and he knows this and he knows that." Dad said okay, and we ended up bidding the job out of California. We were one of five vendors to win the contract. The whole thing was résumés, getting résumés in. There was a little dinky St. Louis motel where we set up shop. We worked the hell out of that place.

The McDonnell win was key for the Yoh Company; it peaked at over two hundred Yoh contractors and led to fifteen years of work. Perhaps—only perhaps—Harold was again using an invisible hand to set up his oldest son for success. The contract also showed that Spike was established as a strong salesman and sales leader. He remembers well the key decision maker at McDonnell. "We'd go out with the customer. He was kind of my age, and his name was Joe Albers. He was probably the best I ever had as a relationship with a customer." Joe was a Notre Dame graduate, so Spike and Mary joined Joe and his wife in South Bend when Notre Dame hosted Duke in football. As anyone who follows college sports would imagine, the home team came out on top. Spike went on to develop strong relationships with many other managers at McDonnell as well.

The McDonnell job introduced Spike to his closest, longest-term industry peer. Another of the winning suppliers was a small upstart company, also headquartered in Philadelphia, called Comprehensive Designers, Inc., or CDI. It had been started a few years earlier by Bill Morris, the former treasurer of Yoh, who saw the cash that a successful staffing operation could generate. One of Bill's first hires was a determined Midwesterner named Walt Garrison. Walt was about a decade older than Spike and had been a natural businessman and entrepreneur since childhood. He eventually became a stress engineer, which is at the top of the heap of technical positions in the aviation business. Over time he built a large network of skilled technical contractors and joined CDI, where he soon became the leader. A true captain of industry, by the time Walt transitioned from CEO to Chairman in 2000, CDI was a $1 billion company with over ten thousand employees. CDI and Yoh have been competitors for over half a century.

In his early years at CDI, Walt recalls how formidable the Yoh Company was and how impressive its founder was. "We were enamored with the Yoh reputation. Profound respect. Harold Yoh was the personification of honesty and integrity. They were not a job shop. They were an engineering services company. It was unknown in that day. They were a real quality operation that we were to emulate." This flattering account of Harold and his business is telling, given the mostly unfavorable impressions Spike had expressed to date. It's reassuring to learn that the son's impressions of his father were not universal.

Walt recalls first learning about Spike around the time of the McDonnell contract. "I got to know about him when I heard that they had a twenty-something-year-old Yoh fella running the West Coast. That's the first I heard of Spike." Walt and Spike met at the small St. Louis hotel that CDI was also using as a local office to recruit engineers. Their relationship developed over the years with Walt introducing Spike to the technical staffing industry's preeminent trade association, the National Technical Services Association, and to Young Presidents Organization. In 1972, Spike followed Walt as the president of NTSA, coincidentally thirty-eight years before I would chair NTSA's successor organization, the American Staffing Association. YPO would become the most important organization outside of his company with which Spike Yoh ever associated.

His years running Los Angeles show Spike not only as a natural leader but as a man with an excellent memory. Recalling another customer opportunity, he says:

> We bid this job for Atomics International in Nebraska. It was in the middle of nowhere. They're paying laborers $2.60 per hour. In California they made closer to $10.00 per hour. We got ahold of a local newspaper and saw the local rates. We bid $4.60 per hour. Everybody else was bidding California rates. We were far and away the low bidder, and we made more money on the job.

Spike was now honing his skills of competing and winning in the marketplace. And his leadership sea legs were gaining strength.

• • • •

While Spike's career was taking hold, Mary opted to stay home, focusing on getting them settled into their new city. After engaging professional opportunities during college and as a newlywed, Mary seemed happy to devote herself fully to marriage and homemaking. Shortly after they arrived in Los Angeles, she learned that she was again pregnant. When it came to family planning and how many kids each of them wanted to have, Spike says, "We never talked about it, never planned it." The apartment they had originally rented when they arrived in the summer of 1960 did not allow children, so once Mary began to show her pregnancy, the couple moved to an apartment on the twelfth floor of a high rise in the Park La Brea neighborhood, between Beverly Hills and Hollywood.

The new parents, with Hal at five weeks old

Harold L. Yoh III was born on December 22, 1960. Despite Spike's relationship with his father, he seemed to value his lineage, in this case by bestowing this name on his firstborn. While Harold Sr. went by "Harold," and Harold

Jr. went by "Spike," Harold III would go by "Hal." Anticipating the birth of her first grandchild, Katharine had flown to Los Angeles in mid-December. Unfortunately, the child was late and Katharine had to fly home before Hal arrived. Sensing the value of a mother figure on the scene, Spike surprised Mary by flying out her mother Marjorie on Christmas Eve to spend the holidays and help her daughter adjust to motherhood.

Spike describes Mary as a natural mother from the start. "She was so organized. She had everything under control. I was really very fortunate. It all just flowed." With Spike's busy work schedule, which included many overnight trips and Saturday office stints, Mary had some help at home. Her mother also made several subsequent weeklong visits as well. "I would ask her," says Spike, who always paid for her airfare, "and she would always come." Spike's generosity didn't end with travel assistance. When the young couple's income began to rise, he was quick to start sharing some earnings with his mother-in-law. "Over time, I helped Mary's mother out with gifts here and there. Nothing was asked for. If there was a need, I would fill it, but nothing ostentatious." Spike's parents' visits were less common. During the growing family's time in Los Angeles, his mother Katharine visited "maybe a couple of times." Harold's visits were even less frequent, despite having his son, a new grandson, and a business operation in the area. Spike's recollection was that, "My dad would only come to see us when he was on some other kind of trip."

During the couple's first full summer in Los Angeles, Mary's brother, Paul, lived with them and took summer courses at UCLA. "I remember playing with Hal and doing all kinds of stuff there," Paul says. "It was a great summer. Barbara came out at one point, and we all went to Las Vegas together." I would imagine that having both of their siblings with them brought joy to Mary and Spike.

In the fall of 1962, Mary's mother arrived for another visit to support her daughter, who was in her final trimester of another pregnancy with nearly two-year-old Hal underfoot. Spike remembers that his mother-in-law "got sick while she was there. She wasn't sick before, but she got sick and had a temperature. We went to the doctor, and he said, 'She's got pneumonia and we have to put her in the hospital.' She didn't want to go in the hospital." Further testing revealed a heart condition that needed immediate attention, and a procedure was scheduled for the following day. According to Spike, "That night, we're in her hospital room and she called me to her bedside, away from Mary. She grabbed my hand and said, 'Take good care of my Mary.'" Spike and Mary left the hospital. Marjorie died early the next morning.

Spike received the hospital's call at work. He immediately realized that his unknowing and very-pregnant wife was about to leave the apartment to see her mother before the procedure. As Spike tells it, "I got in the car and drove home at about a hundred miles an hour and took the elevator up to the twelfth floor. I was about to put the key in the door, and the door opens and Mary is leaving to go to the hospital. It was just the hardest thing, having to tell her that her mother had passed." Unfortunately, I can relate to this difficulty, as over the years I have had to inform my wife, Kelly, of the unexpected passing of two of her close relatives and one of mine.

Mary now had neither parent living. This drew the young couple even closer together. When asked how Mary felt, Spike says, "She never said much about it. It just wasn't something you really discussed back then. She had an interesting relationship with her mother. There wasn't necessarily this close mother-daughter thing. Yet her mother was an amazing woman, losing her husband and then everything she did to raise those kids and get them through school." Mary's brother Paul recalls that "it was a sad time. In our relationship, Mary was still kind of the adult. She took care of things. I helped her pack up Mom's stuff and store it. I mean, it was just a shock that for the first time I realized that now my dad's dead, my mom's dead, and I'm kind of an orphan."

Mary dealt with all of this mere weeks before giving birth to the couple's second son, Michael Hulme Yoh, on November 9, 1962. Months before they had decided on the middle name to honor Spike's mother's family. According to Spike, Mike's due date was two days earlier. Given his love of number combinations and of good luck signs, he admits to hoping that Mike would arrive on "11/7."

Spike remembers how he and Mary wanted to learn how to be good parents. This was particularly important to him, given his own experiences as a child. Because Mary's mother was not local and then passed away, and Spike didn't consider his parents strong role models, the young couple read books. The most famous parenting book of the mid-1900s was Dr. Spock's *Common Sense Book of Baby and Child Care*, which espoused a kinder, gentler approach to raising kids. Spike, however, believed differently. "I can remember reading Dr. Spock. He was supposedly going to help me with my kids, but I didn't buy into his philosophy, nor did Mary for the most part. You couldn't spank your kids, you couldn't do this, you couldn't do that." Needless to say, the young couple eschewed much of Spock's advice. That's not to say that Spike was overly physical, but he did not believe that discipline should be played down to the extent that growing conventional wisdom suggested. Just as he was starting to do in his business career, Spike and his bride were acting on their own instincts rather than drawing on their parents' advice or society's popular beliefs.

Given what a natural mother Mary was, Spike was able largely to continue his hard-charging work routine. He does, however, recall one difference. "I didn't have any fear of flying before I had kids. But now we were responsible for someone else. I continued to fly regularly, but it made me nervous." He says that this fear continued until he retired in 1998 and no longer had large numbers of people relying on him and his leadership. I can relate to this, as I, too, became a nervous flyer once I became a father.

The "natural mother": Mary with Hal in Laguna Beach, California in 1962

While Spike and Mary were dealing with some of the growing pains of starting a family and a career, the fall of 1962 was also a time of heightened tension between the United States and the Soviet Union, first involving the failed Bay of Pigs Invasion, and then the Cuban Missile Crisis. Of course President John F. Kennedy was the central figure in these two related events. Spike, twenty-three years old when Kennedy was elected in 1960, remembers that election as a defining moment regarding his political views. "It made me much more conservative." The young man seemed to discover—or maybe clarify—that he was a dyed-in-the-wool Republican: pro-business, an advocate for lower taxes and smaller government, and socially conservative. Despite his lack of support for the president, Spike was shaken—and impressed—by the Cuban Missile Crisis. "That was scary. That was really scary. The Russian threat. We were talking about radiation cellars and food storage. I remember the two [Kennedy] brothers were hand-in-hand on that thing. They pulled that off, I thought, really well." Spike's praise of the Kennedys' performance demonstrates that despite his strong ideological differences with the famous political family, above all he was—and is—a patriot.

Even with two young children, Spike and Mary prioritized their marriage, hiring a local babysitter so they could continue to go on dates, have dinner with other couples, and take a few out-of-town trips together. They grew deeper in love and genuinely enjoyed their one-on-one time. In addition to Mary joining Spike on a few of his business trips, such as going to see Notre Dame beat up on Duke in football, the new parents also staged a few quick getaways to Las Vegas, which since the construction of the Hoover Dam in the 1930s had become a center for gambling and entertainment. Spike recalls, "We loved going to Vegas. We'd either drive the five hours or purchase $29 plane tickets on Hacienda Airlines. We would gamble, and if we won, we would buy clothes, cowboy clothes or something like that. We just had a great time doing that. We must have done that two to three times a year."

They made one bigger trip together as well, one that Spike almost didn't get scheduled before they moved back East. Spike says of himself, "Old Bozo here, I promised Mary before we moved to Los Angeles that we'd go to Hawaii a couple of times. I thought it was like going to Camden from Philadelphia, you know? Little did I know it seemed more like going to Australia." They did take eventually their Hawaiian vacation; Spike recalls visiting three different islands and having "a wonderful time." He remembers one incident from that trip in particular:

> One time Mary was knitting in the back of a bus we were
> on, and there must have been fifteen elderly people on board.
> We were traveling to see a volcano or something. The bus
> driver stopped suddenly and Mary's basket fell over. A whole

bottle of rum fell out and rolled down the bus. Everybody
assumed we were these sweet, innocent honeymooners, and
then here's this noisy bottle rolling down the aisle.

I'm fairly certain that Spike was mostly behind the stashing of the rum among the knitting supplies, although Mary was certainly an accomplice. The Hawaii trip was the first of dozens—if not hundreds—of adventures Spike and Mary would take together over their more-than-fifty-year marriage, a routine that both husband and wife enjoyed.

Spike's Sigma Nu social chairman persona showed itself in Los Angeles as well. Since his boyhood bets on harness races in Van Wert, he has always liked horse racing. His favorite event is the Kentucky Derby. I always remember him telling us how when they lived in California, he would wake up early on Kentucky Derby Saturday and sneak into a neighboring yard in his bathrobe to pluck a few sprigs of mint from the garden. The mint, of course, was to infuse the simple syrup he boiled for that afternoon's race-accompanying mint juleps. Even if it was just he and Mary enjoying the event, race day was not complete without the appropriate libation.

• • • •

After two and a half years in Los Angeles, Spike had turned the Western Region around, making it the largest of the Yoh Company's three territories. Perhaps more important than business success, he and Mary had had two young boys. Both Spike and Mary, however, understood that a change was needed. "What got me was what I perceived as the moral standard out there. It just really bothered me. I remember being blown away that a few of the girls in Bill Shand's daughter's *eighth-grade* class were pregnant. Maybe that was unusual, but it really affected us as new parents." He tells another story about receiving a phone call one night from the wife of one of his salesmen:

She said, "Spike, do you know where he is?" I said, "He was going out to dinner with a customer. I guess he should be coming home soon." She calls me back about an hour later and says, "Don't worry about it. I just found him." It turns out the salesman was fooling around in the backroom of a bar around the corner from his house . . . with the wife's sister.

Regardless of whether or not these were isolated incidents, they made a strong impression on the young East Coasters. "I got to the point where I couldn't wait to get out of there," Spike continues. "While Mary was not as conservative as I was, she was ready to get back East as well. I also felt like the region was in good shape and Bill Shand would make a great leader. I wanted to sink my teeth into more of the company."

Spike and Mary's brief but professionally and personally rewarding time in California came to an end, and during the 1962 holiday season they decided to move back to Philadelphia. The time they spent in Los Angeles provided important time apart from their families and friends. Alone, they really got to know one other, having only each other to rely on. But Spike also established a cadence of long work hours and business travel, and Mary developed an independence as the mother and primary caregiver of their growing family. These emerging dynamics laid the foundation for much of their future. Their time in California cemented a bond and created a partnership between them that would drive their marriage, their family, and their numerous business and volunteer leadership efforts for over half a century. To this day, Spike will advise any young married couple to move away like they did. Again referencing Spike's thematic *Happy Days* mentality, nothing could hold Spike when he held Mary.

Chapter 5

Foundations Laid

In the end I do respond to my own instincts. . . .
You have to, I think, remain true to what you believe in.
—Anna Wintour

As the calendar advanced to 1963, Spike and Mary prepared to move back East. During the years I lived in San Francisco in my early twenties, I heard this phrase—"back East"—a lot. What I found interesting about it was that even native Californians who had never lived on the East Coast still called it "back East." I mean, for them, wasn't it just "East"? But again, I digress.

As Spike reflects on their justifiably labeled move "back," he notes the uncertainty that lay before them, even with returning home. "We didn't have the slightest idea what we were getting involved in. We had two babies. I had a business that I'd been waiting much of my life to put my hands around, but I really didn't understand the magnitude of it all." Despite some uncertainty, Spike reveals feeling invincible as long as Mary was by his side. In one of my favorite comments from this entire biography, he says, "I was looking forward to my business. Mary was here to support me, and we were so much in love we didn't care. Whatever was going to happen was going to happen, and we were going to stand by each other. We were ready to settle back where we knew we were going to live the rest of our lives and make a life for ourselves."

Spike flew to Philadelphia prior to the move to look with a realtor friend of his father for a place to live. "I looked at houses and narrowed it down to a couple of them." After returning to Los Angeles to wrap up his business dealings and take Mary to Hawaii, Spike drove their car across the country by himself, making the trip in "three to four days." Mary and the two boys then flew home—in first class. Splurging for first-class tickets was not at all the norm for Spike. In fact, he and Mary lived a frugal lifestyle for the most part, particularly in their first two to three decades of marriage. Not until much later in life did they became more comfortable spending money more routinely on things like expensive airline tickets. His decision to send his family home in the front of the plane showed that he was willing to splurge if it eased Mary's voyage, although I'm sure he winced at the price tag. Accompanying them on the plane ride was "Bobbo," the family bird, named after their best man Bob Lynch (which was sort of any odd tribute, if you ask me). While both boys apparently slept on the overnight flight, Bobbo made noise most of the way, much to Mary and her fellow high-paying passengers' dismay.

Spike has a clear recollection of meeting his young family at the airport. "They let me drive out to the plane because I had two kids on it. I pulled right up, climbed the stairs when they rolled them up, and there they were in the first row. This is the way the world worked back in those days. You didn't have all this security stuff."

He then took Mary to look at houses. Little did she know, but the day before he had signed the papers on one of them. He took her there first. "Thank God she liked it. I thought she would and that she would support my decision, but I did breathe a small sigh of relief." I am amazed that he had the *chutzpah* to buy the house before she saw it. I don't think that sort of unilateral decision making would fly so well in a new marriage today. Spike and Mary now owned their first home, on Wooded Lane in Villanova. It cost them $35,000.

Spike, Mary and their first two children, spending time with Spike's family shortly after moving back to Pennsylvania

• • • •

Spike was anxious—both in the excited way *and* in the tense way—to sink his teeth into the broader Yoh Company. Upon his return to Philadelphia, he assumed responsibility for all three regions. As to why his father supported the move east and the promotion, Spike says, "I guess things were looking bad back there, and we were looking pretty good out west." But he also comments that his father "never said a good word to me the whole time. Never." Spike doesn't recall his father ever telling him that he loved him. This lack of expressed affection clearly influenced Spike, as it was not until his own children reached adulthood that I remember him routinely hugging or kissing us boys. We always knew he loved us, but he didn't become a "hugger" until later in life.

Initially, the overall business seemed daunting. "I found out that the company wasn't really making any money, so I knew I had my hands full."

Spike assumed responsibility for the Eastern Region, promoted Bill Shand to run the Western Region, and inherited another manager in the Central Region. Regarding the latter manager, Spike says:

> I went to the Central guy, told him what we needed, and then tried to work with him for a couple of months, but he didn't cut it. So eventually I said, "I want you to know there's going to be some changes in your department." The manager responded with, "But I'm the only one in my department." So then I said, "Yes, that's correct."

Spike always had a way of being direct, particularly in a case like this where he had made his expectations clear and allowed several months for performance to improve. As clever—or cruel—as this exchange was, it was only after employing his dual-pronged management style of analysis combined with firsthand observation that Spike removed the manager.

Notwithstanding this anecdote, Spike was growing into quite the "people person," developing a knack for connecting with his subordinates and making them feel empowered. He would sit with his team members and review their financials and customer information, then agree on a list of actions to improve performance. His people knew what was expected of them, and Spike would provide encouraging words. In parallel, these agreements provided Spike with a means of holding his team accountable, enabling them to "do what they say" they would do. This style was a precursor to the motto "We Do What We Say," which Spike would formalize two decades later. Spike expanded this approach beyond only the regional leaders, applying it to every office:

> I'd go out and I'd ask questions based on the data I had. I went to all the branch offices, often without the regional manager to get my own feel for what was going on. The visits were a great opportunity to pump up the staff and tell them how

much all of us in Philadelphia appreciated what they did. I loved interacting with our folks in the field and visiting customers. I'd usually meet with the regional manager before going home. We'd make up a plan and hopefully I liked his plan. After a couple months, if things didn't change, then either the regional head made a change, or I did. That was my job, and everyone in the region was counting on me to do it.

Spike was putting his arms around the business, and his confidence as an evaluator of talent was growing with each trip into the field.

The Yoh Company was by now a division of Day & Zimmermann, which Harold had acquired in 1961 when Spike was in Los Angeles. Spike was not involved in the transaction but recalls that:

Day & Zimmermann was the big kahuna, and my dad and his team were spending all of their time up at 1700 Samson Street [D&Z's headquarters], and I was down in the Yoh offices on Second Street. That was good for me, because none of the old man's people were standing over me. I got to know the corporate Yoh people and got to know what we needed to make the company stronger. Not that I had any great years of expertise to know what I was talking about, but I knew what I wanted and when I wanted it, and I was an impatient type of person.

Clearly, the self-confident leader in Spike was taking form. It seems that Harold recognized the business savvy and the strong motivational skills that Spike possessed and was more than willing to capitalize on them. It's also possible, however, that Harold decided to give Spike freedom so his son could establish himself at Yoh. Despite his mostly negative comments, Spike remembers his father as being fairly cooperative during this period. "I had to get the old man's approval for any changes I wanted to make. While some of them required pretty lengthy conversations, I actually don't remember him ever saying no to me." It appears, yet again, that Harold's treatment of his son may not have been as universally bad as Spike remembers it being.

• • • •

The merger of the Yoh Company with Day & Zimmermann in 1961 was a watershed moment in Yoh family history. Harold had grown the Yoh Company into a formidable, ethical service provider that spanned the country. But as Spike recalls, "Dad always wanted to get into higher-end engineering work." The principal difference between the services that engineering firms provide versus those that staffing firms provide is that engineering companies perform the actual engineering work themselves and are responsible for certifying, or "stamping," the drawings to indicate that the designs are done properly. With staffing services, the company is providing only the people who do the work, and those people work under the customer's direction. The customer is then responsible for certifying the work quality. So a company like Day & Zimmermann could command higher margins and was perceived to be higher in the value chain than a staffing firm like the Yoh Company.

In the late 1890s, a man named Charles Day graduated from the University of Pennsylvania with a degree in electrical engineering. In 1901, Day teamed up with Kern Dodge and formed the engineering consulting firm Dodge & Day, which initially produced Efficiency or "Betterment" Reports. Today we still employ the term "Betterment" to describe the company's offerings. The two men were later joined by Day's Penn classmate John Zimmermann, the three-man team soon winning a subcontract for the construction of the Panama Canal. After designing an elaborate series of eighty-five-foot-tall towers and eight-hundred-foot-long cableways, Dodge & Day set a world record for hauling concrete, quite an accomplishment for such a young company. The year 1911 signaled two important events in the young firm's evolution:

the awarding of a project with the United States Navy—the first in what is now over a century of contracting with the federal government—and Kern Dodge's decision to withdraw from the partnership, a change that spawned the name "Day & Zimmermann," which then had forty employees. As a point of pride—and at times fastidious zeal—the two surnames that comprise the company name are connected by an "&" and not by the word "and," and the name "Zimmermann" has two "n's" on the end. In my twenty-plus years at D&Z, I saw would-be vendors literally lose contracts because they were not attentive enough to spell our name properly.

The Bensalem Bridge construction project in Philadelphia, won in 1916, was suspended one year into its duration when the United States joined World War I. The work resumed at the conclusion of the war, but the customer insisted that D&Z honor its original—now unprofitable—pricing structure. True to its word, the company finished the job, incurring a loss that nearly bankrupted the company, but also establishing integrity as a cornerstone of our culture. Another precedent-setting project around this time was for the Hershey Chocolate Company, one of whose products was bite-sized chocolate treats, individually hand-wrapped in foil. D&Z's engineers invented a machine that could wrap these treats *en masse*. On the front end of the machine, a row of chocolate dollops was squeezed out of a series of small orifices, creating a "kiss" sound. Thus, the Hershey's Kiss was born, named after the sound created by a D&Z-designed mechanism.

In the late 1920s, John Zimmermann left the business and Charles Day retired. After Day passed away shortly thereafter, the company credited him with being "largely responsible for the high position attained by the organization. Through his inspiring leadership, high professional ethics, sound business principles and consistent optimism, a most valuable heritage has been left." The concurrent Great Depression provided yet another precedent. The company's core engineering and construction businesses were hit hard, but its public utility work and expertise in efficiency studies helped the firm survive. The diversity of D&Z's operations—then and now—has buoyed us through many tough economic cycles. Leaning on innovation also allowed the company to endure, an example being a 1930s contract with Safeway in which D&Z designed a large, stand-alone store wherein multiple categories of food and home goods could be purchased, rather than through different street vendors, butchers, bakers, etc. The modern-day "supermarket" was born.

***WWI veterans welcomed home in 1918 in front of
D&Z's Philadelphia headquarters***

On the precipice of WWII, D&Z designed and constructed a one-and-a-half-million-square-foot aluminum reclamation plant in Cressona, Pennsylvania, which was immediately repurposed as a reclamation center for our Allies' damaged ammunition, or ordnance. The company then won a contract to construct an ordnance manufacturing facility in Iowa, taking the project from design to start-up in an astonishing eleven months, after which D&Z assumed operations of the plant. Hence began Day & Zimmermann's long and proud role as a producer of ammunition for the United States Government.

By the middle of the twentieth century, Philadelphia-based Day & Zimmermann had become an undeniable powerhouse, positioned as a national expert in multiple technical markets, spurring Harold Yoh to set his sights on D&Z as an acquisition target. At the time of the merger in 1961, Day & Zimmermann had a healthy balance sheet with almost no debt and a high equity ratio, showing their high net worth relative to their total assets. Harold's initial purchase offer was rejected, but a subsequent proposal was accepted in early November. Despite Day & Zimmermann having four times the revenue and fifty percent more assets than the Yoh Company, Harold was able to fund the entire transaction with borrowed money. The combined entity, over which he became chairman and president, had revenues of $32 million. The purchase document was incredibly simple by today's standards. Harold made D&Z the parent company and Yoh a subsidiary, which is how the businesses still operate today. A profile in the *Philadelphia Inquirer* said, "The affiliation of the two long-established Philadelphia firms creates one of the largest technical organizations in the United States, with a staff of more than 3,300 operating all over the Free World."

Spike notes that the munitions business, specifically the Lone Star Army Ammunition Plant, for which Day & Zimmermann won the operating contract in 1950 as Douglas MacArthur was leading a fourteen-country coalition against communist expansion in Korea, fueled much of the company's profits. Larry Suwak, an engineer who joined Day & Zimmermann a few years after the merger and went on to have a long career at both D&Z and Yoh, concurs. "The big dog on the block had been the Lone Star plant. I remember early on getting a two-week Christmas bonus because of Lone Star."

• • • •

As Spike further immersed himself in the Yoh Company, he saw talent gaps in the organization—a realization that led to two of the most important hires of his career. Still adamant that growth was of paramount importance, Spike sought additional entrepreneurial leaders, and his focus homed in on fellow engineer, fellow Duke Alumnus, and fellow Ollie Brother, Darryl Copeland. Spike and Darryl had discussed Darryl's joining the company a few times before, but nothing had materialized. This time, things were different. Because Harold still retained formal oversight of the Yoh Company, Spike had to get his father's approval. "I mentioned to Dad about hiring Darryl Copeland. This was when Ford Motor Company and Robert McNamara had their Whiz Kids. The old man thought he would have his own Whiz Kids as well." Given Darryl's incredible work ethic and high intelligence (Spike always says Darryl was much smarter than he was), he fit the "Whiz Kid" model. Darryl's wife Shirley remembers, "We were in Baltimore at the time, and Darryl was with Westinghouse and working towards a master's degree at Johns Hopkins. Spike again approached him and convinced him that he was finally ready." In what would become a common occurrence between Spike and Darryl, neither man knew exactly what the consequences of Darryl joining Yoh would be. As Shirley notes, "I remember that Darryl said to Spike, 'How do I know what to do?' Spike said, 'Well I don't know either, but we'll figure it out.'"

When Darryl joined the Yoh Company in 1964, he was named executive vice president. While he was indeed highly intelligent, what truly differentiated Darryl was his willingness to make bold moves and take risks—the exact entrepreneurial profile Spike wanted. Fellow Ollie Brother Bill Lee corroborates, "Darryl was an idea man. He was always going to take on the world, and Spike [who also liked to take risks] was, strangely enough, the guy who harnessed that." Spike recalls Darryl having an almost instant impact in sales. "Darryl came in and we took off. We had great shootouts with CDI in the process." Darryl would go on to work directly for Spike, first at the Yoh Company and then at Day & Zimmermann, for almost thirty years, until heart trouble forced Darryl to retire in 1992 while still in his mid-fifties. His bold moves translated to a bold lifestyle, one in which he traveled extensively for business and lived by Spike's same work hard/play hard philosophy. Sadly Darryl would succumb to further heart trouble in 2013.

Spike, a twenty-seven-year-old Republican, outside the Democratic National Convention in 1964

Darryl's immediate impact on the Yoh Company was so impressive that Spike was confronted with a difficult decision. An existing member of the management team had worked there for a long time, his role similar to Darryl's but his performance half as productive. Spike didn't need both men, and Darryl was clearly the person to keep. "It got to the point where I had to let the other guy go, which was awkward as hell because he'd been there forever. There were like a hundred people on staff who knew him and here he was being let go." But Spike did what was right, making the difficult personnel decision based on what he deemed best for the company.

Another thing on which Darryl and Spike found early alignment was the commitment to ethical business practices. During many of their "shootouts" with Walt Garrison and CDI, both firms were regularly asked by new customers to transfer existing contract employees from other customers to their projects. Honoring such requests was unethical, but many competitors did it, hence the earlier comment about varying levels of professionalism within the staffing industry. Neither Yoh nor CDI leadership subscribed to this approach. Even if it meant sacrificing profit or losing work, both firms refused to pull their contractors from a customer prior to the end of an assignment.

While Spike continued to hone and grow the Yoh Company, he also got his first exposure to Yoh's sister operations in engineering at D&Z. The science and precision of engineering-related activities drew Spike, much as it had he when was in high school and college. "The beauty of engineering is teaching you the sequence of how to get to an end result. There's a process and then an outcome. I love that methodology."

Spike soon discovered a similarity between the operational leaders at Yoh and D&Z, which led to his other important hiring decision. Both groups were unhappy with their financial reporting. Ever since his realization in Los Angeles that the cost allocation methodology conveyed an inaccurate picture of company profits, Spike knew that reporting needed to improve in both logic and speed. As he settled into Philadelphia, word soon spread that he was willing to challenge the entrenched leaders in finance, who had long had his father's ear. Other business leaders began coming to Spike with their own gripes about the financial information made available. Spike was immune to the toadying leaders in accounting. "Every night they would come down and try to get me to go over to Bookbinder's to have a drink. They'd want to tell me what was wrong [with how I was looking at the numbers]. Once they realized I wasn't going to be persuaded, they got ahold of Darryl and tried to do that to him." Eventually, Spike was ready to take action. "I went to the old man and said, 'Look. This is all screwed up. We need better records, and we've got to get information quicker to our offices.'" This lobbying also showed Spike's "field first" mentality; he knew that the field—not corporate headquarters—was the center of gravity in the organization.

Just as he did with hiring Darryl, Harold approved Spike's request, not only authorizing his son to hire a senior financial leader, but increasing Spike's responsibilities in the process. In addition to continuing to run all three regions of the Yoh Company, Spike was now Day & Zimmermann's vice president of administration, in charge of the financial function supporting both D&Z and Yoh. Again, we see Harold recognizing talent in his son, giving him still greater responsibility. Spike attained this prominent role in spite of privately but consistently claiming, "I'm not a good financial person." Finance was an area, unlike sales, management, or leadership, where Spike's self-confidence was not high. As humble as he may be—and as true as his contention might have been—he *did* have an engineering degree from Duke. And he *did* have an MBA from Wharton. He *had* successfully turned around the financial performance of a struggling Western Region that his father had considered closing. Oh, then he *did that same thing again* with the Yoh Company as a whole. Clearly he wasn't *that* weak where finance was concerned.

Spike was confident in his ability to read people, trusting his intuition as to when changes in personnel were necessary. The year was 1969, and the change in personnel brings us to John P. Follman, or "Jack" as he is known. Jack attended West Catholic High School in Philadelphia, where arguably his biggest claim to fame was having his shot blocked on the playground by Wilt Chamberlain. After earning a degree in economics and accounting from Wharton and playing basketball for Penn, Jack embarked on a career in accounting at Price Waterhouse.

Spike and others went through a hiring process and narrowed their field of candidates to two, one of whom was Jack. Jack remembers being impressed by Day & Zimmermann's strong reputation. Of meeting Spike, Jack recalls:

> I was favorably disposed. He was pretty laid back and didn't try to impress me with how smart he was. He knew that something had to be done on the finance side of the business, and he knew that something had to be done to get more cross-fertilization. Harold fostered keeping things separate, not letting other people know what you're doing.

This initial exchange shows two things about Spike: that he was good at connecting with people and making them feel comfortable, and that he was effective at conveying what improvements were needed.

Jack continues, "I asked Spike something early on. I thought maybe their problem was they were out of money. I said, 'What are your cash balances?' He said, 'I don't know.' I said, 'Well, do you have any problems with creditors?' He said, 'No, I don't think so.' It turned out they had plenty of cash, but they didn't know how much." In Spike's defense, he was brand new to his accounting responsibilities. But he knew enough to know he needed an expert he could trust.

Despite Jack's ability to connect with Spike and quickly zero in on the company's problems, Spike notes that the other candidate, a Harvard graduate, was deemed to be someone who would not "rock the boat" with Harold's loyalists. Harold directed Spike to hire this other man as Day & Zimmermann's first-ever controller, responsible for the financial records and financial processing functions of the company. Apparently Harold didn't abide by his son's recommendations *all* of the time.

It was soon apparent, however, that the new controller was not up to the task. He was unable to effectively navigate the waters between Harold's and Spike's teams, nor could he produce financial records that satisfied Spike's thirst for accurate data. After a brief stint, the controller left. Fortunately, Spike had another option. It took him less than two hours to place a company-changing phone call.

Since the D&Z interview process a few months earlier, Jack had been working with a small group of people trying to take a few private companies public. Unfortunately for Jack but fortunately for Spike and for Day & Zimmermann, the market for public offerings was not favorable and their efforts did not materialize. Spike's call came at an ideal time on a Friday afternoon in early 1970. Jack started the following Monday, with the official title of controller, although he was the de facto CFO—a title he would acquire years later—with responsibility for the company's treasury function as well.

Jack was thirty-two, six months younger than Spike. As they would soon discover, Spike and Jack had gotten married on the same day, June 20, 1959. Both couples honeymooned in Bermuda at the same time, though not at the same resort. Even their wives, who became and remained close friends, had similar names, Mary and Mary Pat. Jack would go on to work with Spike for the next twenty-eight years, until Spike retired. Jack continued as Day & Zimmermann's CFO for another three years and still serves as a member of the company's board of advisors. He even wrote a manuscript entitled *Cash and Carry-on*, which was a financial history of D&Z from 1960–2000. His relationship with Day & Zimmermann has spanned forty-seven years, one year longer than I have been alive.

At the time of Jack's hiring, the economy was weak, Lone Star being the main profit engine. Jack quickly surmised, "We knew we couldn't live off the ammunition business forever. People forget about that recession. The Yoh Company was down to four hundred contract people. Four hundred. The whole engineering department was down to a hundred people. We really took some major hits." Jack's initial impressions of the company's financial functions confirmed what Spike had suspected:

> The company was financially obsolete and out of control—a bad combination. We had a bunch of great, long-term people there—great tickers and tackers who kept the back office running day-to-day—but they were not with the times in their thinking. Nobody was on top of our finances on a week-to-week or month-to-month basis.

Furthermore, the long-term incumbent head of the company's financial operations, one of Harold's confidants, was unwilling to share the financial records with Jack, despite the fact that Jack was now in charge. Unlike the previous, short-tenured controller, however, Jack made an immediate impact:

> We basically redid the accounting department. They had no procedures. They really didn't have any way of doing things. They just did it the way they always did it. They hadn't issued financial statements for almost a year. The audit hadn't even been started yet for the previous year. Spike gave me a free hand. We got that all cleaned up in sixty to ninety days. We started issuing financial statements every month.

Darryl Copeland and Jack Follman, both of whom Spike hired in the span of a few years, would become great teammates and executives for Spike, as well as dear friends. Spike's knack for hiring strong people and empowering them to be successful was now fully evident. This leadership style fueled growth, and equally important, enabled Spike to modify his own business practices at a crucial time when his growing family was beginning to draw more attention.

• • • •

While Spike was entrenching himself at work, Mary was running the Wooded Lane house and taking the lead on raising the family. Their only daughter, Karen Bogart Yoh, was born on August 25, 1964. Her middle name was a tribute to Mary's mother's maiden name. Less than two years later, on June 16, 1966, the couple had their fourth child and third son, Jeffrey Milus Yoh, his middle name honoring Mary's own maiden name.

Home life with four kids under six was expectedly hectic. Spike recalls:

> We had a routine. If I was in town, I'd be home for dinner.
> But I hated all the noise and chaos of the morning routine,
> so I typically left the house at six a.m., before they woke
> up. God bless Mary. She took care of everything. She really
> did. I couldn't have done it without her. She was fantastic. I
> would get into work early and get everything done the way
> I wanted it before the day got going.

The house, a modest split-level at the end of a long residential street, was the family home from 1963 to 1971. Hal, the firstborn, remembers loving the neighborhood:

> We'd always play outside because it was a cul de sac. We'd
> play dodgeball and things like that. Kick the can was a big
> game. There were woods back there, too, so we'd always go
> in the woods and run around. I remember, a neighbor and
> I threw rocks at a beehive once. By the way, don't do that.

Hal also remembers Spike bringing home a telescope and teaching his young sons a bit about astronomy, though in hindsight we all know that Dad likely made up much of his conveyed expertise on the spot.

Holidays were memorable times for Yohs. Both Hal and Mike remember Thanksgiving dinners at Merion Golf Club with their grandfather. While the adults had cocktails before the meal, the kids played dice in the corner of the room. During each of our college experiences, each of my siblings and I developed an affinity for a game called "liar's dice." I think we know when this seed was planted.

Around Christmas, Spike would do his best precursor impression of the character we would later come to know as Clark W. Griswold, the Chevy Chase character from the 1989 hit comedy movie *Christmas Vacation.* "Dad would get up there with his staple gun," Hal says, "trying to line the whole house with lights." These days, much to our wives' chagrin, this there's-no-such-thing-as-too-many-Christmas-lights dogma is yet another trait my brothers and I inherited.

Spike, Hal, and Mike all remember Christmas Eve of 1966 especially well. The family had had dinner at Spike's father's house when a huge snowstorm blew in. Spike says:

> We were in this International Harvester Scout [4x4], but we couldn't get up the hill to our house, which was a half mile away. We got out and I held [six-month-old] Jeffrey up above me, going through the snow that was belt high. Mary was following me carrying Karen, and the two older boys were following them.

An older couple who lived next door observed the young family trudging up the street and came over as they arrived home. Spike remembers them saying, "'What you've got to do is put these kids in the bathtub and give them each a shot of warm Seagram's Seven,' which we did." For better or worse, Hal and Mike remember the night as well—the long walk, the piling into the tub . . . and the whiskey shots. Another era for sure.

Family dinner has always been a particularly important event at the Yoh house. Anyone who has ever visited us knows even today what a big deal dinners are. When are we eating? How many people will be here? What are we having? What time are cocktails beforehand? Worst of all: Who's on dishes? This family custom started early on. While most major dinners occurred on weekends, holidays, or birthdays, every night with a large family presented at least some of these dynamics. Even as a young child, Jeff sensed the importance. "I certainly remember the almost command performance it was to be at dinner. I'm not sure if I appreciated it that much back then, but I appreciate it now having my own family together. So it's a little bit of irony that way." Little did anyone know back then how important command performances would become for us later in life. The older kids even remember the meals. As Hal recalls, "Mom cooked meatloaf. I hated meatloaf. But Dad loved meatloaf." Mike adds, "Whenever we got home from school and there were frozen dinners thawing on the counter, we knew Mom and Dad were going out."

One of Jeff's memories from a few years later underscores the lasting impression that dinnertime made. "The story I enjoy the most was when we'd gone to a country fair and watched a chicken get its head cut off. They had to put a barrel on top of the chicken to get it to finally stop moving. We went home and had chicken that night. We weren't allowed to go swimming or have ice cream without finishing our chicken." Ugh.

Dinners were also a time for teaching life skills. As Mike remembers, "At meals, there was a constant focus on manners like elbows on the table. Dad always liked to do the fork thing in the elbows, if he was close enough. Hal and I used to jockey not to sit too close to Dad—out of fork range." Spike and Mary's focus on manners eventually expanded into lists of chores hung on the refrigerator, and then a swear box. Hal recalls how Dad, the engineer, would make charts of the chores, organized by child. "We would earn allowance money and spend it at the toy store." About the swear box, Mike says, "Basically, if anyone cursed, they had to put money in the box. A few times Dad would sit down, throw a dollar in the box, and announce, 'All right, I'm covered for anything that might come up.'" Later in life, my brothers and I would discover that each of us is also a stickler for table manners with our own children. Although to my knowledge, none of us wielded a fork or implemented the swear box, much less preemptively filled it.

The dynamics among the siblings took shape early on. Hal remembers that it was not always fair being the oldest. "Mike and I would always get in fights, and Karen would be the peacekeeper. Or sometimes, she would start it. Mom would always yell at me because it was my fault, or at least that's the way I felt."

Dynamics between Spike and Mary also made a lasting impact on their young children. The kids always saw them as a united front, but when decisions were being made, it was often more one-sided. According to Mike, "Dad usually ran the show. Mom got to talk and was involved in discussions, but it usually ended up that Mom would agree with Dad." On the nights before trips, says Hal, "Dad would be all packed and ready to go, and Mom wouldn't be [nor would the younger kids]. There would be some yelling and sometimes some tears." Hal then adds with a note of sarcasm, "That was always a good way to start a trip." Based on my own experience and those of some of my married male friends, this pre-travel dynamic was far from unique to Spike and Mary.

On some occasions, Spike would employ his anti–Dr. Spock parenting techniques and spank us for wrongdoings. I recall bringing home a couple of Cs in "General Deportment" from school that led to a few swats on my backside. Spike was, however, willing to bend his own rules. According to Hal, "I remember one day I came home and Dad led me into the next room and asked, 'All right. What did you do?' I explained it, and he goes, 'I'm just too tired. How's this? I'll pretend to spank you and you yell. Okay?'" While I have never spanked any of my own children, I can relate to some nights simply being too tired to do the whole "parent discipline" thing.

In addition to the disciplinarian, Spike was also a prankster, just as he had been at Haverford in the 1950s. Mike recalls, "One night I got in bed and was wondering why Dad hadn't come up to say good night. I finally gave up and turned out the lights. I lay down to go to sleep and he comes out from behind my bed and shouts, 'Roar!' It scared the you-know-what out of me." I have a strong feeling that Spike incurred Mary's redheaded wrath later that night.

Remember Bobbo the bird form the cross-country flight? He was a fixture in the Wooded Lane years as well. Apparently the bird could talk, at times repeating what it heard people say. Bear in mind that Mary was the adult at home most of the time. Says Hal, "Allegedly, Mom never cursed, particularly around us. But somehow Bobbo learned how to curse. I think we know where he learned that. And then one time Dad came home and Bobbo asked, 'Daddy want a scotch?'" With his first-class cabin squawking, his sailor's mouth, and his bartender's disposition, Bobbo was one hell of a pet.

The Wooded Lane years were special times for Spike, Mary, and the four kids. All six made close friends that would last beyond the time they were neighbors. As good as life was on Wooded Lane, fate and biology soon intervened. In the fall of 1970, Mary was again pregnant. Yours truly was on the way, and Jeff's five-year reign as the baby of the family would soon come to an end. Given Spike's earlier comment that he and Mary never planned any of their children, I'm guessing I wasn't. Only my cruel older siblings, though, especially my always teasing sister Karen, would ever suggest that I was a "mistake."

A fifth child simply would not fit in the Wooded Lane house, so in the early months of 1971, the family moved from Villanova to a larger home on Woodleave Road in Bryn Mawr, the next town over. I was born on March 30th, 1971, at Bryn Mawr Hospital, continuing our generations-long hospital tradition. Bryn Mawr, with its 19010 zip code, would be my home throughout childhood, and is now the town where my wife and I are raising our own family. We live, in fact, near to where Spike and Barbara spent their final elementary school years after the Booth School relocated.

The Yoh family, now complete, on Woodleave Road

• • • •

As our family grew, Spike continued to interact, albeit infrequently, with his sister and parents. Having graduated from Endicott College shortly before Spike's wedding, Barbara blazed her own trail. "I wanted to be an airline hostess, but Dad and Spike really didn't like that idea." So she ended up at the Philadelphia School of Office Training and became a legal secretary. While living and working in Philadelphia, she met Al Juda, who was studying to become an orthodontist at the University of Pennsylvania's School of Dental

Medicine. The two fell in love and were married in February of 1962. As to the relationship between Spike and her husband, Barbara says, "They got along okay. But they really didn't have much in common. Two very different backgrounds and personalities." Spike had grown into an outgoing, big-personality businessman, while Barbara remained more quiet and reserved. Understandably, she married someone more like her. Also, Al was a sole practitioner, while Spike worked in a senior management position in a large organization. Their lives and interests were quite divergent.

Barbara and Al had the first of three daughters, Leslie, in February of 1963. Al was serving in the air force and was stationed in Japan, where they all lived until 1966. Once they moved back to the Philadelphia area and Al started his own orthodontics practice, the Judas saw little of Spike and Mary. "We were all busy having babies, busy with schools," says Barbara. "We weren't the couples who would have each other over for dinner. We didn't do that kind of thing." However, they would begin a tradition of getting together for major holidays, something the two families continue to do half a century later.

While his sister seemed pleased with the life she established, Spike's mother was faring less well. When Spike and Mary returned from Los Angeles, Katharine was living alone in an apartment building across the street from the Baldwin School in Bryn Mawr. What Spike recalls of his mother during this period is that "she didn't do much at all. She really had nothing." This is a stark contrast to the subsequent marriages, children, business career, and world travels that filled her ex-husband Harold's life.

One thing Katharine did do, however, was resume her efforts to indoctrinate her daughter-in-law to life on the Main Line, introducing Mary to the Devon Horse Show, a ten-day-long, world-renowned competition held annually in May. It is today the oldest and largest outdoor equestrian competition in the country. Mary was such a student of her mother-in-law's social expertise that she would go on to chair the fund-raiser that takes place at the county fair and runs concurrent to the competition. The fund-raiser benefits Bryn Mawr Hospital and, given the importance of the hospital to our family, Mary's dedication seems apt. Spike also recalls that his mother "loved the grandchildren." Hal recalls him and Mike visiting her and spending the night at her apartment.

A few weeks shy of Spike's twenty-ninth birthday in 1965, he and Mary and the three children (Mary was pregnant with Jeff) met Harold and Esther at Merion Golf Club for Thanksgiving dinner. Spike recalls the club manager coming to the table to tell him he had a phone call. His cousin Carol, Katharine's sister's daughter, was on the line. As Spike tells it, "She said, 'Your mother hasn't shown up for dinner, and I think you ought to go check on her.' I excused myself from the table and made the short drive to her apartment. She didn't answer, and I was now really starting to worry, so I kicked the door in. She was in the bathtub, motionless at the bottom of the water." His mother was dead.

He immediately called Harold at Merion and then called the police. It's surprising but also comforting that in his time of need, Spike reached out to his father. Katharine's death certificate lists the cause of death as "acute alcoholism." She died from drink, just as two of her three siblings would. Spike's sister Barbara was still living in Japan at the time and did not find out until the next day. Sympathetically, she assumes the experience for Spike must have been "very traumatic."

Despite the piercing clarity with which Spike remembers finding his mother, of the funeral he says, "I don't remember a thing." He does know that the service was at All Saints Episcopal Church in Wynnewood, near where Katharine had lived for so many years on Loves Lane. Given the somewhat perfunctory nature of their relationship, Spike believes that her being gone didn't impact him much. "We had a good relationship, but not deep. It was more of a friendship than anything."

Shortly after Katharine passed away, Spike would again see his father divorce his wife and take a new bride, his fourth and final. Harold's three younger children—Robert, Teddy, and Marianne, whom he had had with Mimi—were now teenagers. Esther had done a good job raising her stepchildren, but Harold had been introduced to Mary Catherine "Kitty" O'Hey, who had been previously married as well. Spike recalls the night he and Mary went out to dinner with Harold, but not Esther, just after Spike and Harold had returned from Van Wert to settle up some of the family's Ohio affairs. "We were seated downstairs," Spike remembers, "and the next thing I know, he's gone for a while. I went upstairs and found him sitting at a table. Kitty was there along with another couple. That's the first time I met her, and they were together from then on."

Harold soon divorced Esther to marry Kitty, who was blonde, attractive, and younger. Spike had grown to like Esther, respecting her for stepping in and raising the children like she did. When Harold told Esther they were through, she was in disbelief. As Spike recalls, "She couldn't believe the old man was going to divorce her, so he asked me to go over and explain it to her, which I did. And then she said, 'Oh, he's serious?' And I said, 'Yes he is.'" Spike, in his late twenties with a wife and family of his own—not to mention having recently dealt with his own mother's death—had to explain to his second stepmother that his father was divorcing her. This sequence of events is one of the more poignant ingredients of the gloomy impression Spike has of his father. Yet again, Spike's resilience was being both tested and built.

• • • •

As his family and work responsibilities grew, Spike recalls how his priorities and time management changed. "I was working long hours. I traveled a lot. I spent a ton of time on the road, right through the 1970s. I was missing most of my older kids' sporting events, and looking back, that was crazy." Mary would occasionally travel with Spike on business, but more often she attempted to pin him down for important activities with the kids. Spike remembers her saying, "You have to be here for this. You have to be here for that." He then learned how to take advantage of being in charge at work. "It was just a matter of getting the family things on my calendar. As the boss, I could then work my schedule around what I wanted to do without really losing a beat. I still traveled a lot, but I was smarter about when I did it."

The Yoh and Juda cousins with their grandfather and his fourth wife, Kitty

Beyond scheduling improvements and starting to attend more of his young family's activities, Spike also started giving back to his communities. "I saw how much these various organizations were doing for our family, and I wanted to start helping out." He first decided to join Mike, who was ten, at his Boy Scouts meetings. Spike was immediately drawn to scouting and the life skills and experiences it afforded young people. While all of us participated in Boy Scouts and Girls Scouts, Mike and Jeff both achieved the rank of Eagle Scout, which is one of the strongest extracurricular accomplishments, even today, that a young person can achieve.

Within months of joining Mike at his meetings, Spike had displayed both his leadership prowess and his penchant for assessing talent and found himself appointed the head volunteer of the local troop. He accepted the position only under the condition that the troop replace the scoutmaster, whose performance was weak, but about whom no one else had bothered to comment. Before long, Spike would be running the whole Philadelphia sector. Later he would hold several regional and national roles as well. His affiliation with scouting would last more than forty years, earning him awards and formal recognition at the local, regional, and national levels—a rare feat for a scouting volunteer.

Spike's realization that he had to carve out more time for his family and community coincided with an acknowledgment that his business would be more successful if he shared more of his responsibilities. Both of these recognitions led to a change in leadership style.

> Delegating allowed the people who had talent to do a better job without me hanging over their head. In the beginning I was a detail guy. I was in everybody's business and I didn't think anything of it. Then I realized that if you have the best people, let them do their job. If they tell you they're going to do something, make a note, and then when they do it, say, "Congratulations." It was an interesting process, and I think my direct reports enjoyed it. When we would all say, "This is what we're going to do," I left the room and it was their job to do it. I would follow up and provide support as needed.

Spike would never completely shed his thirst for minutiae, but this point in his career signaled a deliberate attempt to limit his control of the workplace. He further elaborates on how to coordinate everyone's efforts. "You use the people you have and take advantage of their best assets and position them in the right spots. That's the kicker. You've got to make a team. You've got to make a team that's coordinated and likes each other, and then it works."

• • • •

In the late 1960s, the Jersey Shore would again surface as an important place for Spike. A few summers after returning from California, Spike rented a house for his young family in Longport, where he had spent so many summers with his mother. But his good friend and best man, Bob Lynch, told Spike, "'You've got to try Avalon. It's like what Longport used to be, except it's modern and cleaner.'" Spike took Bob's advice and rented a house in Avalon for a month. Fast-forwarding two years to 1968, Spike and Mary purchased a beachfront lot, built a six-bedroom house, and furnished it. They did all of this for $90,000, the inheritance Spike received when his mother passed away. Those who know current-day property values and construction costs at the Jersey Shore will surely gawk at this level of required investment.

During construction, Spike and Mary met a doctor from Delaware named Church Franklin and his wife Mary, who owned the house across the street. The Franklins and Yohs would become lifelong friends, raising their families together during the summers. We still refer to them as Uncle Church and Aunt Mary. While the Franklins are our closest friends on the block, many other couples socialize regularly during the summer season as well.

Mary and Spike's first Avalon house, constructed in 1968

One custom that many homeowners at the Shore follow is naming their houses. Mary and Spike decided to do this in the 1980s, selecting "Sea Dunes," given the property's beachfront location. When the letters were laid out on the sidewalk, Hal and Mike decided to rearrange them. Fortunately, Spike noticed what they were doing before "Nude Ass" could be nailed to the side of the house for all to see.

In 1990, Spike and Mary decided to build a new home on their Avalon lot, so they sold the original house . . . for $1.00. Of course this is an unthinkable price, but it was because the new owner was going to move the house off the property, enabling Spike to avoid the demolition and clean-up fees. Like a scene right out of a Monty Python movie, a work crew came on site, inserted a giant steel I-beam under the home (shore houses are built on cinderblock walls to guard against flooding), hooked the structure to an ancient-looking tractor trailer cab, and towed it to another lot eight blocks away, where it still stands. Spike and Mary then constructed a larger, three-story home on their beachfront lot, completed the following year. That home was substantially modernized in 2011 and remains a busy summer thoroughfare for family and friends.

● ● ● ●

In the ensuing years, Spike settled into a real groove both personally and professionally. He entrenched himself more and more in the activities of both Yoh and Day & Zimmermann, while he and Mary continued to raise their children in Bryn Mawr and Avalon.

Spike's working relationship with his father never improved. According to Spike, "I don't think he had too much to do that was right. I would typically do the opposite of what he did in treating people. It seemed to me that if he liked you, he would go along with anything you said, even though it might be wrong. It seemed kind of crazy." Others had a similar, albeit toned-down impression of Harold. Mary Pat Follman, Jack's wife, recollects the first time she met Spike's father. "I said, 'Oh, that man is really tough.' I was scared to death of him." Maybe predictably, given Spike's determination to be unlike his father, this is the opposite first impression that Spike Yoh makes on nearly everyone he meets.

While Harold would leave a poor impression on some, his reputation with others was not as dismal. Recall Walt Garrison referring to Harold as "the personification of honesty and integrity." After being pressed about his father in our interviews, Spike did concede that "he had to do something right, I guess. I've thought about this a lot. I don't know." Further evidence of Harold's good qualities is a thoughtful introduction he penned for a commemorative book written in 1966 entitled *Sixty Five Years with the Men of Day & Zimmermann*. Harold says, "We are the fortunate offspring of a spiral of success . . . I am very proud of Day & Zimmermann and the men who make it go . . . My associates and I shall continue to respect the strength and courage of the men who founded the company. Like our forebears, we shall move forward to new ideas, new horizons." A likely observation involves the references to "men," which seems limited through today's emphasis on gender equality in the workplace. Ironically, two of the nineteen executives pictured early in the book are female.

Despite their rocky relationship, Harold and his son, along with their respective teams, oversaw strong growth in the business. Leading the way was the munitions industry, which was booming as a result of the United States' increasing involvement in Vietnam. According to Jack Follman, "The ammunition business was dominating in terms of cash flows and profits. We had thirteen thousand people working at Lone Star, seven days a week, three shifts per day." In 1970, Day & Zimmermann expanded its munitions footprint, securing the operating contract for the Kansas Army Ammunition Plant in southeastern Kansas. Lone Star and Kansas remain key parts of Day & Zimmermann's portfolio today.

Harold and Spike at a 1960s business function

Munitions was far from the only successful part of the business. In 1971, Day & Zimmermann secured a large valuation project to assess the assets of the recently bankrupted Penn Central Railroad. This huge effort involved 320,000 acres of land, 20,000 bridges and 150,000 rail cars. The total valuation of the railroad's assets was over $2 billion. The Yoh Company continued to grow its aviation business, which had expanded into aerospace after President Kennedy's 1961 declaration that America would put a man on the moon by the end of the decade. One of the Yoh Company's largest contracts at the time was for Lockheed, and it dedicated the majority of its Second Street headquarters to the project. Day & Zimmermann and the Yoh Company continued to interact more, consistent with Spike's strategy of cross-fertilization. One relevant project involved a massive modernization project for the United States Postal Service in the early 1970s. D&Z oversaw the project for the USPS's northeast region, while the Yoh Company provided more than 250 technical personnel nationwide to bolster the effort.

As a result of Spike's growth philosophy, the company started making acquisitions. The largest of these was the mass land appraisal company Cole-Layer-Trumble, or CLT, in 1975. CLT had pioneered a computer-assisted technology that could appraise large municipalities for tax assessment purposes. The Yoh Company provided people to the land appraisal industry as well, and the combined entity was the largest firm in its market in the country. Darryl Copeland was instrumental to the deal, spending much of the next several years commuting weekly to CLT's headquarters in Dayton, Ohio. Darryl, an avid golfer, allegedly enjoyed the carpet of his office there, which was cut in the shape of a putting green with a mock hole that afforded practice time while working.

• • • •

Spike's early years in Philadelphia were a time of growth and early success. He and Mary completed their family, and Spike became better at balancing his work and home obligations. He brought changes to the management team of both Day & Zimmermann and Yoh, and fostered the first efforts of meaningful, lucrative collaboration between the two entities.

As the calendar approached 1976, the nation's bicentennial year, Spike decided it was time to revolutionize his professional life. He committed to a course of action to buy the company from his father. He accomplished this by forging his fellow executives into a buyout group that then became a committed team of entrepreneurs, destined to lead Day & Zimmermann to unprecedented growth and success.

His cheerful philosophy on life now in practice, Spike recalls, "I really went with the flow. I was an upbeat guy. I still am. Every day's a good day. I never felt pessimistic about anything. If something's wrong, it's my fault and I've got to fix it. There's nothing that can't be fixed."

Chapter 6

Coming Into Form

Do not go where the path may lead.
Go instead where there is no path and leave a trail.
—*Ralph Waldo Emerson*

Coming out of the early 1970s recession, Day & Zimmermann experienced strong growth, with total revenues at the end of 1975 of $126 million. While Spike continued to ramp up his commitment to the business, his father was ramping his down. As Jack Follman observed in *Cash and Carry-on*, "Spike realized that his father's heart was no longer in the business, and he was only interested in maintaining his lifestyle." More recently, Jack recalls his and Spike's alignment on the path forward, "I thought we were on the same page. We had to do something to change the mentality of the company. To do that, Spike came up with the solution that he had to buy his father out."

As it turns out, Harold was interested in selling the business, but not necessarily to his son. Spike recalls how in 1975, a broker came into the office to discuss a potential buyer for Day & Zimmermann. There were two firms interested in the company. Not surprisingly, given the strong performance of the munitions plants, both were in the defense industry. The broker first met with Spike and asked him about Day & Zimmermann's interest in being acquired. Because Harold still retained 100% of the stock—never having transferred any to his son or management team—Spike said to his visitor, "I'm not the right person to ask. Go upstairs and talk to my dad. By the way, tell him also that I'd like to buy it." The fact that it took a third-party liaison to trigger this conversation illustrates the distance that existed between father and son, even though they bore the same name and—ostensibly—worked together. Spike recalls that only twenty minutes later, the broker came back to his office and relayed, "Your dad said to put a proposal together." Spike then went to see his father and learned that Harold was, in fact, ready to sell.

Harold presiding over a management meeting late in his career, with
Spike seated front right

Spike now had an official expression of interest from his father. The first step was taken. But there were still three major hurdles to overcome: Spike would need the support of the management team, he would need to borrow several million dollars, and he would have to pay market price for the company. Harold was not interested in facilitating a discounted deal for his son, again illuminating the divide between them.

To clear the first hurdle, Spike began talking with other members of the senior management team. The most important of these was Harry Perks, the vice president of the company and Harold's right-hand man. Spike decided up front that he wanted a 60% stake, so he approached Harry and offered him 40%. Much to Spike's surprise, Harry turned him down, informing Spike that Harold had also told Harry that he could buy the business. Undaunted, Spike approached five other key leaders one by one, offering each a 5% stake. Showing their faith in Spike's leadership, each one signed on. The group included Jack Follman, Hugh McCullough, Bill Moseley, Marvin Nadel, and Frank Vitetta. However, between each of these conversations, Spike returned to Harry to offer him whatever percentage remained. Harry turned him down each time. Finally, between his 60% and the other five men's combined 25%, he went to Harry one final time. As Spike recalls, "I think Harry finally realized what was happening, and he took the 15% that was left." First hurdle cleared.

Per the new shareholders' agreement these executives would sign, each would sell his ownership stake back to the company upon retirement, thereby increasing Spike's control. Darryl Copeland was not one of the initial members of the buyout team but was subsequently granted a 5% stake when one of the initial team members left. When Spike retired over two decades later, only Jack Follman was still working. Per Spike's commitment, Jack was bought out at the same time and at the same share price as Spike, even though Jack continued to work for three more years.

As far as finding a bank that would participate in such a significant transaction, D&Z at the time had no debt and no ongoing banking relationships. What it did have, however, was Harold's position on the board of directors at Continental Bank. Continental was neither large nor well known, but it was a perfect fit for D&Z. The bank's chairman, Roy Perino, and its vice chairman, Jim Morris, were entrepreneurially minded and had populated their board with risk-taking business leaders like the young Spike Yoh they were now getting to know.

According to Jim Lynch, today a well-known banking executive in Philadelphia but at the time an entry-level banker at Continental assigned to the Day & Zimmermann account, D&Z had become a great "lifestyle business" for Harold, meaning that he took a lot of the profits each year to fund his travels, his large homes in Haverford and Palm Beach, and his generally grand way of living. Even after adding these expenses back to the bottom line, Jim recalls, "I did the analysis and concluded, based on the numbers, that we should pass on the transaction." Perino and Morris conceded that Jim's analysis was accurate . . . based on the numbers. Fortunately, however, they decided to move forward in support of Spike and his management team anyway. They were indeed risk takers as well.

Of the transaction, Jack says, "We called it in those days a bootstrap acquisition." This was still about a decade before Michael Milken would popularize the term "leveraged buyout." As Jack explains:

> Basically, you use the company's assets as collateral to buy
> the company. That's pretty much what we did. The problem
> we had was, based on the price we had to pay, we were going
> to end up with negative net worth. In those days in particular,
> if banks and surety companies saw negative net worth, they
> didn't want anything to do with a deal. It became a tough sell.

Fortunately, Continental was willing to take the risk, albeit with expectedly onerous terms for D&Z's new majority owner. Spike had to collateralize all of his personal assets, including his family home on Woodleave Road. When asked about Mary's awareness of or involvement in the negotiations, Spike says, "She knew we had an offer, but she had her hands full at home. She trusted me and I trusted her." However, when it came to pledging all of their assets—including the house—to the bank, Spike adds, "I did clue her in on that one." As would become common practice when business matters or philanthropic efforts were concerned, Mary supported her husband. Second hurdle cleared.

To get over the final hurdle, Harold's sale price, Continental agreed to fund a portion of the purchase amount provided Harold take a note from the company for the balance, which had to be paid in seven years. In a rather awkward series of negotiations, Harold pushed for as high a price as possible, flaunting the potential of one of the outside defense contractor's ability to pay more. But eventually a deal was struck, and the father's business could become the son's. Shortly after the buyout, Jack and Spike established the company's first-ever line of credit, also with Continental. The terms of that arrangement, meaning the interest that D&Z had to pay on any money it borrowed from the bank, were more favorable than the terms they had in place with Harold on his note, so Spike opted to pay off his father ahead of the original seven-year time table. This outcome likely surprised Harold, who—according to Spike—had previously expressed doubts about his son's ability to be successful enough to honor the agreement.

The final piece of the company purchase puzzle was Spike's informing his sister Barbara, who recalls Spike coming over to her house one evening. "It was a short conversation. He said he had just bought the company from Dad and that he had to pay top price. He had to outbid other people. I could tell from the look on his face that he was mad. I thought, what a shame."

In 1976, father and son finalized a stock purchase agreement for the transfer of ownership of Day & Zimmermann. The formal closing was in late August, just days after Harold's sixty-ninth birthday. Harold, the first in his multigenerational family of farmers to attend college, was now a retired millionaire. His son Spike, four months before his fortieth birthday, was now a much-in-debt, but much-destined-for-greatness leader of his own business.

Despite their differences and the animosity that Spike felt for his father, the Yohs were in a win-win situation.

Harold Yoh, a true rags-to-riches story

• • • •

There was no big fanfare around Harold's retirement, nor around Spike assuming the leader role. But there was much work for the new ownership group to accomplish. The economic winds in the late 1970s again turned unfavorable due to rapidly increasing interest rates and high inflation. Despite government attempts at wage and price controls, D&Z's commercial businesses—those not tied directly to government spending—struggled. Complicating this climate was the fact that the company's balance sheet was "upside down" due to the high borrowings and negative net worth situation described above.

Fortunately, however, Spike and his team were up to the dual task of growing the business and putting in more and better controls. Continental Bank stayed by the young management team's side with much-needed working capital to fund growth, and Spike set to work on forging a high-performing team to guide the business. He recalls how this teamwork philosophy led to new business wins. "Everybody got excited about growing, particularly Darryl and me. From there, things kind of just snowballed." A highlight project during the late 1970s was a fixed-price contract award to design and build ammunition production lines in Taiwan. Given the management team's penchant for taking risk, this became the largest fixed-price contract in the company's history, requiring enormous effort by Jack and the finance group to secure necessary financing.

Spike and his team also ramped up the company's acquisition efforts. A highlight of their deals was the 1977 purchase of MDC Systems Corporation, a business that provided management and oversight of high-profile government and commercial infrastructure projects in the United States and abroad. Almost immediately after the acquisition, MDC won a contract to oversee the construction of a $3 billion pipeline in Saudi Arabia. Clearly, growth and diversification were coming to fruition.

In addition to these advancements, Spike and Jack also instituted several efforts to improve the balance sheet and financial controls of the business. One such move was the divestiture of the company's long-standing line construction business, a service offering to public utility customers. While line construction was once a cornerstone of D&Z's portfolio, this area had struggled to make a profit, and it occupied significant amounts of cash that could otherwise be used to finance growth or pay down debt. With this "prune to grow" strategy, the company got smaller by selling a nonperforming business but was then positioned to grow because its business mix was healthier.

Another challenge facing Spike, Jack, and the management team was bonding their growing list of projects. Performance bonds, which are somewhat like insurance, ensured that D&Z and their customers could recoup their investments on a project if something went grossly awry. Only through Jack's tireless networking and marketing to lenders and surety agents, coupled with Spike's ability to convince these partners that he and his team had the wherewithal to succeed, did the young team secure the bonds necessary for their projects.

Around the time of the buyout, Spike and his team decided to consolidate the Yoh and D&Z Philadelphia offices to one location, 1818 Market Street. This move reduced the company's rent and provided better oversight of operations, as well as facilitated Spike's vision of a more integrated, cross-fertilized company. "1818" would remain Day & Zimmermann's headquarters until 2008.

These many growth tactics and financial controls led, in 1979, to the company's first profitable year since Spike had bought out Harold. By 1980, D&Z's revenues were $162 million, a 29% increase since Spike took over. The debt they incurred to fund the purchase continued to come down as well. The risky, scary, exhilarating late 1970s had passed and the business was again profitable. Spike's leadership style had come into its own. Spike relaxed as a leader, and a calmer, more confident demeanor emerged. He could now shape the culture of the entire company without his father's shadow casting over him. His growth as a leader manifested itself in a newfound humility and level of trust. "I took the attitude that everybody was smarter than me. I didn't care. I didn't want to go challenging anybody on anything until I knew what the hell was going on." This approach made his managers feel empowered, and it gave them freedom to speak their minds more readily. Because they felt more relaxed, Spike's team provided him with more and greater insights without him having to personally dive into the minutiae of each operation.

John O'Connor joined D&Z's MDC Systems in 1980, where he experienced firsthand the latitude and entrepreneurial opportunities Spike afforded. "I learned so much about so many different types of projects in a shorter period of time than I could have ever done. I crammed ten years of experience in that first five years with MDC. It was just a great, great experience." John would go on to work at Day & Zimmermann for almost twenty years. Today he contends that joining D&Z was "easily the most significant thing I did in my career." John's first time meeting Spike, a few days into his tenure at the company, showed how warm and welcoming Spike's style had become. "It was probably six thirty in the morning," John recalls, "and I had a box or two of papers and a big roll of drawings in my arms. I pushed the elevator button, and this guy comes on and says, 'Here, let me give you a hand.' I didn't know who he was. He says, 'Hey, I'm Spike Yoh.' And I say, 'Well, nice to meet you, Spike. I'm John O'Connor.' And that's how I met him." John recalls Spike using this unassuming style all the time. "When he went to a project, and it could have been anywhere across the country, he would walk in and start with the person who was sitting at the reception desk and say, 'I'm Spike Yoh. How are you?'" John says that Spike "never felt compelled to make a big impression or anything of that nature. It's relaxing. He made people around him feel relaxed."

Anthony Bosco joined the company in 1979 as a junior-level auditor on the Saudi Arabia contract. Today, thirty-eight years later, he is a senior executive. He recalls his first interactions with Spike, which were to review the expenses on the large overseas project. "There was a lightheartedness to him, but with very direct questions. He never made you feel intimidated, and he always made you feel like what you were saying was important. He wanted to hear what you had to say. If he didn't understand, he would go at it again, but in a very welcoming way." John Stetson, Spike's aforementioned Haverford classmate and D&Z team member, has a similar impression. "While Spike was very much hands off and worked through his top staff, typically not micromanaging below that level, he was always accessible to anyone that interacted with him." Mike Adelman had joined the Yoh Company in 1978, where he would work for over twenty-six years. He recalls Spike making a similar connection with him in their first meeting only a few weeks after he started. "We did talk about some of the companies that I'd called on. But I had a sense he wanted to learn a little about me personally. It wasn't just a business relationship. He wanted to know who you were. The funny thing about that meeting is that I remember it to this day, almost forty years later. I thought it was great."

Spike's easygoing style and ability to connect with people at all levels served to inspire larger groups of employees as well, as Anthony recalls from his first time hearing Spike give a speech at the annual holiday party. "He had this presence about him that was larger than life, even though he was a regular guy. He made you feel like you were part of something in a very good way. He made it about you, not about him. You felt like he had his arms wrapped around you."

While Spike developed this more relaxed leadership style, his direct management style could still create stress for his managers, particularly as his presence and the size of the business grew. As Spike recalls, "Mary would always tell people, 'Spike doesn't get stressed; he gives it.'" His difficult upbringing may have hardened him to the physical, mental, and emotional havoc that stress can wreak, but that did not insulate others—both at work and at home—from experiencing the tension from knowing that Spike Yoh was counting on you. So there was—and is—a dichotomy in Spike. He can be magnanimous and comforting, but also blunt and pressuring.

Two final trademarks of Spike's leadership style surfaced more noticeably during this period as well. The first was his high level of vigor and cliché "work hard/play hard" philosophy. Shirley Copeland, Darryl's widow, recalls, "Spike always had this excess amount of energy. He was always the last one to bed and the first one up. But he always seemed to have a plan. Even with all of the late nights and everything that went on, you could tell that he always had a plan."

Spike's ever-present pocket tools

Spike's other trademark, as distinctive as the black, thick-rimmed glasses he had worn since childhood, were the small pink notepads he always wrote on with little green golf pencils. Anyone who has spent a decent amount of time with him will recognize these ubiquitous accessories. I've mentioned already how Spike would make lists with his managers then use these to follow up on performance. He further elaborates on his love of lists, both at work and elsewhere. "I started every morning making a list on my notepad, and then I'd see what I had to do and when I had to do it. I'd cross things off as I went along." Spike liked the size of the pads and pencils because they "fit in any pocket I wore." As to why he used pink (the man was certainly no Lilly Pulitzer devotee), "Pink was chosen by the mail room. When they knew that I wanted to have little notes sent out, they thought that pink would get the most attention." The green golf pencils usually said "Merion Golf Club" on them, reminding Spike of his most enjoyable pastime.

● ● ● ●

Spike knew that the success of the business was paramount, for him and for his family. "If the business didn't work, nothing was going to work. During some of those days, family had to come second. The matter of balancing family and business was a tricky one, and it always varied. Mary was my big guidance on that because she knew the lay of the land and what needed to be done at home and with the kids." Mary knew the lay of the family "land" so well because she was tilling it every day— by morning a short-order cook with Cat-in-the-Hat lunch making speed; by day a home-managing, laundry-folding, school-volunteering Energizer Bunny; and by night a dinner-for-seven-preparing, homework-checking, tub-supervising mom, usually still with bandwidth to catch up with Spike when he was in town. Even with Jean Bright helping out a few days per week, the energy Mom put into the family was herculean and constant.

Notwithstanding the demands of work and home, Spike says, "I realized that it was time for me to help my community even more. My role at the company put me in a position to make an impact." Having already embarked on efforts with the Boy Scouts, he now set his sights on the Philadelphia business community. "I felt like Philadelphia needed all the help it could get. It had done so much for so many, including the Yoh family and Day & Zimmermann, and for so many of our employees who lived there." Charlie Pizzi, who held several public and private sector leadership roles in Philadelphia, saw the by-product of these connections firsthand. "Spike was such a major employer in the city. Even though he lived in the suburbs, he always had a deep and abiding love for Philadelphia. He took a very responsible approach to being a corporate citizen. If you asked me to identify what good corporate citizenship looks like, I would say, 'Spike Yoh and Day & Zimmermann.'" Charlie, like many of the other local business and civic leaders with whom Spike worked, remains a close friend to this day.

As with any busy person, time was Spike's most precious asset. He realized that with greater volunteer engagement, finding room in his schedule was crucial. "It became a matter of time allocation and where am I going to take that time from? Most of the things I got involved with early on were city things, which I could do during the day, so it was easy to participate. The more I could contribute and volunteer with local Philadelphia activities, I didn't really lose anything work-wise or home-wise."

Spike learned the key to balancing his rapidly growing list of business and family endeavors. "I kept everything simple. My idea was to enjoy anything and everything I did. There wasn't a day at work that I didn't enjoy, and there wasn't a day at any of the volunteer groups that I didn't enjoy. Because if I didn't enjoy it and I couldn't change it, I'd leave." Many times Spike could—and did—change things so they became better (and therefore, more enjoyable). But this life view also shows how important it was for Spike to have fun in whatever he did, another by-product of his childhood. Even if this "keep things simple/enjoy what you do or leave" philosophy is a bit simplistic or revisionist, his ability to boil tasks down to their essence and to bring joy to all he did enabled him and those around him to be productive, to be engaged, and to derive satisfaction from their joint efforts.

Spike's ensuing multiyear involvement in Philadelphia included a stint as the vice chairman of the Philadelphia Industrial Development Corporation, an economic development organization managed by the City of Philadelphia and the Greater Philadelphia Chamber of Commerce. PIDC's long-time leader Walt D'Alessio recalls working with Spike in the early 1980s, saying how he was "very decisive and focused. He wanted to get to an answer quickly, and if people were slow to come around, he would sort of cajole them into line. He had a big personality and a good sense of humor. It was hard to resist his enthusiasm." The pinnacle of Spike's civic efforts occurred in 1985 when he was named chairman of the board of the GPCC. His commitment to community, along with his passion for commercial growth and engagement, rang loudly in one speech he gave as Chamber chairman. "We must address issues that affect our community as a whole. Without more sales, without growth, and without people working, nothing can function." Spike's becoming chairman coincided with the Chamber hiring a new president, Nick DeBenedictis. Nick's recollections of working for Spike echo those of Spike's D&Z colleagues. "I felt very comfortable. There were no airs about Spike. I always felt I could be straight with him." In 1985, D&Z had grown to a $344 million company, but Spike's down-to-earth style belied his company's stature. As Nick puts it, "I didn't realize how big the company was. Spike was very unassuming." As testament to Spike and D&Z's enduring legacy, my brother Hal later followed in his footsteps as chairman of GPCC as well.

These latest forays into volunteer leadership roles also showed Spike's proclivity for being in charge. He often says, "Don't get involved in any activity you wouldn't want to chair. If you don't feel strongly enough about it to run it and make it better, then it's not worth getting involved." While not everyone has the aptitude or desire to be a leader, Spike certainly did. Many not-for-profit organizations over the course of his life have been fortunate beneficiaries of his experience, passion, and leadership.

● ● ● ●

As Spike's volunteer leadership efforts expanded, so did the pressures he and Mary experienced raising five children. Mary continued to get more and more involved in the kids' schools, most notably chairing the parents associations and major fund-raisers for both Karen's school, Agnes Irwin, and the boys' school, Haverford. Spike got better and better about attending each of the kids' sporting events, as well as Karen's choral performances, an activity she pursued extensively through high school. Around this time, Spike had an epiphany about how he prioritized his time. Both Hal and Spike remember it well. Day & Zimmermann had season tickets to the Flyers, and Spike had invited his oldest two sons to a game. Hal remembers, "We were excited about going, but then a day or two beforehand, Dad said, 'Sorry. I've got to take some clients.' But the day after the game, he said, 'I will never do that again.'" Spike also recalls that incident, with both clarity and guilt.

Despite his regrettable Flyers decision, Spike imbued in all of his kids a love for Philadelphia's sports teams, to which D&Z had a special connection as well. In the early 1970s, the company provided construction management services during the building of Veterans Stadium, the home of the Eagles and Phillies until 2003.

What stands out the most for me were Eagles games. Attending Eagles' home games, which happened only eight Sundays per year, was a true ritual for our family. We would first go to church and Sunday school, after which Dad would usually make a scrambled eggs breakfast. His frugal side would come out, as I remember having only half an English muffin and exactly two strips of bacon per person. Given Spike's lifelong love of Frank Sinatra, the kitchen's AM/FM radio would be tuned to *Sunday with Sinatra*, a weekly program hosted by Sid Marks, a hall-of-fame disc jockey who has been hosting Sinatra programs for sixty years. (Incidentally, our weekends were kicked off with Sid's other weekly show, *Friday with Frank*.) Soon after breakfast, while the fall sun poured through our tall, multipaned kitchen windows, Aunt Barbara and Uncle Al would arrive, my uncle's six-foot-five frame usually covered in Eagles-green plaid pants and coordinating Izod V-neck sweater. Lipton sour cream and onion dip was prepared to bring along with bags of Fritos corn chips. You could bring food to the games in those days, and Spike valued how much cheaper it was to bring at least some of your own. Finally, Bloody Marys would be ritualistically mixed—for adults only, of course. With the family recipe of Gordon's vodka, Mr. & Mrs. T's Bloody Mary mix, horseradish, Tabasco sauce, Worcestershire, black pepper, and a stalk of celery, these Sunday libations were specifically and consistently made the same way, week in and week out, year in and year out.

We would pile into the family van at eleven thirty sharp, and though commutes to and from sporting events may not be memorable for every family, we Yohs—with Spike at the wheel—certainly remember ours. He had a knack for getting us into, and more urgently, out of the stadium parking lot faster than nearly anyone alive. I'm sure we beat the mayor's motorcade on a few occasions, and he had a police escort. On these commutes, I remember lots of lane switching, horn honking, eyes covering (by Mom), and even older sibling summoning. The last of these happened one time after Dad accidentally clipped a guy with his side-view mirror and the situation looked like it might escalate. Spike's first instinct was to call his older boys to the front of the van for backup, but fortunately nothing came of it. While I have never summoned my own sons from the back of the car in such a situation, I have—much to my wife's and our guests' dismay—inherited Spike's maniacal drive to get out of stadium parking lots as quickly as possible. My sisters-in-law all concur that my brothers share this defining characteristic.

As kids, we were fortunate to attend many regular-season games and occasional playoff runs of all of Philadelphia's professional sports franchises, making us "four-for-four" fans. I will always remember seeing Tug McGraw's final pitch in the 1980 World Series, Wilbert Montgomery's forty-two-yard touchdown run against Dallas in the January 1981 NFC Championship Game, and Dr. J.'s windmill dunk against the Lakers in the 1983 NBA Finals. My dad and Day & Zimmermann made each of these moments possible.

When the Phillies won their next World Series in 2008, I was again in the D&Z seats, only this time with one of my own sons, who was eight years old. After the final pitch, I grabbed his small scarf-wrapped face with my glove-covered hands and shouted over the euphoric din of the stadium, "You will remember this moment for the rest of your life!" He gave me back a blank stare. But someday he'll get it.

When weekends were not filled with sports outings, Hal recalls that "Mom and Dad always loved to play bridge, especially with friends. I always remember they'd have people over and play bridge all the time." Entertaining friends, going out to dinner, and periodically taking Mary out of town were ways that Spike invested in his local friendships, as well as created opportunities to connect with his wife, away from the demands of his business and the oft-insatiable demands of five children.

Spike and Mary found time to take their children on trips as well. Jeff painted a pretty good picture of what our family of seven was like traipsing through other cities. "I remember getting to places and taking over the airport. All these bags and golf clubs would be coming out. We'd have like fourteen of them. Dad would be off getting the rental car, and all of us, like ducklings, followed Mom to the curb."

For an entire month in the summer of 1977—only one year after he purchased the company from his father—Spike took the family across the country and back in a plush Coachman van he had purchased. His work involvement on the trip was limited to a few office visits and periodic collect calls to headquarters from hotels and pay phones. Spike was putting his empowerment management style to the test early on. It was important to both my parents that their children see and appreciate our country and that we do it as a family. Though I was only six at the time, I remember many of the places we visited and the people with whom we stayed. I recall our making lunches almost every day in the van. I'm not sure I've had another bologna-and-yellow-mustard sandwich since. The van had an eight-track tape player, on which we played Shaun Cassidy's "Da Doo Ron Ron" over and over. A child of my times, I loved that song. My siblings remind me of that anytime they can. Maybe you're humming it right now?

Spike and his children at the Lone Star Plant during the family's 1977 cross-country trip

Unfortunately for me, the most memory-seared moment of the trip was the night I threw up on the shag carpet of the Durango, Colorado, hotel room into which we were all crammed. Unlike the one-time-only first-class tickets he purchased for Mary and the oldest two boys on their flight from Los Angeles, Spike's frugality while traveling prohibited him from splurging for more than one hotel room for his family of seven. We'd move mattresses so someone could sleep on box springs as well, quilts and sheets distributed widely. What made the shag moment so memorable was Spike running to my aid, only to slip in my vomit and fall, which sent my siblings into hysterics. With Dad in a daze, me covered in spew, and those four bullies laughing, Mom started yelling. All hell had officially broken loose. As the baby of the family, I'm still scarred. At least I can take solace in the fact that my daddy was trying to comfort me.

When we were not traveling, Hal recalls home life as being "hectic and fast-paced, with a lot of things going on and a lot of energy." He noted the unique version of democracy that Dad would employ when it came to making family decisions. "There were seven of us, and often we would take a vote about some excursion or other family activity. But Dad gave himself seven votes. The rest of us ended up losing many votes seven to six." Jeff corroborates, "Dad was certainly the domineering one, without a doubt." As I have mentioned a few times, both Spike and Mary had tempers, and though we kids were at times the target, they occasionally unleashed on one another. "I do remember one fight in the basement," Jeff says, "where they really got into it, top-of-their-voices type stuff. After they settled down, we all were kind of saying, 'What the heck was that?'" But Jeff is quick to point out that their disputes were mostly "just arguing back and forth or nitpicking each other. They had total devotion to each other. They showed that to us. There was no chance that either of them was going to split up from the other." All of us agree that their love and commitment never waned, their special bond evident even to young children. Adding to this dynamic, Spike's experience seeing his father married to four different women created a deep-seeded pledge not to put his children through such an ordeal.

Much like his approach to business, Spike's view on decision making with his wife was simple, with strong emphasis on personal accountability. "Everything was my fault. It didn't matter. And Mary loved to agree with me on that," Spike says with a chuckle. "But then we would get into a second round of discussions and it would be different. We would again agree, often with her going along with what I wanted. I was really lucky like that." So his formula reveals itself: put Mary at ease by having her think he was taking the blame and then rehash and rehash until she would acquiesce. Mary Pat Follman picked up on this dynamic. "Mary was wonderful for Spike. She could shut him up if she had to. But most times she was very good for him and went along for the ride."

On the Saturday mornings when Spike had to go into the office, he would often take a few of us kids with him. Hal and Mike both remember being temporarily entertained by the C5-A and F-5 model airplanes and other customer tchotchkes in his office, but mostly being bored and wanting to go home. Spike, always efficient and wanting to help out at home when he could, created these trips both to get some extra work done and to give Mary a brief respite from all five kids. While I only vaguely remember these weekend office visits, I distinctly recall Dad piling all five of us into his baby-blue Cadillac Eldorado convertible, lighting up one of his cheap cigars, and taking us to Sears and Roebuck. Again, he could accomplish a dual purpose: get his own shopping done (usually Craftsman tools or toys for himself like walkie-talkies or a CB radio), and more importantly, give Mary a few moments to herself.

Karen, the only daughter in a male-dominant household, was cheerful and ever present. Jeff recalls her being "sweet and smiley. Just a big smile and just sweetness." Because Karen had no sister, Jeff and I both recall her dressing us up as dolls with makeup and all. Jeff, however, was only two years younger than Karen, not the seven years that meant that I had to endure being brought to her school for "show and tell." Fortunately, I was a baby and have no memory of that. Hal remembers Karen as "always having a bright smile and really enjoying her position in the family. She loved being the only girl." Mike, two years older than Karen, recalls her as "driving togetherness. I think even a few of Mom and Dad's arguments were cut short because they knew how much Karen was about togetherness. That reminded them to chill out and figure things out calmly." Mike saw Karen as "bright, engaging, and sometimes a bit manipulative—but not necessarily in a bad way. She could be an instigator who knew she might not get in trouble as the only daughter." He recalls Spike telling him, "It's your job to protect your sister." Jeff reflects,

"I remember Mom and Dad being really supportive of her. Dad hated cats, but he broke down and got her a cat. Karen was so excited and so happy."

Karen and Spike enjoying a cheery father-daughter moment

Spike recalls that "Karen was so sweet." He felt like he tried to make a point to spend one-on-one time with her watching TV or talking about her day at school. In his mind, he spent more time with her than with the boys. But he also concedes not really knowing how to raise a girl. "I guess I pushed a lot of that responsibility on Mary. I said to her, 'I don't really know what to do, and maybe I'll be overly strict.' So Mary dealt with a lot of things. Sometimes, though, she would turn her over to me when she got out of line." The reality is that Spike didn't have a strong female role model from childhood. He was barely a teenager when his sister and he were split apart after the divorce, so he didn't observe much in the way of parenting techniques for girls either.

Spike tried to be a good father to Karen, and as much as he could tell at the time, he was.

• • • •

The household chores that had begun years earlier continued, setting the foundation for our strong work ethics and future careers in business. Spike even instituted a management structure among the kids. Mike recalls how "Mom and Dad started to delegate. It was like, 'All right, you older ones, you teach Billy how to set the table. If Billy does it wrong, it's your fault.'" (Yes, I went by Billy back then. To this day, you can tell if someone has known me since my childhood; they'll more than likely call me "Billy," a name I now enjoy.) Jeff remembers Hal's role evolving. "Hal became the supervisor, bossing us around and seeming like he was not actually doing any work. He would say, 'I'm the oldest, I get to be the supervisor.'" I'm sure Hal did some of the chores as well, but perceptions are reality, right?

Our chores eventually became summer jobs, mostly at the company. Mike recalls Mary and Spike—particularly Spike—instilling the need to work hard. Jeff agrees, "We were obviously all brought up with a very strong work ethic." Unlike today when so much of young people's summers are filled with overly prescribed sports schedules, our summers focused on work. If summer league basketball games or off-season football workouts were permitted, they took place early in the morning or after work in the evening.

Hal's first job, at fourteen, was to sort through thousands of resumes to purge duplicates and any that were out of date. Mike's first role, also around fourteen, involved delivering drawings on foot to nearby clients' offices for D&Z's architectural company, the Vitetta Group. Jeff began working at a slightly younger age, starting out in D&Z's accounting department on an adding machine. His second summer was in engineering, where he decided that he wanted to major in the field during college. After that, he mostly worked in the Yoh Company, which instilled in him a passion for the staffing business that carried well into his professional career. My first work experience, at fourteen, was not at the company; I picked up trash on the beach at the Shore before the lifeguards arrived each morning. I spent about half my summers working at D&Z and half working elsewhere. I suppose that as the youngest of the family, I wanted to blaze more of my own trail. Dad seemed okay as long as I was working hard.

As the family grew, college came into focus. Hal started his senior year at Haverford in 1978 with a strong sense of what he wanted to study. "I knew I wanted to be an engineer because of everything I was good at, math and sciences. I enjoyed them." He applied to Princeton and Duke. Spike was a proud Duke graduate but was not yet meaningfully involved in the school. Hal remembers Mom as his main partner in the application process. "She was fabulous. We worked all the way through them." Hal was accepted to Duke, so he withdrew his application to Princeton. A trend had unknowingly begun.

Spike and Mary were good about showing their children many different colleges, often piling some or all of us into the family van and canvasing the Eastern Seaboard looking at schools. Much later in life, Spike will confess to a subtle tactic to encourage his kids to head south to Durham. "I may have scheduled a few of the New England visits when the weather wasn't so nice up there."

Mike, two years behind Hal, said, "I had a love of architecture and the art that came with it, as I had worked in architecture at the company. And I also had the mathematics that I was doing at Haverford that lent to engineering." He applied to Duke's engineering school and to Cornell's architectural school. He got into Duke and was deferred at Cornell, so his decision was made.

Karen's admissions process may have been the most eventful of us kids. On the day the early decision letters were to arrive, she stayed home from school to get the mail. The postman came and went but delivered nothing from Duke. Keep in mind that in the early 1980s, a letter could always take a day longer to arrive than planned, so many people may have resigned themselves to waiting another day. Not Karen Yoh. She located the phone number of the Admissions Office and called them directly. The self-advocacy she had developed growing up wedged between four boys was showing itself. By that point Spike had gotten more involved with Duke, so he had already heard confidentially from the Admissions Office. Karen had been accepted, but he and Mary did not want to spoil the surprise of her finding out on her own. The combination of Karen skipping school, the letter not coming, and her calling down to Duke made for quite a spectacle for Mom and Dad. Fortunately, the news their daughter received over the phone was positive and she matriculated at Duke in the fall of 1983, a few months after Hal had graduated. It was becoming clear that once Karen put her mind to something, she was not to be taken lightly.

One by one, Spike's kids all found their way to Duke

For Jeff, only a year behind Karen, Duke also seemed ideal. All of us were smart, did well in school, and brought athletic successes and other extracurricular activities to our applications, not to mention serious family momentum. According to Jeff:

Deciding on college was pretty clear. We would visit my
brothers at Duke, and I just thought that it was the only place
I wanted to go. Pretty much from the beginning, all I ever
wore were Duke shirts. It was enough so that my girlfriend
in high school gave me a shirt that said, "This shirt doesn't
say Duke." Of course, the irony is that the shirt did in fact
say "Duke."

As you'll soon read, my decision five years later to attend Duke would not
be so straightforward.

• • • •

As Spike's professional, community, and family activities accelerated, he
also ramped up his involvement in what he would refer to as "the single most
important organization I've ever been involved with." He attributes much of
his growth as a business leader, a husband, a father, and a person to Young
Presidents Organization.

YPO, the only true source of ongoing mentorship that Spike Yoh had, was
founded in 1950 and has 25,000 members today in over 130 countries, which
makes it the largest network of business leaders in the world. To qualify, a
person must be the leader of a company with at least fifty employees by the
time he or she turns forty years old. YPO's website describes its membership
as "peers who share in common the achievement of success at an early age;
a commitment to learning as a lifelong adventure; and a desire to connect
authentically in an environment of trust and confidentiality."

Spike first joined the organization in 1973, thanks to his competitor and
friend Walt Garrison. Spike would go on to hold numerous leadership positions,
both with his local chapter in Philadelphia and at regional and national levels.
In the early 1980s, he and Mary chaired YPO's most ambitious and successful
international family conference to date. The event was a weeklong Caribbean

cruise for almost nine hundred people from all over the world. Later, Spike was a member of two partner organizations that YPO members join when they "age out" at forty-nine. Mary was also active in many spousal activities and networks, including the small group of spouses that served as the initial advisory panel for spouse forums.

A forum is a small group of YPO members who meet monthly to discuss both personal and professional issues as a means of helping each other solve their problems and improve their lives. Spike has always referred to his forum as the board of directors of his business. Given that there had never been a fiduciary board in place at D&Z, this small group served a crucial role. I take this characterization of his forum one step further, however, and claim that they acted as the board of directors *of his life*. This group of colleagues was what most drew Spike to YPO and what he credits as the most beneficial element of the organization. Two of my brothers and I have also had the chance to be in YPO, and we can each attest to the value that forum can bring. None of us, however, has had the connection to forum that Spike has had over his forty-four-year (and counting) affiliation. Spike says, "I credit them with anything I really became, like how to be a better husband, father, and leader; how to motivate; and even how to give a speech. I immersed myself in it. YPO did so much for me, including the friendships that I made, lasting friendships."

Confidentiality may be the most critical aspect of forum. What is discussed cannot be shared with anyone, including spouses. As such, Spike and I were careful when discussing his forum, as were his forum-mates and I when I interviewed them. In fact, the only member of his forum to whom I assign attribution for any quotes is Walt Garrison, because he and Spike had a business relationship prior to and outside of YPO. Spike and Walt have been in forum together for over three decades. On being fierce competitors but also forum advisors, Walt says, "Spike and I never talked direct business. It was always leadership issues and personal stuff." Walt shares Spike's attitude toward the forum:

> We have nine or ten other people. Most of 'em are smarter than I am, and most of 'em have built bigger companies than I have. Most of 'em have accomplishments I've never been able to accomplish. They all say it like it is, not what you want to hear. You'd say, "Give me the real answer," and they'd give you the real answer. And you'd listen to it.

Walt and Spike share not only this humility about their respective accomplishments but also a reverence for how forum contributed to their successes.

For as highly as Spike speaks of his forum, his fellow members give him equal, if not greater, accolades. One of them remembers Spike as helpful during his own YPO application process in the mid-1970s. "Spike took the lead. He had a very calming effect. I came away feeling very good. I still remember how he made me feel." According to another forum-mate, "Spike was fun to laugh with, but he had definite ideas. And his ideas were black and white. He had his view, and he conveyed it as the correct view of the world. But he was able to tell you why he felt the way he did. He never just winged it when giving advice." This is the first time we see Spike as an advice giver. He was never a mentor in the Socratic meaning of the term; he did not excel at asking people a slew of questions to help them sort through their issues. His success strategy as an advisor was, and still is, for folks to give them all their data, after which he'll give them his recommended course of action.

● ● ● ●

Relationships have always mattered to Spike, whether they be familial, professional, or social. No matter how busy life has gotten, with a wife and five children; with a large, growing business; and with his numerous and time-consuming volunteer leadership roles, Spike has invested continually and meaningfully in his friendships. No group of friends demonstrates this better than his beloved Ollie Brothers. The Ollies remained close throughout their child-raising years, through divorces, career changes, and health scares. They continued to go to Duke sporting events together, attended each other's children's weddings, and visited each other's vacation homes.

A real highlight for all of us in the extended Ollie family are the Christmas cards that Zook Mosrie and Rob Townsend send out every year. Each fall, the two of them get together, dress in ridiculous coordinating outfits, take a photo, and create a card to send to the Ollies and their families. Among the hundreds of cards my wife and I receive each December, theirs is the one to which I most look forward.

Rob and Zook in one of their annual Christmas card classics

Around 1980, Spike and Mary were visiting Darryl and Shirley when they felt the need for more formal get-togethers for the five Ollie families. As Shirley remembers, "It was Mary and Darryl's idea. Mary announced to Darryl and me, 'You two are hosting the first one.'" So in the summer of 1981, the five Ollie Brothers, with their wives and children, all descended on Barnegat Light on Long Beach Island in New Jersey. Thus began the tradition of the Ollie Reunion. These memorable gatherings took place every other summer starting in 1981, and continued for thirty years. Each Ollie Brother took turns organizing and hosting, either in his own vacation town or at a family-friendly park or resort. The four-day gatherings encompassed upward of seventy-five Ollie family members, further deepening the relationships. They bonded the Ollie wives together as well, mostly under the common banner of having to endure their oft-inebriated husbands' rehashing of all the same old stories. The reunions also forged connections among Ollie children and grandchildren. As with my siblings and me, some other Ollie children followed in their dads' footsteps and attended Duke. A few even roomed together and were in each other's wedding parties.

Ironically, the large Ollie Reunions also gave each individual family some quality "family time." As Bud Copeland, Darryl and Shirley's oldest son points out, "A real benefit was that we each got the chance to see everyone in our own family as well, which is not something we could do very often." I agree that one of the best things about the gatherings was that we Yohs were together on a somewhat regular basis.

Ollie Reunions were truly special events, and Spike, as in college, was the leader. According to Shirley, "He was the one that really kept it together. I could see when we were all together that he was the one people most looked up to and listened to." Bud agrees. "For the reunions, it became more and more organized. A lot of that was Uncle Spike. Things grew from 'Hey, we're going to have a party on Long Beach Island' to having family directories and monogrammed shirts, towels, and cups."

Unfortunately, with the Ollie Brothers all getting longer in the tooth, it was decided that Ollie '11, the sixteenth installment, would be the last formal reunion. Fittingly, the final gathering took place at Zook and Caroline's home on Boone Lake in northeastern Tennessee, the Ollie families' favorite destination. Perhaps some of us Ollie children will be motivated to restart the tradition. More likely, though, it's a revered event whose time has passed for good.

***The Ollie Family, gathered at an Ollie Reunion in 2007 hosted by
Mary and Spike***

● ● ● ●

As the first half of the 1980s progressed, our family saw less and less of Spike's father. After the buyout in 1976, Harold and Kitty spent almost all their time in their beautiful, Italian-inspired Palm Beach villa just off famed Worth Avenue. Harold purchased a restaurant a few blocks from their house. Symbolic of the keen wit that Spike inherited from his father, I remember a brass plaque over the door of the restaurant that read, "For Members and Non-members Only."

In 1984, Harold was diagnosed with an acute form of leukemia. By March of 1985, despite visits to the National Institute of Health, Harold was beyond recovery. Spike visited him in the hospital, essentially to say good-bye. Most importantly, he told his father that he loved him. Even then, in his final moments, Harold did not reciprocate.

Barbara, Spike's only full sibling, recalls visiting their father shortly after Spike had, and by then their father's condition had worsened. She was with her youngest daughter, Elizabeth. "It was very hard. He barely knew I was there. I held his hand, gave him a kiss, and said good-bye. I knew that would be the last time I would see him." That night, Barbara received the call that her father had passed.

The funeral was on April 4 at a Presbyterian church in Palm Beach unknown to even Harold and Kitty. Spike delivered the eulogy. With a voice and presence that enrapture his audience, as well as a talent for knowing what to say, he has always has been a great giver of speeches. His remarks at his father's funeral were no exception. Playing the dutiful son, Spike reflects, "That's what you're supposed to do." From the pulpit, he referenced Harold's "thoughtfulness and humor," as well as his "strength, real power, and vision, coupled with a kindness and gentleness." A lifelong lover of unique number combinations, Spike expounded on the significance of his father's dying at seventy-seven years old. "If '7' is lucky, then indeed my dad was a great symbol of luck. The best are always the luckiest." Spike also referenced how Harold had played football in college, when his favorite contemporary was the future hall of famer Red Grange, who wore the number 77. But the tenuousness of the father-son relationship came through as well. Spike spoke of how his father "made you earn his respect and love." While he did say, "I am very proud to be his son," he continued, "I am sure I never achieved the goals on the level that he thought I should." He concluded by reciting the opening of Frank Sinatra's "My Way," including the lyrics, "And more, much more than this, I did it my way." Spike paid tribute to his favorite singer but also conveyed his belief that his father did things his own way, often placing his best interests first.

Spike, at the age of forty-eight, was now an orphan like Mary. But since his college years, he had lived as if he already were one. His adult relationships with his mother and father were amicable, but not close or meaningful. His father did more good things for him than Spike realized, but perceptions are again reality, and the reality of this relationship was tenuous at best. More than anything, these dynamics spurred Spike to forge more intimate relationships with his own family, with his close friends, and with his trusted colleagues.

The first ten years of D&Z ownership brought more growth and early prosperity for Spike, both at work and at home. He remained always the optimist, his glass brimming, his actions focused on what was best for those around him. He summed up his father's life philosophy as "My Way." This characterization stood in direct contrast to Spike's own ethos and priorities, which—while almost always framed by circumstances he dictates—have produced a lifetime of thinking of the group, not himself, first. Spike's way was—and always has been—"Our Way."

Chapter 7

Dream Team

Everyone wants to live on top of the mountain,
but all the happiness and growth occurs while you're climbing it.
—*Andy Rooney*

Day & Zimmermann's 1985 revenues were $344 million but would increase to more than $1 billion by the time Spike retired in the late 1990s. The factor he most credits for this incredible growth was the management team he built, whom he empowered to grow the company in the entrepreneurial, values-driven fashion he revered. Fast-forwarding briefly: in the lead-up to the 1992 Summer Olympics, the international body that oversees the sport of basketball amended its long-standing practice of not allowing professional players to compete in the Olympics. As a result, the United States assembled a "Dream Team" made up of NBA stars for the Barcelona Games, where they won gold—beating their opponents by an average of forty-four points per game. Ahead of his time, Spike assembled his own team of stars at D&Z in the 1980s. About his executives, whom he called the Chairman's Council, Spike says:

> These guys were heavyweights. They were pros. They'd been around the block so many times. It allowed me to breathe. The following they had and the people they could call on were

incredible. That was special. Many customers did business
with Day & Zimmermann because of them. It was something
that's hard to forget, coming from our humble beginnings.

Both then and now, the gratitude that Spike felt for such a strong team is evident. This group was not averse to taking risks, behaving like true entrepreneurs despite working in a large, long-standing business.

The Chairman's Council already included Darryl Copeland and Jack Follman, as well as Marvin Nadel, who was one of the initial shareholders at the time of the buyout from Harold. While Marvin had been a key member of Harold's team, he adapted well to Spike's leadership style and continued to serve in an executive role for more than a decade. He advised Spike on operating groups' strategic initiatives, while also leading due diligence on many acquisition targets. Marvin was a great singer as well, a talent he showcased at company retreats.

To augment the Chairman's Council, Spike hired retired three-star army general Eugene D'Ambrosio to run the munitions business. Gene's major accomplishment during his active duty career was to revamp the army's supply and logistics operations, organizing and implementing new and more efficient ways to keep our troops well equipped and battle ready. This background, coupled with his extensive network and keen business acumen, was a perfect fit for D&Z's interests in the Department of Defense. The two men grew close, Spike referring to "General D" as "the big brother I never had."

Another equally impressive executive hire was Floyd Walters, who had been president of Catalytic, a large, publicly traded, Philadelphia-based engineering and construction company. While Floyd was preparing to retire from Catalytic, Spike was parting ways with Harry Perks, who carried the title of president of Day & Zimmermann, although his principal role was running the company's engineering and construction business. He still had his 15% ownership stake. When Harry left, Spike eliminated the overall president title and assumed the running of engineering and construction, but he knew he would have to hire from the outside to get the kind of leadership necessary to grow the company's longest-operating business unit. Spiké knew of Floyd's strong reputation as an industry leader, but it was Mary who provided the introduction. Mary was friends with Floyd's wife Linda, both couples having daughters at the Agnes Irwin School where Mary and Linda were active volunteers. Spike called Floyd at home one weekend to ask the Walters to join Mary and him for Sunday brunch. "My call to Floyd was totally out of the blue," Spike says. "I had no idea he was in the process of retiring from Catalytic. I just knew he had a great reputation and seemed like a really good person."

The two couples met at Merion on a blustery winter Sunday afternoon and instantly hit it off. Spike and Floyd subsequently met one-on-one, and Spike asked Floyd to join the team. Linda remembers Floyd telling her, "Spike told me he's going to make me an offer I can't refuse.'" As it turned out, Spike did . . . and Floyd didn't. He retired from Catalytic and immediately joined D&Z. For Spike, the sequencing of these two meetings—one with spouses and with just the prospective new hire—would typically occur in reverse order; he would size up the candidate first and then meet the spouse. Given Mary's unwavering support, Spike had by now developed a deep appreciation for the importance of an executive's husband or wife. As a result, he had made it a habit to get to know a potential hire's spouse before extending an offer. In this case, however, because Mary was so instrumental to the introduction, the four-person interaction occurred first. The Yohs and Walters developed a close personal relationship, a common practice involving Spike and his key managers, the Copelands and Follmans being just two other examples.

I had the chance to interview the Walters in their quaint, remote farmhouse in Chester County, Pennsylvania. Refreshingly, it is one of the few places I know for which GPS directions do not help; you won't find their home without the Walters' personalized directions. Seated at their Little-House-on-the-Prairie-worthy dining room table, I had a great conversation with Floyd and Linda. But my visit also afforded me the chance to do a little impromptu modeling. Not only had Floyd taken up goat farming and the production of goat cheese in recent years, Linda continued to be one of the area's best freelance photographers. Given Linda's talents, the Walters have created a unique rite. As owners of an authentic J. Peterman "Horseman's Duster" jacket—I'm embarrassed to admit that I thought J. Peterman existed only on *Seinfeld*—Floyd cleverly decided that Linda would photograph visitors wearing the coat. An entire wall in his tractor barn is covered with portraits of visiting friends donning the garment. I'm proud to say that I now have my place on that wall of fame.

Once he joined D&Z, Floyd immediately noticed the newfound freedom and flexibility that working for a private company afforded:

> My prior experience had always been with public companies. You always had this, "What are the shareholders going to do, and what are the analysts going to say?" You might spend a lot of money and time on something, but when the analysts got hold of the information, they'd ask, "Why are they doing that?" With Day & Zimmermann, you didn't have that problem. You had to be able to satisfy the management team, and Spike in particular, but it wasn't a matter of solely answering, "How soon will it pay off?" That was a big difference.

Being a private company has always been something our family considers a competitive advantage. Spike was often asked, as is our generation, why we don't take the company public. There are many reasons, but most fundamentally we believe it would change our culture, including how we compete and our value proposition in the marketplace and with our employees. While it's true that being accountable to public markets might instill more consistent discipline (e.g. Floyd's comment above about payoffs), we have always believed that being private allows us greater flexibility and autonomy to attract and engage great employees and great customers.

Spike (far right) and members of the Dream Team

Reflecting on his hiring strategy, Spike says, "I would always try to hire the smartest people I could, and I'd put them in charge and tell them to protect my ass. I would hold them accountable to deliver." Floyd seconds this approach, adding his voice to the many that relish Spike's hands-off approach. "One thing that Spike used to say, which is what made him a good manager and a good owner, was, 'If I have to make those decisions for you, I don't need you.' That gives the individual a freedom that you don't find in most public companies, where you're always being second-guessed by somebody."

The dream team's roster included other key players over the years—too many to list in total. Like Marvin Nadel, Fred Brown also spanned both Harold's and Spike's leadership tenures. Excelling in consulting and marketing, Fred carried the nickname "The Glide" because, according to Spike, "He could smooth out any rough situation. He was a true professional in every way imaginable." Fred and Spike shared the birthday of December 12. Each year they would send one other a birthday card "signed" by their fellow 12/12-er, Frank Sinatra. Ben Pellegrini, another retired army general, joined the Chairman's Council and ran a number of different businesses at D&Z, adding to our proud history of employing retired military officers who have gone on to successful private-sector careers at the company.

Under the leadership of the dream team, Day & Zimmermann grew to unprecedented levels, through new project wins and myriad acquisitions and partnerships. One example of this growth was a large project the company bid with Bechtel to oversee a major expansion of the Miami International Airport. John O'Connor remembers Spike's participation in the proposal process. "Spike came down and I thought it was going to be a ten-minute overview. But he was like a dog on a bone. He asked us a hundred questions about why we were doing things this way as opposed to that. It was like catnip for him. He just loved it." Spike then participated in the customer presentation, and the Day & Zimmermann team won the contract. A job of that magnitude, with the much larger and better-known Bechtel as a partner, helped establish D&Z as a formidable player in the market.

In the late 1980s the company identified an emerging, untapped market in the nuclear power industry. After two decades of active construction of nuclear power plants in the United States, two events—at Three Mile Island in Pennsylvania in 1978 and at Chernobyl in Ukraine in 1986—heightened public opposition to further growth. Construction efforts were largely halted, and the companies that had designed and built the plants transitioned to providing maintenance to the nuclear utilities that owned them. A few people, including Floyd, saw opportunity in this transition. Understanding that there were major differences between building power plants and maintaining them, Floyd encouraged Spike and the Chairman's Council to enter the maintenance business. The company identified a small power plant maintenance business, NPS Energy Services, and acquired it in 1988. As Floyd recalls, "We were not afraid to try new things. We had a sense of what was needed, and we built a good reputation." Spike's risk tolerance and trust in his team were starting to pay off.

Darryl Copeland's now-proven record of taking on new ventures and successfully growing them meant that he was charged with running NPS. The company—NPS specifically but D&Z more broadly—was buoyed by a strong influx of talent from Catalytic, many of whom followed Floyd Walters and his stellar reputation. This influx included Barry Buechner, a brilliant, Harvard-trained executive-level analyst, and Joe Ucciferro, a civil engineer with a PhD in applied mechanics with extensive experience designing and overseeing the construction of nuclear power plants. On a personal note, both Barry and Joe would become important mentors for me early in my career. The influx also included Mike McMahon, who today runs all of D&Z's engineering, construction, and maintenance businesses. For the past decade, Day & Zimmermann has been the market leader in the United States for nuclear power plant maintenance. The seeds of this success were sown by Spike's dream team.

Another start-up success story under Floyd was Life Sciences. Again leveraging his experience and network from Catalytic, Floyd and his team saw an emerging market trend. As he explains:

> The production of pharmaceutical products changed significantly. It had become about growing cultures then harvesting the items that you wanted out of the material. They had to be in a sterile environment with constant temperature and gentle agitation. You would grow them, and they would multiply. You had to put nutrients in there, and you had to get rid of

the waste. That's why Life Sciences grew. No one before us
had figured out how to do it well.

At ninety years old, Floyd can still explain the nuance and complexities of
this technical business.

One of the key leaders brought in to run this business was Bob Giorgio, who
joined D&Z in 1987. According to Bob, "Floyd said, 'We have the financial
resources, the infrastructure, and the engineering. We'll back you. You can
form the company as you want.' I always liked Floyd and trusted him." Bob's
impression of Spike was equally positive. "He was very cordial, friendly, and
warm. He told me, 'Floyd wants to do this, and I'll back it. You guys can do
what you want. We're very entrepreneurial. I'd love to have you guys come
aboard.' It was a very positive initial meeting." Bob and a team of experts
moved to D&Z and began executing a business plan for the new venture.

Almost immediately, their former employer levied a lawsuit to prevent
the new business. Bob remembers being nervous when meeting with Spike
about the potential legal proceeding. "I thought he'd be very concerned. But
Spike said, 'No, this is a good thing.' I said, 'What do you mean this is a good
thing?' Spike said, 'It means we've got something that they want.' It was just
the opposite view from what I thought he was going to have." Spike's intuition
told him that they were onto something big.

With Life Sciences, Floyd's vision and Spike's hunch proved correct.
The lawsuit never amounted to much. The business plan called for heavy
up-front investments and a profit to be made in year three. However, only
three months into the new venture, the team secured a $30 million contract
with a pharmaceutical company in New Jersey. The new business had instant
validation from the marketplace. A series of additional early wins, followed by
flawless execution on the projects, meant that Life Sciences turned a profit in
year one. The business would go on to have a successful run into the mid-1990s.
As competitor companies caught up to D&Z and the market shifted, however,

Life Sciences closed a decade after it was launched, collapsing almost as quickly as it had grown. Such is the journey of an entrepreneurial enterprise.

Another key growth initiative was the 1992 Yoh Company acquisition of Salem Technical Associates. Larry Suwak, mentioned earlier, had worked in engineering at Day & Zimmermann since the mid-1960s. In 1986, Spike asked him to become president of the Yoh Company, recognizing Larry's strong leadership aptitude and core values. Yoh Company's revenues were $92 million at the time. Larry remembers meeting with Spike about the new opportunity:

> He asked me if I'd be interested in running the Yoh Company. I was so excited and so flattered. I thought, "This is *the* family business. The family name is on it." Most times I would say, "Well I'm going to have to talk to my wife about this." But I didn't hesitate. I jumped at the chance. Quite frankly, the highlight of my career was when I was with the Yoh Company.

Larry reported to Darryl Copeland, but he attributes the culture of Day & Zimmermann principally to Spike. "Spike was a cheerleader. He surrounded himself with good people. He encouraged them and made them feel important and feel valuable." Mike Parente, who joined Yoh in 1982 and spent over twenty years there, concurs:

> Spike always preached entrepreneurship. If you could get it done, he would allow it, as long as you could prove you would produce results. Taking the risk, the autonomy he gave you, the entrepreneur spirit—it all flowed down. And he had a big thing about trust. In any organization, when it's successful, it starts with the owner.

Because Larry had worked at the company for such a long time, however, he also remembers that Spike had to grow into his role as cheerleader. "In his early stages, after he bought the company from his father, I would go to some of these sessions with Spike and I used to think, 'He's not a very good speaker.' Some of the things he would say would be awkward. But as he matured, he became much, much better. He became a real motivator in his communications." I attribute this improvement in Spike's communications skills to his more relaxed leadership approach after his father retired, as well as to his involvement with YPO.

Larry remembers the Salem acquisition as being particularly influential. "It was a game changer for Yoh, but also a game changer to teach D&Z how to do deals." Salem was the largest acquisition the company had ever achieved, adding close to $50 million of revenue. Equally important, it brought twenty-one new branch offices. Many of these branches were in the same cities as Yoh offices, and Larry embarked on a bold evaluation process whereby the strongest leader in each city was appointed head of the new combined office, regardless of the company from which the person came. He further integrated Yoh and Salem by appointing two of Salem's leaders as regional managers, though Spike was not initially in favor, given that one had won the job over someone close to the CEO. Larry recalls that "Spike was upset with me because I didn't make his son Jeff the manager. But I thought, 'Darn it! I'm trying to do the best thing for Spike's business, and I think Jeff is still too new.'" Larry was vindicated, as Jeff learned much from his Salem manager and would eventually succeed him. The boldness of this move, coupled with his core values and how effective he was at growing the Yoh Company, are the reasons why Spike holds Larry in such high regard to this day.

Critically successful hires, new ventures, and acquisitions led to strong double-digit annual growth for Day & Zimmermann from the mid-1980s into the 1990s. However, not all of Spike's growth initiatives bore fruit. One effort that failed was his 1989 entry into the plastic recycling business. As Jack Follman recounts in *Cash and Carry-on*, "We analyzed the potential of plastic recycling as a means of reducing the valleys in the professional services group's income stream and using our technical background to serve ourselves." However, he further states, "As time would tell, our market intelligence and recycling assumptions were proven defective." The business, Day Products, was sold in 1993 after sustaining sizeable losses over its brief lifespan. A silver lining of this endeavor, however, was the operating and leadership experience it provided for Hal, who was eventually put in charge of the venture to minimize its financial impact. Jack credits Hal with "ably negotiating the sale [of the company], which provided sufficient cash to liquidate the liabilities associated with the business."

Work hard/play hard: Spike and Mary with members of the Dream Team

In the early 1990s, Spike challenged his management team to aim for even more growth. A fan of both motivational slogans and giveaways, Spike articulated the challenge by designing and distributing drink coasters that said, "Grow to a Billion." Despite the bullish leader that Spike had now become, this ambition stunned his managers. As John O'Connor recalls:

> Spike told everybody he wanted us to be a billion dollars. At
> the time, I couldn't even think about a billion-dollar company.
> But he said it. He actually had the road map of how to get
> there already figured out. To me, that was sort of a seminal
> moment. Not that his style changed or anything of that nature,
> but that's when I saw the visionary side of him. Maybe it had
> been there before, but I didn't appreciate it until that point.

While this audacious challenge was inspired and motivating, it compelled some D&Z company executives to adopt a "growth for growth's sake" mentality, creating a disconnect between sound growth initiatives and the inclination to pursue any work that could add to the top line.

Bill Hamm, another Catalytic employee who had followed Floyd Walters to D&Z in the role of general counsel and would go on to be a member of the Chairman's Council as well, experienced this tension firsthand. The company won a project in Egypt that led to significant financial losses, while also requiring talented people like Bill to focus their energies on minimizing damages rather than maximizing gains. As he recalls somewhat ironically, "I remember we had our fun in Egypt trying to extract ourselves from what turned out to be a very troubling project. I traveled back and forth to Cairo a lot. I was over there one time for like twenty-one straight days." Spike's leadership and charisma fostered this kind of dedication from his senior leaders. As Bill remembers, "We'd always call Spike and Jack in the afternoon Cairo time, which was in the morning Philadelphia time, to brief them on the day's events. During one of these calls, he gave me a battlefield promotion, which made me the first senior vice president, as far as I know, at the corporate level." The way Spike empowered his people, with added responsibility and the reward of job titles, demonstrates what an adept motivator he had become, knowing that delegation led to growth, as well as to more flexibility in his schedule.

The Egypt job, coupled with the financially disastrous performance of a recently acquired construction company in the Southeastern United States, led to the only year in almost two decades in which Spike Yoh's Day & Zimmermann lost money, 1996. Ironically—or appropriately—that same year company revenues almost eclipsed, for the first time, $1 billion. Jack provided an appropriate postmortem on the "growth for growth's sake" movement. "We allowed our management to enter businesses and contracts for which we lacked adequate controls and dependable management. Being entrepreneurial and imaginative is fine, but you better have the people and financial resources to execute as well." Every strategy has its shortcomings. The company grew and many careers were advanced, but financial results and personal sacrifices resulted as well.

Spike's tenets of growth and diversification, fueled by implicit trust in his people, had another shortcoming as well. At times people took advantage of Spike's hands-off approach, either by not working as hard or as ethically as they should have. Spike simply did not have the visibility or checks and balances to inspect everything that was taking place. Mike McMahon, who joined Day & Zimmermann in 1994, took note:

> Spike would stay on the surface, it seemed. He had many, many people that, because their mothers raised them right, were working hard and doing the right things. But he had a few other people who were taking advantage of him. I would see a few people that were executives, and I would say to myself, "You're not giving this company half of what you should."

When asked why he thought this happened, Mike offers, "It could be the family thing. Spike made you feel like you were part of a family. But you might not hold family members accountable like you would someone else. He probably had a small piece of his brain that said, 'No, they wouldn't screw me. They just wouldn't.'" John O'Connor surmised that "the point at which a personal quality moves from a virtue to a vice can be a very thin line. Spike was extraordinarily personalized. But you can take personal loyalty too far." Anthony Bosco offers a slight variation: "I think that ultimately Spike knew it [was happening], and he understood it. I think he thought it was just a cost of his approach to business."

Regardless of the degree to which Spike was aware of these dynamics, he made two changes in the 1990s to emphasize more scrupulous behavior: a shift in the organization's reporting structure and a heightened focus on integrity.

Concerning the change in organizational structure, prior to the 1996 losses each business unit was organized as a stand-alone operation, wherein all support functions such as finance and human resources reported directly to the business unit president. Said another way, these functions had "solid line" reporting to their president. They also had secondary, or "dotted line" reporting to the corporate CFO, Jack Follman, as well as his corporate peers in human resources and other areas. This structure gave significant autonomy to the presidents, including their being the primary conduits to Spike regarding their financial performance. As Bill Hamm recalls:

> Basically, the fight was over control, whether or not a business
> leader should be the sole point of contact for the CEO about
> what's happening in the business or not. Spike's philosophy
> and the way he grew the business had been sort of the Johnny
> Appleseed approach: "I'm going to sprinkle these seeds on
> the field. I'm going to create a lot of individual P&Ls with
> individual leaders who are accountable for the performance
> of those businesses. Give them president titles and let them
> have their own brand." So in effect, it wasn't stock ownership,
> but it was a pride of ownership of the different businesses.

Jeff Yoh recalls one business unit executive telling him how much it meant to him to be given a "president" title when he joined the company. But Jeff adds,

"Once the guy started working, he noticed that there were a lot of presidents floating around and he didn't feel quite so special."

The downside of this reporting structure was that the presidents alone had formal connections to Spike. After 1996, Spike implemented a visible and understandably unpopular (with the presidents) change. Each business unit's controller became "solid-lined" to Jack Follman and "dotted-lined" to the president of said business. This provided Spike's corporate staff advisors with much greater visibility into operations.

Spike's other, perhaps more impactful change was to increase the company's commitment to unwavering integrity. Bill Hamm contends, "The thing that was consistent about him from day one until the day he retired was his focus on values. For him, the principal value was integrity." Spike's increased emphasis on integrity was best embodied by the creation of the company's motto, "We Do What We Say ®." However, unlike the "Grow to a Billion" phrase, this collection of words had a universally positive impact on D&Z's culture.

Spike saw a need long before 1996 for more accountability throughout the company. In the late 1980s, he coined the phrase, "I Do What I Say." He had "I Do What I Say" lapel pins made and signs hung in the elevator lobbies of headquarters and field offices. "I was trying to get everybody to believe that when they said something, particularly to an employee or to a client, that they'd mean it and they'd do it." Hal recalls that the idea germinated from a lunch discussion when Spike took his eldest son out for his birthday. Showing the tension that the new motto exposed, Hal remembers, "At night some of those signs would be torn down by those who didn't want to abide by Dad's more visible approach to accountability. We would have the signs replaced the next day."

Ever since that father-son lunch, the evolution of this slogan has been a topic of friendly debate among company executives and the Yoh family. It is yet another example of John Kennedy's quote that "success has a thousand fathers." Several people, including Hal, Mary, Karen Lautzenheiser (the former head of our corporate marketing group), and even me—while I was in high school—could each have been responsible for telling Spike that the "I" really should be "we." Regardless of who actually got through, he remembers recognizing that a change in pronouns would make a substantive improvement. "We ought to just say, '*We* Do What We Say.' We are one company. It should be 'we.' So we changed it. It was now not just personal, it was more group oriented."

Spike soon put the phrase into action with one of our important government customers during a rebid presentation. "In my opening remarks, I pulled out a slide from the beginning of our contract term three years earlier that summarized the four primary things we were going to do. I said to the customer, 'You know what? We did every one of them. And you graded us well on all four. What more can you ask of us as a contractor? Our slogan is, 'We Do What We Say.'" His words were intended to show the customer what we believed, but also to demonstrate to his employees that he was serious about integrity and accountability. D&Z retained the contract.

Today, "We Do What We Say®" is as synonymous with Day & Zimmermann as anything we do or anything in which we take pride. Its power is in its simplicity: commit to what you will do ("say" it), and then do it. It compels us to think hard about our future plans, making sure that everyone is aligned, and then deliver on our word. "We Do What We Say®" applies to big, important efforts like customer proposals and banking relationships, as well as to more routine activities like telling a coworker you will call them back.

Unfortunately, an accident occurred in 1989 that spurred Spike and his management team to heighten their focus on another of our core values, safety. Day & Zimmermann was—and still is—in high-risk businesses, including manufacturing large-caliber ammunition, working extensively in nuclear power plants, and providing armed security services for government facilities central to the country's national defense efforts around the globe. Even in the Yoh Company, where the majority of our services are low-risk professional functions such as information technology and engineering, almost all of our thousands of Yoh employees work in customer facilities under the customer's direction, so we have little day-to-day control over their well-being.

As Jack explains in *Cash and Carry-on*, "There was an explosion of a submunition on the Kansas CEM (Combined Effects Munitions) production line that caused three deaths. This event was devastating. An exhaustive investigation involving the FBI and DIS took place, which determined that the accident resulted from human error." From then on, Spike and his team put much more emphasis on worker safety. Mike Yoh corroborated the impact of this event, given that he had previously worked in that exact spot.

Today, the emphasis on safety has increased, serving as Day & Zimmermann's number one priority and company value. We are very proud of the track record we have established for performing hazardous work safely, something that is widely agreed to be one of our core competencies. While we will not be satisfied until we achieve zero injuries, our safety performance regularly receives customer and industry awards and recognition.

Another important cultural evolution of the company in the 1990s was the heightened priority of equal treatment of women in the workplace. Spike's early career took place during the initial days of the feminist movement when disparities in the treatment of women versus men were far greater than today. In 1991, the much-publicized case in which Anita Hill accused her then-boss and future Supreme Court Justice, Clarence Thomas, of sexual harassment brought significant visibility to the need for gender equality and women's rights. In *Leadership Looks Back*, which D&Z produced for our 110th anniversary in 2011, Karen Lautzenheiser, a twenty-five-year company veteran, recalls being tasked by Spike to examine the treatment of women at D&Z:

> Soon after the Clarence Thomas/Anita Hill lawsuit, Spike asked me to find out about sexual harassment at Day & Zimmermann. So I convened a caucus of forty-eight women [from various levels of the organization]. As it turned out, there were no real problems. Even still, I think Spike learned a lot. A big part of my job was educating people about women in the workplace and fostering a positive culture.

This sequence of events likely awoke Spike's childhood proclivity to protect his mother and his sister and undoubtedly stemmed from his deep admiration for Mary and the fact that his only daughter was climbing the company's managerial ranks.

● ● ● ●

While growth, empowerment, integrity, safety, and equality all defined Spike's corporate culture, so did the notion of family. As Larry Suwak recalls, "One of the things that Spike did was talk about the importance of family—both at home and at work. We all felt like we were part of this big family with Spike at the helm. I never had that experience anywhere else I had worked."

One of the ways Spike showcased and developed the family feel at Day & Zimmermann was with routine social get-togethers and corporate retreats for his executives and their spouses. Larry's wife Joan remembers the trips as a unique phenomenon. "It was very unusual. With all our friends who worked at different companies, I don't think any of them ever had anything like it." Many of these retreats were to The Greenbrier, a beautiful resort in the Appalachian Mountains in West Virginia. To augment his focus on family, Spike would have his adult-aged children attend as well. During these every-other-year trips, the company managers spent mornings discussing longer-term, strategic topics, with afternoons and evenings devoted to team building on the golf course, in the outdoors, at themed dinners, or in The Greenbrier's bowling alley. Seeing dozens of us in tuxedos and evening gowns bowling late at night was always a spectacle.

The pinnacle of these getaways was a weeklong Day & Zimmermann ninetieth-anniversary cruise in the Caribbean in 1991. Spike rented a small cruise ship for his top fifty executives and their spouses. In addition to The Greenbrier trips and the cruise, Spike would occasionally take the Chairman's Council to other resort destinations as well.

Spike, his family and the D&Z management team and their partners on the 90th anniversary cruise

During the retreats, Spike would hire guest speakers on topics that appealed to the spouses as well, symbolizing his recognition of how important a manager's partner was to his or her career. Mary's influence was undeniable. In their case, the old adage, "Behind every great man, there is a great woman," was slightly altered. Mary was not behind him, but right next to him. At virtually every event Spike ran or attended, whether a company retreat, Philadelphia business community function, or YPO trip, Mary was at his side. Mary Pat Follman remembers, "Mary was such a good person. You could feel that when you were with her. She tried to make you comfortable. When I first met her, she had to know I felt very nervous, and she made me feel relaxed. I had nothing but good times when we were with her." Walt D'Alessio (from

PIDC) recalls that "Mary was always at the events. She took an active role in discussions. Everybody saw her as a gracious hostess. If you had the opportunity, you'd like to sit next to Mary and engage her." Floyd Walter's wife Linda, an accomplished singer who would often perform duets with Marvin Nadel in the evenings at Greenbrier, has similar recollections:

> Just recently, I found a wonderful quote by Gandhi, and it was so true of Mary and Spike: "Happiness is when what you think, what you say, and what you do are in harmony." They were that way, absolutely. You didn't have Mary on Monday being one person and Mary on Wednesday being another. And Spike was the same. You could count on them. They were consistent.

In a remembrance written for the 1995 Greenbrier trip, Barry Buechner and his wife Suzanne say, "Our first Greenbrier trip will always be among the most special. For the first time, we got the chance to know the spouses of the D&Z team. What a wonderful group it was (and is)! No understanding of D&Z, a family-oriented company, is complete without knowing the spouses." Bill Hamm seconded this observation:

> I think it goes back to the approach that Spike had that this was a family business. We would get invited over to Spike and Mary's house around Christmas. And we would go on these spectacular trips that we wouldn't have been able to take on our own. It was a very welcoming environment where you and your significant other felt like you were all part of the same team. Spike would go out of his way to say something nice about you in front of your spouse.

Emmett McGrath, who joined the Yoh Company in 1985, feels similarly. "I always found Spike and Mary to be genuinely interested in my wife and me.

Greenbrier was one of the most fantastic times in our lives. And I don't think I'll ever beat that cruise. We've been to a lot of nice places, but I've never had a chef serve me caviar in the ocean surf again."

Company events also gave Spike the opportunity to share one of his greatest passions—golf. Eschewing competitive strategies that might create discomfort, Spike always awarded the best golfing prize to "Mr./Mrs. Average Golfer," the person whose score was the mathematical average of the entire field of players. Whether it was at The Greenbrier, Merion, Oakmont, Pebble Beach, or a number of other renowned courses, Spike's company outings were meant to be fun and relaxing.

Spike was not averse, however, to a little friendly competition between the golfers and the tennis players. For Spike there existed a caste system for sports, with tennis players below golfers. In the same collection of 1995 remembrances, Jeff and Suzanne Yoh lightheartedly wrote, "Obviously, golf is very important to Day & Zimmermann. We are surprised that golf has not become a company value." Not to be outdone, Floyd and Linda Walters remark that "tennis players have bigger balls!" Needless to say, Spike's managers were relaxed and enjoyed each other's company.

Beyond fancy trips, Spike had other ways of connecting with and motivating his team, such as attempting to make his employees feel like his equal. As Joan Suwak recalls, "I remember one time Larry and I were somewhere and Spike said, 'I work *with* Larry.' He did not say, 'Larry works *for* me.' That phrase said a lot about Spike." Similarly, Joe Ritzel, Day & Zimmermann's CFO since 2001, recalls first interacting with Spike while still working as an external auditor in the early 1980s:

> At the end of the independent audit every year, there was this big dinner at the Union League. Jack and Spike would come, along with the whole audit team. Here I am, a twenty-two-year-old kid from Pottsville, Pennsylvania, and I'm thinking,

"This is pretty cool!" I remember Spike. He had this presence and this voice that projected. But he was so down to earth as well. I was taken by how friendly he was to everybody. I still remember that. It was fabulous.

Joe relates another story involving an employee and his forty-hour work week:

My wife Linda worked in payroll at D&Z when we met. She reminded me of a time when somebody called headquarters to report their hours for the week. But there was a new receptionist who accidentally transferred the call to Spike. His secretary wasn't there, so Spike answered the phone. The person said, "I have thirty-two regular hours and eight overtime hours." Spike didn't say, "Let me transfer you to so-and-so in payroll." He wrote down the hours and walked the paper over to the payroll department. Not only did he go to this effort, but he also didn't say, "You goofball! I'm the chairman of the company. What did you call me for?" He didn't embarrass the guy.

Interestingly, Joe added that Spike asked the person in payroll how the employee could have eight hours of overtime if he only worked thirty-two hours of regular time in a forty-hour work week. No job might have been beneath him, but Spike also insisted on ethical business practices, his knack for watching details paying off.

Spike speaks to how he derived success by leveraging every person in the organization:

Some people became pretty set in their ways, particularly, it seemed, former engineers in management roles. I remember we had a problem with a production line at Lone Star. We sent some industrial engineers from Philadelphia to go out and study it. After all this high-priced analysis, we hadn't come up with anything. Finally someone went out and talked to the machinist on the production line that was doing the work. The guy said, "Look. If we do this and we do that, the line will work right away." Nobody had thought to ask the darn machinist doing the work how to fix the problem.

Spike had developed a way both to lead an organization that employed sixteen thousand people and to recognize and value the contributions of every one of those workers.

The D&Z headquarters team and their partners,
celebrating at the Franklin Institute

Spike's final method for making an impact on his coworkers was likely less intentional, that of occasionally appearing to doze off in meetings. Joe recalls:

> One time Jack and I were in Spike's office, and while I'm talking I see his eyelids close. I think, "Oh no! I'm boring the guy!" I keep talking, and I'm thinking he's not listening. I'm say to myself, "Jack! Do something!" It felt like twenty minutes. Then Spike looks up and asks me three questions that were right on point. He heard every word about the topic. Whatever happened during that period, he was still listening.

Two walls of Spike's office consisted mostly of windows, and by early afternoon the sun would create a warming drawer effect for Spike and any meeting participants. I am one of several people who have experienced this panic when it seemed we put Spike to sleep.

Not only did Spike try to be down to earth with his employees, but he also tried to personally support the local economies around many of D&Z's remote operations—sometimes with unintended results. This was most notable with the munitions plants, including an ammunition storage depot in Hawthorne, Nevada, where D&Z has had the operating contract since 1981. To give a sense of the scale of this facility, the town of Hawthorne is only one-and-a-half square miles, while the plant is 230 square miles, 153 times larger! This is the equivalent of a five-cent nickel being placed on an 8.5"x11" piece of paper. Adjacent to the town are the picturesque landmarks of Walker Lake and Mount Grant, whose snow-capped summit stands over eleven thousand feet tall. One of the few places to spend the night in Hawthorne is the El Capitan Lodge & Casino. Staying at a casino enabled Spike to pass a few evening hours with his fellow travelers gambling, another of his favorite pastimes. But as his son Mike recalls, sometimes his intentions backfired. "Dad would gamble to try to put some money into the local economy. Ironically, many times he would end up winning. In those cases, it kind of had the opposite effect." Spike would never bet much, so he would never win much. Win or lose, he always meant well.

• • • •

As the 1990s progressed and the dream team gradually retired, Spike realized it was time to plan for his own transition. In 1996, at only fifty-nine, he initiated a two-and-a-half year succession of company leadership. Even though he was relatively young, Spike was acting on two major observations he had made over his career. The first was knowing when it is time to move on, something he had learned from D&Z's history of operating munitions plants for the United States Army. While the majority of the people working at these facilities were D&Z employees, our management team reported to a small contingent of active-duty military personnel and government civil servants. The base commander, usually a lieutenant colonel, would be assigned to the location for a finite amount of time, typically two years. When that period ended, the officer would move on to another assignment and not return. As Spike puts it, "I knew from the military that when you finish a command, you're out of there." This form of transition felt right to him so there would be no ambiguity about who was in charge.

Second, Spike had seen too many patriarchs of other family businesses stay in charge so long that they stunted the professional growth and leadership experience of the next generation. Of another family-owned firm, he says, "The two sons run the company. The father comes in at the end of every month and gets a check. And then at Christmastime, he comes in and gets another check. He still owns all the stock and won't give real authority to the kids." Spike knew his children were getting older, and he preferred to err on the side of leaving a bit early rather than staying on too long.

As he had with so many other important decisions, Spike actively engaged his de facto board of directors, his YPO forum. Two decades later a forum-mate recalls how importantly Spike treated these advice sessions:

When Spike requested advice, his description of the issues
was highly organized. It was written down, it was evidence
based, and it was clearly presented. After a full discussion
of the group, there generally was a consensus. What pleased
me, but also modestly alarmed me over time, is that Spike
would take our advice and he would usually act on it. As I
saw this repeated time and time again, I began to be aware
of the sense of responsibility we had.

Spike's request for advice in this case was not a one-time effort. "For two
years, I worked with my forum on how to make the transition. I would come
to the meetings with charts and stuff. They would give me good input about
the different thoughts I had in trying to make it all work."

He also spent a lot of individual time reflecting. "I did a lot of my thinking
at night, lying in bed." Undoubtedly, many of those late-night, one-person
brainstorming sessions would end with Spike swinging himself out of bed,
feeling his way through the dark to his closet, turning on the light, grabbing
his pink memo pad and green golf pencil, and jotting down whatever wisdom
had come to him.

After these two years of deliberation and reflection, Spike decided to make
a move. He had always been certain that he wanted his children to own and
run the company after he did. But he also knew that one person had to be
in charge. So in late June of 1996 he decided to promote his oldest son, Hal,
to president of Day & Zimmermann, reporting directly to him, launching
a two-and-a-half year succession plan for company leadership. Hal would
assume responsibility for the entire company, except finance (Jack Follman)
and legal (Bill Hamm), which would continue to report to Spike. As to why
he chose Hal, Spike says:

He was the oldest, and he was the one in engineering, which
was a sophisticated market and our oldest business. He had

had the most diverse background. For a family business, we've all got to learn the hard way. Obviously I was hoping that I could help him in the coming years. I remember Mary asking me if I thought he was ready. I said, "I don't know if he's ready, but we're going to find out."

Spike knew that any decision he made would have risks, but he was confident in his and his son's abilities.

The specific timing of Spike's decision to promote Hal was the result of a reorganization that one of his group presidents was contemplating, a move that would alter Hal's responsibilities. Spike says, "I went into the Chairman's Council meeting and told them, 'This is what I'm going to do. I'm going to announce Hal as president in charge of everything but law and finance. And I'm going to be retiring sometime in the near future.'" I'm sure that at that moment, you could have heard a pin drop on the carpet of the board room.

While the leadership team was shocked by Spike's news—several paid him individual visits after the meeting—Bill Hamm, with a bit of hindsight, surmised that the timing made sense. "Once the dream team started to retire, it became a challenge for Spike." The proverbial times were a-changin', and Spike sensed it was time to start the transition.

At this point, the soon-to-be company president was unaware of the announcement that had just been made several floors above him at 1818 Market Street. As Spike recalls, "Hal didn't even know about it. I met with him that afternoon." Hal's recollection of that moment is clear. "I was in a meeting, and someone came in and said that my father needed to see me right away." Like it would for most people, Hal's mind was racing. "On the elevator ride up, I was thinking, 'What the heck did I do? Why did he pull me out of a meeting?'"

According to Spike, "Hal came in, and I told him, 'I've decided to make some changes. I'd like to announce that you're going to become the president of Day & Zimmermann effective July 1.'" Hal was obviously caught by surprise—this was certainly not one of the scenarios he had played out on the elevator—but the two men talked it through and agreed to move forward.

Working directly for his father presented Hal with a host of opportunities to learn, as well as a few challenges to clarify and share responsibility with the man who had guided Day & Zimmermann for two decades. One immediate challenge involved the person to whom Hal had reported before the promotion, a person who now worked for him. According to Spike, "The group leader couldn't really accept Hal's new role. The two of them were disagreeing over the path forward, and Hal got to the point where he felt like a change was needed." Before any change could take place, however, Spike asked Hal to canvas a number of current and former company leaders to ensure there was consensus. After a few weeks of what Hal describes only half-jokingly as "torture," Spike acquiesced and Hal removed the leader. This move demonstrated the extent to which Hal was empowered from the start.

Spike and the final iteration of the Dream Team and their spouses shortly before his retirement

Hal has much positive recollection of partnering with his father. "It was the best time I ever had with Dad. I really enjoyed it. I got to see and hear all the rumors. Everybody thought Dad was distant from the business, but he really did know the facts and figures, and he understood everything that was going on." Spike's recollection largely echoed Hal's. "My oversight was not constant. It was not overbearing as far as I was concerned. I would ask him occasionally, 'How's this going?' or 'How's that going?' in my typical needling way." An example of their collaboration was at a company leadership conference when the two were preparing to jointly address the attendees. As Hal recalls, "He and I sat in a room and went through these 3x5 index cards with questions people had for us. We discussed who would answer which one and what we would say. It went really well."

Hal learned a lot from his father, especially about decision making. "He would tell me that you don't always have to make a decision today. Even though people are typically looking for a decision that day, don't do it if you don't have to. Be patient, gather the facts you need, and make sure you get some opposing points of view." My brother Mike and I, who have both worked for Hal for extended periods of time, can attest to how effective Hal became regarding this leadership skill.

Hal also recalls early advice from his now-fellow Chairman's Council members. "People said that once you report to Spike, you've got to be on your 'A' game. You might not think that Spike was always on his 'A' game because he's so jovial and nice and all that. But, oh, he's on his 'A' game. And you'd better be on your 'A' game with him." This was sage advice, as well as keen insight into Spike's continued engagement even late in his career.

Hal relates one final, slightly amusing dynamic that arose between father and son early in Hal's presidency:

> Dad always had an open-door policy, so people got to know
> what type of meeting it was. In his office, it was always an

open-door meeting, so the discussion topics were typically
lighter. My office became for closed-door meetings, where the
things we said might have been more sensitive or confidential.
People quickly understood what was going on, and they
learned what to expect depending on where the meeting was.

In 1997, about a year into Hal's new role, an initiative emerged that would
ultimately convince Spike that it was time to retire. Day & Zimmermann
continued to operate as a diverse set of businesses, each running on its own
systems to track employees' time, project costs, and other key data. Hal and
an emerging crop of new leaders recognized that this model was untenable,
both from a growth perspective and from an oversight and control perspective.
According to Spike:

> One of the projects led by Hal was looking at a new computer
> system. They came up with this SAP thing that would cost
> more than $40 million. I didn't understand computers and
> didn't see why we had to spend even one dollar on them. I
> couldn't see how it was ever going to pay for itself. But a lot
> of smart people thought it was a good idea.

The system was intended to improve controls, support future growth, and
spur further integration among the businesses. Bill Hamm saw how Spike
struggled with the recommended investment. "SAP was one thing that was
hard for him to put his arms around. I think that kind of enterprise approach
to managing the business with more centralized influence was something with
which he was less comfortable." Reflecting on this balance between Spike's
laissez-faire style and the need for more control, Mike Yoh recounts how
"the entrepreneurial spirit was alive and well, but everything needs controls,
and there were not sufficient controls in place." The project was eventually

approved—the largest capital investment in the company's history—with Hal as its executive sponsor.

As a result, in the early fall of 1998, Spike knew that the end of his D&Z tenure had arrived:

> I decided I had to leave at the end of the year. Don't ask me why I picked it. I thought I'd been there long enough. Hal had had a chance to grasp the job. We had had a lot of conversations about family businesses during that time. At times I wondered if he'd ever be fully ready, but that's the thought you have about anybody taking over for you. It was time.

I can still vividly remember the time and place of Spike's announcement. A management dinner was being held at the Union League, whose motto is, "Love of Country Leads," fitting for Spike. As attendees entered the meeting room, we passed by a twelve-foot-tall Thomas Sully painting of the great leader and patriot George Washington—again fitting. After drinks were served over informal conversation, Spike silenced the room with his bellowing call for attention, which we were all accustomed to heeding. His remarks were nothing extraordinary. He simply stated that the time had come for him to retire, and that at the end of the year Hal would become the new chairman and CEO. I remember my heart beating fast and my eyes welling up when he spoke. While everyone at the company knew that this day would come, no one was prepared for it to arrive.

A priority that fall was to finalize the stock purchase agreement between Spike and the five of us kids, particularly regarding how Spike's shares would be valued. He did not want to force his kids to pay "top dollar" as his father had done, but he did want to ensure that he and Mary would have the financial wherewithal to maintain their lifestyle, while also preparing for potential future medical needs and greater philanthropic commitments. It was determined that Spike would receive favorable tax treatment from the IRS if, after the transaction closed, he had no involvement with the business—cut ties cleanly and completely. For Spike, of course, this would not be a problem.

During Spike's final week in the office, the days leading up to Christmas Eve, I had the pleasure of taking him to lunch at one of his favorite haunts, The Happy Rooster. A staple for wet lunches and happy hours, The Happy Rooster was a small, dark city tavern with a handful of booths and a limited menu of red meats and crab cakes. We drank Dewar's on the rocks and talked about what life would be like for him after he retired. He was excited but stoic, only mildly melancholy about his transition.

On Christmas Eve, the office closed at noon and the management team headed back to the Union League for an annual holiday luncheon. After we returned to and exited our building's parking garage, Spike ceremoniously handed me his access card, saying, "It's not like I'll be needing this again." I kept that card, even long after it had been rendered useless by a change in the garage entry system. After December 24, 1998, he never again set foot in 1818 Market Street. A few days after Christmas, he and Mary headed to Florida where they spent the ensuing winter season. They would soon become Florida residents, the change in their driver's licenses and voter registration cards symbolizing the huge transition in their lives.

Several executives have reflected on Spike's retirement. Bill Hamm was impressed with his equanimity:

> The thing that was maybe the most surprising was how smoothly it went regarding any emotions that could have been conflicting for Spike. Obviously he identified with the company, he loved the company, and he appreciated the role that it created for him in the community. But he was ready to go. Once he left, he was gone. A big part of that was because he was turning over the company to his kids, which is what his vision had always been. He handled it superbly.

***Spike and Mary during a retirement dinner, surrounded by their
children and their spouses***

Joe Ritzel embodied what many executives felt. "I was shocked at the way
Spike turned over the keys and walked away. You knew he loved Day &
Zimmermann and put everything he had into it. That had to be hard. Maybe
he didn't want to do what happened with his father, where the transition wasn't
smooth by any stretch." As Jack Follman's right-hand man, Joe understood
the IRS requirements for Spike to sever involvement, but he wishes Spike
could have retained some connection. "People still wanted to see Spike. They
missed him. Many still wished they could say, 'Let's go say "hi" to Spike!'"

In 1998, Spike's final year, Day & Zimmermann's revenues were $1.1
billion. The company was almost nine times as large as during the final full
year of his father's career in 1975, having experienced average annual growth
of over 10% during Spike's tenure. D&Z employed over sixteen thousand
people and provided income and livelihood to thousands more who came
and went with the ebbs and flows of the company's business cycles. Equally

important, Spike had built a values-driven family culture and had maintained a strong entrepreneurial spirit despite the size of the enterprise. Ultimately, he transitioned the business to his children in a collaborative, intentional way, juxtaposed to the distant and doubting way in which his father ceded control to him.

Jerry Smith worked at the Lone Star plant in Texas for an incredible forty-seven years, plus a few additional years as a consultant. He had a particularly close relationship with Spike, effectively summing up his impressions in *Leadership Looks Back*:

> Spike Yoh. He worked hard and played hard. Exceptional leader and family man, integrity without question—all adds up to why Day & Zimmermann has been successful. I was impressed with how Spike treated all employees the same. He took time to talk to anyone and everyone. We provided a BBQ dinner to 1,500 employees during one of his visits. Spike joined the staff as we served food in the serving line. With our D&Z aprons on, we served every employee. Folks will never forget Spike dishing out the goods.

This final sentence by Jerry applies just as well symbolically as it does literally.

• • • •

When Spike retired, his five children each became 20% owners of the company. We siblings, our average age thirty-three, assumed an awesome responsibility, but no one assumed more of it than Hal, our CEO—a role he still holds today. He stepped into the shoes and literally moved into the office of the larger-than-life leader who had guided D&Z for twenty-two years. Below is an overview of how company ownership and culture have evolved since Dad hung up his spurs in 1998. We think that he and Mom prepared us well.

A few years before Spike stepped away, he had the foresight to instruct the five of us to start meeting formally as a group. He knew that we would have to get to know each other far better than typical siblings if we were to be an effective ownership group. The consummate delegator, Spike was hands-off in the transition other than determining the value of his and Jack's shares. As a result, the five of us siblings focused initially on building stronger bonds with each other and assessing how our individual goals and aspirations jibed with the future needs and objectives of the company and each other. We discussed our childhood relationships, resulting in some interesting breakthroughs. For example, as the youngest of the five kids with an age gap of five years between me and the next sibling, I always had the sense that the four of them excluded me or teased me (recall the shag carpet incident on the cross-country trip in 1977). They, in turn, shared that they had felt I acted aloof, thinking that I was better than they were. Discovering and digesting these (mis)perceptions was just one way the five of us connected more closely in preparation for our ownership role.

We also developed a system of metaphorical "hats," wherein we would be conscious of which "hat" we were wearing. At times we were owners. Sometimes we were employees. At others we were just siblings. Of course, the hats frequently overlapped. Hal has had a particularly demanding task with this as CEO; he is responsible for meeting the expectations of the owners, a group to which he belongs. All of us are good at compartmentalizing, but fortunately, Hal is the best.

To facilitate the transition to a much younger ownership, we developed and implemented three strategies designed to show our employees, particularly our senior managers, that we were committed to their continued involvement and career development. Assuring our executives that we were much in need of their expertise was of utmost importance. The first of these efforts was a phantom stock program, wherein senior executives who were not actual shareholders had the ability to participate financially in the appreciation of the value of the business just as the shareholders do, thus aligning all of our interests. An evolved version of this program is still in existence today, continuing to serve as both a motivator and a retention mechanism.

The second strategy, primarily implemented by Hal, was to form a Board of Advisors, composed of Jack Follman and a group of external, seasoned business executives. We also annually rotated one of the other four family shareholders to sit on the BOA. Still in existence, the BOA provides Hal and the leadership team with feedback and advice regarding financial performance, strategy, and talent development. Over the years, it has provided us with the proverbial "grey hair" experience that such advisory bodies can give. Although by now we owners have developed plenty of our own grey hair!

The final measure we put in place was something known in family business circles as a "meritocracy" process. To further demonstrate to our management team that we Yohs needed their continued engagement, we assigned the BOA the key role of approving any management promotion involving a Yoh family member. Each of Spike's children is highly ambitious, and each of us has always been compelled to embrace professional challenges. However, we also knew that this ambition to reach for the next rung on the corporate ladder could be at odds with what was best for the company. Over the years, the BOA has at times recommended against a family member getting a new job, demonstrating the teeth this process has.

These safeguards against nepotism appear to have worked, given that we experienced no voluntary turnover in the executive team following Spike's retirement. A few of those senior leaders are still with us today, almost two decades later.

After the initial transition years, my siblings and I entered a second phase of ownership in the early 2000s, one that focused more on growth strategies and how the ownership group could support expansion. Our third (and current) phase has focused largely on family business succession and governance, including revision of our shareholders' agreement, creating a trust to hold our voting stock, and generating development tools for future owners, like shareholder education materials, a family employment policy, and a series of communications guidelines.

Spike's children and some of their spouses accepting the National Family Business of the Year award shortly after his retirement

As one might expect, some facets of company culture and our priorities evolved after Spike retired, while others remained much the same, most notably our steadfast commitment to our core values and motto, "We Do What We Say®." Joe Ritzel, whose D&Z tenure has spanned Spike's and Hal's CEO-ships, states, "The values-driven side of our business is just as important today as it was with Spike." Jack Follman agrees. "The idea of 'We Do What We Say' and the importance of every employee's contributions are still such priorities. Nowadays this is almost unheard of in many businesses. Everybody will say it, but very few companies actually do things to ensure it's a priority. Spike and Hal will forever share that legacy." Under Hal's leadership, safety has assumed an even greater emphasis as our number one value. Larry Suwak comments, "The heightened focus on safety was really important. That was one of the outstanding things that Hal did."

Also consistent from Spike's tenure to Hal's is a commitment to growth. As the owners of a business that depends on the quality of our people, we have always believed that to attract and retain the best people, the company must constantly be growing to provide them with more challenging opportunities. If the company does not grow, great people will leave for bigger opportunities elsewhere. This growth mindset, coupled with a recognition of the importance of a diversified set of business offerings, has been a key facet of Day & Zimmermann's strategy since its founding in 1901.

Demonstrating the strength of relationships among the management team at Day & Zimmermann, many company leaders and their spouses have remained close long after they have retired. Among them, the Follmans, Walters, and Suwaks, to name a few, still get together regularly to break bread and reminisce. Spike and Mary were involved in many such gatherings as well. Since Mary's passing in 2015, each of these couples, along with many other D&Z alumni, have made a point to reach out to Spike and spend time with him.

Perhaps the most notable evolution from Spike's time to today has been the heightened emphasis on not just top-line growth, but bottom-line performance as well. Joe Ritzel comments on how this played out:

> Our performance culture escalated and the bottom line improved in terms of our returns. Right after the transition, with all the debt we assumed from buying out Spike and Jack and installing SAP, this focus was on steroids. We became much more data driven. This effort to become a performance culture certainly started during Spike's tenure, but it accelerated under Hal.

Larry Suwak concurs. "The shareholders had a lot of debt to pay off, so the business had to be profitable and earn the money to get stable." Mike McMahon says, "Things certainly became more execution oriented under Hal. He is much more focused on the details than Spike was. Hal also led an effort to reduce the number of businesses we had to something more manageable. Things became more structured in the ensuing years. Not only has our performance improved, but our growth has accelerated as well."

We have also developed different ways of executing company initiatives, including taking what we call a "three-pronged approach," the three prongs being people, process, and technology. You need great people, you need to develop and execute with the best processes, and you need to harness the right technologies to be efficient and scale the operation. Bill Hamm remarks how this approach varied from how Spike led things. "Spike was all about the people. He was less comfortable with the other parts, particularly the technology. Today the company has evolved to be an integrated enterprise, and we're approaching $3 billion in sales largely as a result."

Finally, our focus on family as a defining characteristic has evolved. As with many organizations today, we promote diversity and inclusion, recognizing the importance of attracting and retaining a diverse, talented workforce. Bill Hamm sees a bridge between the prior culture and today. "We've evolved from a family culture to a culture of diversity, which is sort of an emphasis on a greatly extended family. Now we want to focus on each person and what can make him or her the best, not just on assuming that everyone wants to be part of the same family."

Today Spike expresses great pride in what his children have achieved since he retired. "It amazes me how much the company has grown and how seriously my children have taken their roles as owners. I never envisioned the kind of success they and D&Z have had."

Chapter 8

Chairmanteer

The greatest leader is not necessarily the one who does the greatest things.
He is the one that gets the people to do the greatest things.
—Ronald Reagan

In January 1999, Spike and Mary were living in Florida with zero affiliation with Day & Zimmermann. In reflecting on his huge professional void, Spike recalls, "My YPO forum was concerned about that because I like to be hands-on and keep busy. I like to . . . I don't want to say *control* things . . . but to influence and to make things better." Spike's not fooling me, or by now, any of you. He lived to control things! The early 2000s would serve as the first of two phases of Spike's retirement. During these years, he did what many retirees do, particularly those who are relatively young. He got busy. What ensued were chairmanship roles encompassing unprecedented scale, visibility, and accomplishment. Combined with his earlier volunteer experiences, Spike honed a pro bono leadership style that made him the consummate "chairmanteer."

In reaction to his retirement and to fill his time-and-talent void, Spike joined the board of a fellow YPO member's company. As he remembers, though, "I found out that I had little in common with the owner and couldn't relate to his business or markets, so I dropped that. It taught me a lesson to wait and to breathe and that I didn't have to rush into things." After this brief foray into the world of corporate boards, Spike realized that his true passion lay with the education- and community-based organizations for which he had such strong affinities. I teased him a few times about this, referring to him as a "community organizer," just as Barack Obama was referred to when he campaigned for office. Needless to say, the devout Republican in Spike did not appreciate the analogy.

Tracing back to the early 1970s with the Boy Scouts and carrying through the 1980s and 1990s with the Philadelphia Business Community and YPO, Spike's interests were clear. "Like with schools, the Boy Scouts had to do with family and young people, and that's what I really love to get involved with." Spike's volunteer roles in scouting spanned from chairman of the local troop in Pennsylvania, to regional chairman of the Northeast, to several roles on a national level, including the National Executive Committee. Dick Marion, Scout Executive for the Philadelphia Council, said of Spike in the early 1990s, "He is one of the most dynamic and enthusiastic leaders I have ever worked with. He is a great family man who is devoted to the youth of our region." According to Spike himself:

> The Boy Scouts is an unusual operation in that the local councils and troops run themselves. They are not dictated from up above, so the local scout executive has a lot of control. Obviously, it gets political from the viewpoint that there's always people who support an individual and those who are against him. The keys are the solvency and growth of the local troops. So much depends on the council leader and on the scout masters.

Spike married this keen understanding of how the Boy Scouts functioned to his pride in seeing all of his children participate in scouting, two of them earning Eagle Scout.

Those knees!

Spike also spent many years fund-raising for the United States Olympic Committee, which oversees both the summer and winter games. He was the state chairman of Pennsylvania and then the Mid-Atlantic Regional chairman. "It was a matter of expediting and improving our fund-raising abilities, trying to outraise my predecessors and the other regions. That was my goal." Spike has always been competitive, but his attraction to the Olympics also reflected other priorities. "I love the Olympics. We got to deal with young people and athletics, as well as competition. And I love our country. The Olympics brought all of that together for me." Spike is unapologetic about some of the perks that came with his commitment:

I was able to attend national meetings at USOC headquarters in Colorado Springs and to meet some of the athletes on the national team. Sometimes, when one of them won a gold medal, we would parade them all over the country. In most cases, they were the all-American girl, all-American boy types. They would wear their medals and make speeches. It was really fun. I also got to meet President Reagan . . . for the second time! God, did I love President Reagan.

In 1989, Spike became the thirteenth chairman of the board of trustees of The Haverford School, the Philadelphia-area, all-boys independent school from which so many in our family have graduated. He served as board chair until 1994. In each of his other volunteer efforts, Spike engaged with the organization first then brought Mary in as his partner to plan and co-host events. Haverford was the exact opposite. While their four boys were students there, spanning almost twenty-five years, Mary was extremely active in her aforementioned roles there and at Karen's school, Agnes Irwin. Her intimate knowledge of the school and the school's reciprocal familiarity with and respect for her talents were part of why Spike was asked to join the board. Due to extenuating circumstances, he was asked to become chair after only six months of service.

Spike's time as the chair of Haverford demonstrated what would become a common element of his chairmanteer efforts. He oversaw and helped implement significant changes in the institution's governance and some of its major focus areas. When he started his tenure at Haverford, enrollment was declining and a divide was growing between the administration and some of the long-tenured faculty. Jeff Yoh recalls overhearing a telling conversation. "I was sitting in the DuPont Theater and heard these two Haverford moms talking behind me before the play started. They were saying how Haverford was such a mess but that Spike Yoh had just taken over, so things would get fixed." The "fixing" at Haverford would include the development of the school's first modern-day campus master plan and capital campaign, as well as the beginnings of what later would become a complete overhaul of the school's faculty evaluation and compensation processes. More than twenty years later, the same master plan is in use, the school has raised over $125 million through capital campaigns, and the above-referenced faculty processes are considered best practice in the field.

Dr. Joseph P. Healy, the school's headmaster during the second portion of Spike's chairmanship, characterized the time period when he and Spike served together. "From my point of view, it was a turnaround. Enrollment had dropped to around six hundred, and the school had just changed headmasters." With respect to changes in faculty compensation, Joe says, "That was a big change. That generated a lot of push back. Some faculty that were used to huge, above-market raises all of a sudden weren't getting them. Spike worked in the background to try to get everybody happy again. Those kinds of efforts changed the dynamics inside the school." Spike's knack for reading people and knowing how to influence groups and individuals paid dividends.

Joe echoes one aspect of Spike's D&Z tenure as well, namely the increased focus on gender issues in the 1990s. Citing their efforts to hire more female teachers in the high school, Joe says:

> A big challenge was the boys' school thing, because girls' schools were popular, and girls were deemed better in math and better in this and that. Boys' schools were looked at like they were left over from the Middle Ages. The school had made some progress, but there was only one female teacher in the upper school. It was a big change, and Spike really had my back through the whole thing.

One of the female teachers hired during Joe Healy's tenure, albeit in the lower school, was a young double-degreed Villanova graduate named Kelly Green, my future wife. Ironically, Kelly met Spike before me when she shook his hand at graduation a few weeks before she and I were introduced in 1994. Today, over 40% of the high school teachers at Haverford are women, as well as two department chairs and the dean of faculty.

Joe is effusive in his praise of Spike as a leader:

> As a board chairman and with the management of the board and the increase in the caliber of our trustees, he was very effective. The meetings were well organized, and they got their business done. He really controlled the conversation so people didn't go flying off in a hundred different directions. Spike didn't necessarily have all the technical knowledge about the school or the faculty, but he had a strong sense of people. And he was not a BS-er. He thought something through, and he came in and he told you what he thought.

Joe surmises, "His success was largely because he ran a family-owned company, as opposed to a corporate entity with thousands of shareholders and all kinds of people on the board. He could decide at a certain point what needed to happen, and he could make that decision, for good or for ill. You had to stand by it and stand with it." Even the company motto, "We Do what We Say®," made its way into Spike and Joe's relationship. As Joe recalls:

> Spike gave me one of his lapel pins with the motto on it. I used to wear it. To be honest with you, that was him. That motto captured everything there was to say about that guy, because he never minced words. If he wanted to tell you that you were acting like a jerk, he told you. He's not a guy that's afraid to give you his opinion. In fact, even if you don't ask for it, he gives it to you!

Most impressively, Joe says, "Spike Yoh was one of the most important people in my life. I just loved the guy. I learned a lot from him. He was a force of nature."

**The thirteenth chairman of the board of
The Haverford School**

As with many of Spike's nonprofit involvements, Mary played a key role as the spouse of the board chair, even after the two decades of her own volunteer leadership efforts at Haverford had passed. Joe says, "Mary was a saint. She was just in another universe, and she was the perfect partner for him. Also, they used to lend my family their shore house in Avalon. Mary would say, 'Go down and spend a week there.' So we'd go down to Avalon."

In a fortuitous confluence of circumstances, Spike and I had the opportunity to sit next to each other on stage for graduation in June of 1990. He was there as the board chairman, and I was there as the prior year's senior class recipient of the "Key Man" Award, tasked with announcing that year's recipient. Today I'm honored to be following in his footsteps as the eighteenth board chair at Haverford.

• • • •

Spike's next major chairmanship—the first during his retirement—was with the board of trustees at Duke University, the alma mater of our entire family. Beyond his routine gatherings with the Ollie Brothers, Spike had not been particularly involved at the school until his children started attending in the early 1980s. The first area with which he engaged was his school of study, engineering, where he joined and soon became chairman of the Engineering Council, a group of engineering alumni primarily focused on fund-raising. Earl Dowell, dean of the engineering school from 1983 to 1999, and current faculty member, relays—in his sweet Southern accent—Spike's impact:

> Spike is a sort of larger-than-life personality. He's a very force-
> ful, direct sort of person. And when we would be discussing
> an issue, he would say, "Here are the facts, folks, and here
> are the choices. Let's get to it." I think that's a characteristic
> of engineers in general. I think Spike epitomizes that style,
> which I appreciate very much.

Earl also speaks to Spike's role in elevating the engineering school. "Duke is now recognized as having a fine engineering school by our peers across the country. Much of that is due to what Spike did and what other alumni, faculty, and students have done over the years." Earl also cites the importance of Spike later becoming board chair—one of only two engineering alumni to hold that position—in further elevating the status of the engineering school.

Spike's involvement in engineering soon led to a broader impact on Duke's fund-raising efforts. John Piva is the former senior vice president of Alumni Affairs and Development. Today he remains a special friend to Spike. John recalls Spike's role in a 1980s capital campaign:

> We were planning for the first endowment campaign directed to the Arts and Sciences. People were getting pretty excited about the concept. Spike, who was chair of the Engineering Council at the time, stood up and said, "Engineering is an undergraduate school, and the focus should be on all undergraduate schools, not just Trinity College [Arts and Sciences]. If you do that, if you include that, I will take a leadership role in raising money." From that conversation, a whole series of conversations took place. It moved from a campaign for Arts and Sciences to a campaign for Arts, Sciences, and Engineering.

That campaign, which initially targeted $200 million, ended up raising over $564 million for endowment. John reflects further, "The campaign results established a pattern where Spike would always stand up and say, 'I'll do it.' He always raised his hand. I guess it was the Boy Scout in him."

During my interview with John in the solarium of his and his wife Kathy's suburban Durham home on a beautiful June morning, he showed me a handwritten letter Spike wrote when John retired from Duke in 2004. The letter reads, in part, "John, Thanks for your leadership! You brought all of Duke 'together' with you! But most of all, thanks for your friendship . . . You always made Mary and me feel at home and part of something very big and special . . . Duke is a much greater place because of you, and Duke's future is a lasting tribute to you." Spike developed close relationships with many administrators and development professionals during the 1980s and 1990s, and his love for the institution grew deeper and deeper.

Symbolic of that love, Spike created "Duke rooms" in each of his homes, fully decorated in school paraphernalia. With Duke blue carpeting bulls-eyed by replica inlays of Cameron Indoor's wooden jump-ball circle, each room's walls (and portions of the ceilings) are filled with Duke pictures, posters, and magazine covers. Duke chairs, desks, trash cans, and even golf putters complete the decor.

Spike's involvement at Duke culminated in his ascension to the chairman of the board in 2000, a little more than a year after he retired from D&Z. "Having gone to Duke, it was one of my obvious favorite places. I knew so many of the people there. And there were challenges that I could look forward to on a large scale." Given that Duke's operating budget the year Spike became chairman was $2.14 billion and the endowment was $2.65 billion, the size and scope of Duke's board chair's responsibilities were large indeed.

Duke's president during Spike's chairmanship was Arkansas-born Dr. Nannerl O. Keohane, an accomplished scholar, educator, administrator, and author. Spike and Nan developed a deep, mutual admiration. Spike says, "I was blessed to work with Nan, who was one of the best executives I dealt with in the nonprofit world. She was able to guide her staff in a very indirect but positive way. We were really opposites in so many ways, but from a Duke viewpoint, we saw so much together and saw things so similarly." And yet they were so different. From their home states to their educational and career backgrounds, political leanings, and even genders, these two were about as dissimilar as two people could be. In their case, opposites really did attract, the pair combining into a formidable board chair–president duo.

Allison Haltom, then vice president and university secretary acting as liaison between the board and the senior staff, had a firsthand perspective on the partnership:

> When I initially thought about Spike as chair with Nan as
> president, they seemed so different. You would almost think

that it would be oil and water. But what grew was a mutual respect, I would say almost a love, between the two of them. Nan thought as highly of Spike as he thought of her. I would bet that initially that may have been a surprise to both of them.

John Piva seconded Allison's observations:

Spike and Nan couldn't have been philosophically from a wider spectrum. But they both had so much respect for one another, and there was a civility there where they would always listen to one another's viewpoint. They wouldn't always agree, but they would always listen. Sometimes Spike would change his mind, and sometimes he wouldn't. It was fascinating.

Bob Shepard, who succeeded John in 2004, also had ample opportunities to see the chair and president interact. He recalls one story in particular. "One time Nan said to Spike, and she was sort of teasing him, 'Spike, why do you like George Bush so much?' Spike said, 'Because I love his core values and what he stands for.' That kind of quieted the room."

My interview with Nan, who casually perched her docksides-clad feet on the coffee table in her home adjacent to Princeton University where she and her husband Bob now work, was a true highlight of this biography experience. It was also humbling, as I realized over the course of our discussion how much research and memory-bank tweaking she had done in advance. Just like Joe Healy and the other not-for-profit executives who had reported to Spike in his earlier roles, Nan appreciated the special attention Spike showed for her role. In her deep, Southern drawl, she recounts:

I remember sitting beside him as chair and feeling that he was more focused on how things were working out for me and how I felt about the way the discussion was going than some of my other chairs, who seemed to be largely focused on the board itself, wanting to get things moving. It wasn't that Spike was neglecting his larger duties as chair. He just had enough peripheral vision to recognize his job was partly to support the president. He was able to do that without taking his eye off the ball. That's a real gift for a chair. We became very close colleagues, and I relied a great deal on him. Spike was a wonderful chair. I remember him with great affection and admiration.

Continuing her reflection, Nan comments on Spike's ability to work a room:

The serious, open, frank, candid discussions about significant, ticklish issues were often held around the executive committee table. Spike was always so helpful. He didn't jabber on all the time, but when he spoke, he had thoughtful things to say. His perspective was always that of a deep Duke loyalist who also had some strong business expertise. It was very helpful.

Spike has always been a meticulous preparer. As his YPO Forum has already showed, one of the reasons he was so good in meetings was because he prepared for them ahead of time as well or better than anyone else. As Allison recalls:

Spike did incredible work as a trustee. He never came to a meeting unprepared. He had read everything, even more than what was expected. We sent him volumes of material. I was struck by how after almost every meeting he would send some kind of communication to either Nan or me or to both of us about the way we could improve something, as well as questions that he had that were unanswered.

In meetings, Spike would sometimes pass notes to Nan, often because his boyish, engineer's humility compelled him to ask for an explanation. "If you ever saw me slip her a piece of paper, it was typically not some meaningful, far-reaching Duke vision, but a request for a definition of some fancy word she had just used. She usually looked back at me with a sympathetic smile because I had probably misspelled the word to boot." While Nan contends that Spike understood pretty much everything she said, she does concede that "maybe passing notes was part of not understanding certain words, but the communication before, after, and even during our meetings was much closer and less formal than with some of the other chairs I had."

Spike remembers another mid-meeting message that was passed between them. While one of the school's senior administrators was addressing the board, Nan passed Spike a note saying that the person currently had job offers from two well-regarded universities. It turned out that Spike was not particularly fond of this person, so he scribbled back, "I would be pleased to write him a letter of recommendation," causing Nan to smirk somewhat uncomfortably.

When asked about Spike's shortcomings, Nan touches on a theme mentioned by many others before her:

> I don't think he had many shortcomings as a leader, frankly. But he was sometimes a little more blunt than some people might have preferred. He didn't have the kind of ingratiating Southern courtesy that some trustees expected to lubricate a difficult situation—to pave the way with sweetness rather than saying, "Well, this is what we've got to get done." However, I thought it was great that he was so direct.

These reflections show yet again how "humble, self-deprecating Spike" and "bullish, straight-talk Spike" often coexisted.

Under Spike and Nan's leadership, the board and the school accomplished many significant tasks. One of these was the *Campaign for Duke* capital campaign. Although its initial goal was $1.5 billion, an incredible sum in its own right, it had amassed an even more incredible $2.4 billion when it closed in 2003, both the largest fund-raising campaign in Duke history and the fifth largest in all of American higher education. Nan was in a great position to speak to the role Spike played:

> He was the perfect chair to be in place at the close of the campaign because he focused the attention of other trustees. Sometimes board chairs were a little reticent about stressing the importance of providing wealth as well as wisdom. Not Spike. He would say, "We need this for Duke. We all need to be in it together." He did it in the most natural, gracious, but firm way. It was with his wonderful humor and directness. Plus with his and Mary's own generosity, he had the moral authority as well. That was essential to the snowballing success of the last years of the campaign.

*Nan and Mary acknowledging Spike for one of his many
accomplishments at Duke*

Sterly Wilder was a Duke classmate of my brother Hal's. Currently the associate vice president for Alumni Affairs, she speaks to Spike's ability to be lighthearted, even regarding the usually serious subject of fund-raising. "One time Spike sent us just one dollar as his annual fund contribution because I had been a pain in the butt about getting him to give to Trinity [the liberal arts college] as well as to engineering. His letter said to split his contribution 50/50 between Trinity and engineering. Oh my God. It was hysterical." Sterly still has the 1997 formal, typed letter, as well as a photocopy of the $1.00 check. Spike's letter reads in part, "Dear Sterly, Having been continually harassed by innuendoes, phone calls and threats, I am reluctantly forwarding my $1.00 contribution to the Annual Fund and hope it will be more judiciously used than in the past." Needless to say, Spike upped his gift shortly afterward.

The second major effort Spike and Nan undertook echoed a theme from both Day & Zimmermann and Haverford: a heightened emphasis on women's roles. As Nan recalls:

> In talking with Spike and other people, I thought we really needed to pay more attention to this issue. Since the men's and women's colleges at Duke merged [in 1972], there had not been the same focus on the centrality and strength of Duke women that there was before. We launched a commission on the status of women. Spike was very supportive.

Nan recalls how his energy in this area carried over to his inclusive facilitation style:

> Spike recognized that it was a pretty male-dominated board, in terms of both number of people and loudness of voice. I remember several times when Spike would say, "Okay, we've heard from you and you and you. I'd like to know what X or Y or Z thinks." Among them, there would be at least one woman. He recognized that most of the women—and this is true of any board like that that I've ever known—were a little

more reticent about speaking up until they had really formed their ideas, by which time six men had already expounded. Spike was aware of that, and he was very clear to draw the women in.

Allison points out that Spike's respect for women transcended the walls of the boardroom:

> One of the things about Spike was how kind he was to the women who worked in my department [there were no men]. These women were obviously lower down on the hierarchy, but Spike was just as kind and respectful to them as he was to the president. One of my colleagues recalled how "he was kind and thoughtful and made me feel important." He made the people around him and who worked with him feel important. He was never a big shot.

Spike's inclusive leadership style did not apply just to women, but to anyone—male or female—who may not have been comfortable contributing to a discussion. Again, Allison explains:

> He was not someone who was out front with his thoughts before anyone else had a chance to speak. The best leadership I have seen are those chairs who provide that kind of facilitation, who make sure that people feel included in the discussions, that their comments—both positive and negative—are heard so that the chair is not out there pushing his own agenda. Spike did that as well as anyone.

While today he is not in as many leadership situations as he once was, Spike continues to excel at garnering a good "sense of the room" and making the uncomfortable feel comfortable. Corroborating Allison's point of view, Jack

Winters, assistant director of athletics and leader of the Iron Dukes, the booster
club for Duke Athletics, offers:

> When I think about Spike, the two words that I come up
> with are "confidently humble." It starts with him, but Mary
> was this way too. Confident in who they are, comfortable in
> their own skin. And at the same time, humble. Spike would
> have a conversation with me the same way he would with
> the president, and the same way he would with somebody on
> the housekeeping staff. The way he treats everybody is the
> same, with respect across the board and with sincere interest.
> I mean, to be who he is but at the same time not flaunt it?
> That's very respectful.

These reflections illustrate a common practice of Spike's, wherein he would
attempt to make the least comfortable people in a room comfortable. Whether
it be a woman or two on the Duke board or a D&Z employee who seemed
nervous during a company town hall, everyone became more relaxed, and
the tenor and depth of the discussions improved.

Spike's third and final major accomplishment at Duke involved the relationship between the university and its health system—the burgeoning
collection of hospitals, education and research centers, and physician practices
operating under the Duke name. Nan describes the impact of Duke Health
System as "huge. It was as important as any part of Duke, and it was better
known in some circles than the university." Supporting Nan's comment, the
health system's operating budget at that time was over $1.1 billion. Today it
is close to $3 billion and accounts for over half of Duke's total expenditures.

The health system had its own leader and its own board, on which Spike—the
consummate volunteer—sat as well. While Duke's bylaws stated that the health
system's leader and board were accountable to the university's president and
board, the reality was that prior to the early 2000s, the health system had

operated largely autonomously. Recognizing both the governance challenges and economic inefficiencies of this dynamic, Nan decided to address the situation. She engaged her board chair to get it done:

> That was one of the few instances, over twenty-four years as president of two institutions, when I went to the board and said, "This I cannot do by myself. I need your help." After saying this, I can still see Spike drawing himself up to his full height and saying, "We've got to take this on. Here's how we're going to do it." We eventually got things cleaned up, but it was Spike who really made it happen. He knew it was the right thing for Duke. He knew it in his bones. He also wanted to support me. I will never forget his leadership in that. Duke is a far better place because of what he did there.

Even as chairman, though, Spike would still exhibit his at-times unavoidable knack for diving into details. Tallman Trask, Duke's executive vice president overseeing all business and administrative activities, recalls:

> One day we were in a trustee meeting and Spike says to me, "I need you to order new pencils." I say, "Why's that?" He holds up a basic No. 2 lead pencil that says "Duke University" on it and tells me, "Because Duke is not the number two university. Duke is the number one university. I want number one pencils." I said, "Spike, you know that the number refers to the type of lead, right? Number one pencils are really soft and they smudge, and that's why nobody uses them." But he still wanted number one pencils. I never did order them, by the way.

In wrapping up Spike's role as board chair, Nan uses a term that resonates with me. "In addition to building communities, he also was an *institutionalist* in his love for Duke. It's the traditions, it's the history, and it's what it stands for. It's a community magnified into an institution. That's how Spike saw Duke."

Even with his tenure as chairman ending in 2003, Spike remained involved at Duke in various capacities, perhaps none bigger than his effort to philanthropically jump-start the struggling football program. Successful up until the mid-1960s, Duke football had experienced a long drought since then, except bowl game appearances in 1989 and 1994. During one eight-year stretch, Duke amassed not one, but two, of the ten longest losing streaks in college football history.

Earl Dowell was one of many people who thought that trying to improve the program was a fool's errand. "I recall trying to convince Spike that engineering was a better investment than football." Shirking Earl's and others' counsel, Spike and Mary made the lead gift to a campaign that culminated in the construction of a state-of-the-art football building bearing the "Yoh" name. According to Spike, "If I had to pick one thing that I've done at Duke, it has been helping reestablish football." Dick Brodhead, who succeeded Nan as Duke's president in 2004, says, "I associate Spike with the pains and the glories of Duke football because of the building, and because I know that he was on the board when the board revisited the question of whether Duke would even have football." Much as Mary is co-credited with the idea of starting the Ollie Brother Reunions in the early 1980s, she is similarly cited as the ultimate push behind her and Spike's gift to the football program twenty years later. Kevin White, who came from Notre Dame in 2008 to become Duke's athletic director, says, "Spike was very quick to tell me that the Yoh Center was Mary's idea." Again we see strong alignment between husband and wife.

Not satisfied with his initial gift, Spike remained focused on ensuring that the program continued to receive the attention needed to achieve greatness. Jack Winters recalls a telling comment Spike made after a round of golf with other members of the athletic department. "The Yoh Center had just been completed. I mean, the paint hadn't even dried yet. The next thing I know, Spike says, 'Okay, what's next?' He had just funded one of the biggest projects to date in Duke athletics, yet he's already asking, 'What's next? What do we do now?'" Since Spike and Mary's gift in the early 2000s, Duke football has experienced a renaissance, appearing in bowl games in four of the last five seasons, with a win in 2015—Duke's first since 1960.

The Yoh Football Center is the crown jewel of Spike and Mary's philanthropic efforts

Beyond football, Jack goes on to discuss how Spike's efforts helped promote the importance of athletics overall, which were not always appreciated for their value by some of the more intellectually oriented departments on campus:

> Politically, the support that Spike provided to the athletic department, the voice that he gave to a cross-section of the Duke community, was huge. He would talk about the value and the importance of intercollegiate athletics to the school and about the exposure that our athletic department has provided for the university to help raise all budgets.

Jack, a deep-talker with a quick wit, was full of praise but also willing to shine light on a few of Spike's much observed but infrequently voiced shortcomings. "So you ask what Spike could have done better? Well, there are two things. First, he needed a lot of help with his golf game. And second, he needed help with his wardrobe." On the latter shortfall, Sterly Wilder says, "I'll always remember commenting to Spike one time about how much Blue Devil gear he was wearing. So he motions to his belt and says, 'You want to see my Duke boxers?' I'm like, 'Oh no no no! No one wants to see your boxers!'"

Spike's wardrobe isn't simply a result of his engineering—let's call it his *nerdy*—demeanor. His dress actually entails a lot of intentionality. Sometimes, he does combine the right button-down with the right slacks or shorts and the right socks and shoes. But other times, oh my. On some mornings, Spike clearly decided that the day would be a "green" day. All of his clothing would be green. Decent idea, right? But the golf shirt would be one shade of green, and possibly patterned, while the shorts would be another shade of green, and possibly differently patterned, and the socks would be yet another shade. Hunter green, kelly green, lime green, never-heard-of-it green. And he might have thrown on a white belt and white patent-leather loafers to round things out. I would argue that his style has come even more "into its own" since Mary's passing in 2015, given that there is no discerning eye or finger wag sending him back up to his closet. Ahhh, Spike. To know him is to love him.

Sterly's bubbly personality facilitated another only-Spike-could-pull-this-off story. As she explains:

> On my first day of work running Alumni Affairs, I get this blue Tiffany's box. I open it up and it's two silver balls. The note says, "Good luck. You're going to need these—Spike." They still sit on my desk today [nine years later]. Every day I look at them and I'm reminded that I need those. I love it

because it makes me think of Spike and how he thought to
do that for me.

In Sterly's defense, she has keen observations that go beyond one-dollar annual
fund gifts and boxer shorts:

> Spike is a great leader, and the world is not full of great
> leaders. They just don't make them like him anymore. He's
> also a great mentor, maybe not in the traditional way, but in
> the little things he does, like the way he values other people.
> One time he was throwing a surprise party for one of the
> other Ollies, and he went out and bought everything himself
> from the Party Store. He was a great mentor to learn from
> just by observing that someone that important would take
> the time to do the little things and add the nice touches, as
> well as be such an extraordinary family man. I learned a lot
> just by watching him.

Many others at Duke have fond memories of their interactions with Spike
as well. Tom Coffman, who started as the deputy director of athletics for
development and planning after Spike's chairmanship had ended, is as close
to Spike today as anyone at Duke, regularly visiting him in Avalon and in
Florida. Spike chose Tom to speak on behalf of the university at Mary's
funeral in 2015. Tom recognizes how many people perceive Spike upon first
meeting him, but he also knows what lies beneath the veneer. "Spike has this
tough-guy persona. Maybe that's from his dad or somewhere along the line.
He's got a certain bravado that if you didn't get to know him or if you only
met him a couple of times, you'd never realize just what a softie he is and
how big a heart he's really got. He doesn't always let that out." One of Dick
Brodhead's first memories as the new president of Duke involved Spike and
the Ollie Brothers:

There's a popular photograph of me, the new president, taken with the Ollie Brothers outside of the Washington Duke Hotel. That was a great way to first experience Spike because so much of him was invested in his friendships. To see that Spike and these men had been best friends for fifty-some years reminded me that I'm coming into a story that's been running for a long time.

Two aspects of the "story" to which Dick refers are tradition and ambition, which I touched on at the end of Spike's undergraduate years. I asked several Duke representatives what they thought made Duke unique and how that uniqueness related to Spike Yoh. According to Bob Shepard:

Duke, more than many universities, has this sense of community. With all of our differences, our disagreements, and our dysfunctionality, there's a sense of civility here that allows us, at times, to transcend our differences. I think that's how Spike views his own family—it's okay to be different, but keep that sense of community strong. Also, Duke is younger and scrappier than many other schools, and it's maybe a little more entrepreneurial and a little more nimble. I think we have a respect for our past, but we're not bound to it. That's a lot like the Spike Yoh that I know, too.

Dick adds to Bob's sentiments. "Great universities like Duke create inordinate affections. They catch you in such a formative moment of your life, and then your world opens up for you, and then people develop a devotion to it, this kind of indescribable devotion. Spike has that in spades." Kevin White cites Duke's "swagger and its adolescence, which make it such an aspirational place. Duke doesn't develop the financial capacity that it has unless it's also very entrepreneurial. All these things have now become pitted in our DNA." Each

of these people draws clear connections between these university attributes
and Spike. Tallman Trask does as well:

> Spike was part of a very interesting group of trustees who
> all went to Duke, but if you ask them why they give so much
> time and resource to Duke, none of them can really explain
> it. They'd become very affectionate about the place and they
> tried to make it better. I think at most other places that people
> think might be like Duke, a lot of folks believe that they're
> already so good that they can't get any better.

Kevin White says, "I categorized Spike as a leader's leader. He was strong
and determined, with equal parts humility and selflessness. A visionary, he
could see around the corner. He was a classic example of a person who was
manufactured in the Duke factory."

Mary and Spike with the Duke Blue Devil at a festive award ceremony

In wrapping up Spike's involvement with Duke, I'll quote from the speech
he delivered upon his retirement from the board in 2003: "Like most of you,

my circle of life includes family, God, country, and friends. But to me, Duke University has always been at the center of my circle, for it has touched virtually every positive and successful happening I have lived and achieved."

• • • •

In 2004, after his Duke chairmanship but still in the "I'm not really retired" phase of his retirement, Spike was named the chairman of the board at the Ocean Reef Club, his and Mary's winter home in Florida. Ocean Reef, or simply "The Reef," occupies the north end of Key Largo. Founded in the late 1940s as a fishing camp, it has grown considerably, the resort accommodations and amenities now encompassing over 2,500 acres of pristine but fragile natural habitat. Today the club has 4,700 total members and an annual operating budget in excess of $100 million.

Spike relished this new role, knowing it would present at least one unique challenge as compared to the other leadership positions he had held. When he ran D&Z, he would go home at night. While chairing any of his previous volunteer boards, he was usually around other stakeholders only while in meetings or on campus. At Ocean Reef he lived in the same neighborhoods, shopped at the stores, dined at the same restaurants, and attended the same events as the almost 1,200 "equity" members whom the board represented. Compounding this dynamic was the fact that most of Ocean Reef's members were or had been CEOs of successful businesses, managing partners of successful law firms, or had held other similar positions of authority. Spike recalls, "Even if the board passed something that we knew had ninety percent support, it still meant that there were about a hundred ex-CEOs that disagreed with what we had just done." Spike looked forward to being in the middle of everything—and everybody—all day, every day. He also knew that the major topic he and his fellow directors would address could have a lasting impact on the community. "My Ocean Reef chairmanship was going to deal with a big change to the membership levels and a consolidation of membership classes.

That was probably the biggest challenge I confronted in all of my nonprofit efforts. But I was looking forward to it."

In the early 1990s, a change in ownership set off a series of events that significantly altered the club's trajectory. The new ownership group endeavored to expand the demographic attraction of The Reef and made many alterations, including new management and significant renovations to the property. The latter changes were perhaps the most bothersome to the longer-established members. Gone were many of the thatched-roof structures, the old, quaint facades, and the natural, bohemian settings of some of the more popular locations. Unhappy members saw what they dubbed "Pepto Bismol Pink" become the central color pallet. To me, it seemed like The Reef went from being a natural-looking tropical escape to a large studio set for *Miami Vice*. All that was needed was for Crockett and Tubbs to come thundering in on a large, multicolored cigarette boat to complete the transformation. Some of these changes were intended to draw new members and increase conference business. However, the few new members who were attracted did not fit well with Ocean Reef's more established, conservative clientele. Making matters worse, the club's governance provided longtime members little influence over operations or major decisions.

Into these divisive developments charged Hurricane Andrew, a category 5 storm, on August 24, 1992. With wind gusts exceeding 160 miles per hour, its eye passed just north of Ocean Reef. The storm ravaged the area, generating an estimated fifteen years' worth of trash in four hours. Ocean Reef saw significant destruction with power lines felled, trees and irrigation systems uprooted, almost every roof and dock on the property destroyed, as well as indoor furniture strewn all over the grounds. Spike and Mary's house lost most of the roof tiles and screens, as well as suffered extensive damage to outdoor living spaces. The wind breached just one door and one window, but these small openings allowed outside debris to enter virtually every room of the two-story home. A breakfast room chair somehow wedged its way through a small window into the yard.

With all of these challenges, Ocean Reef's membership went to work. They were by no means shrinking violets, and many had amassed considerable wealth. In late 1992, a small group expertly negotiated the purchase of the club by the members. They raised an astonishing $52 million *in cash* from the membership in a mere six weeks. The purchase was funded by 250 "patron" members, who contributed $100,000 each, and by 900 "charter" members, each of whom provided $30,000. Both of these groups were called the "equity" members, with the patrons positioned to receive more and better perks for their higher investment.

When the membership buyout closed the following March, the club was losing $100,000 per month. After a top-flight management team was hired and significant focus was placed on both revenue and cost, the financial picture was largely corrected in just two years, the property restored to its glory. Gone were the pink walls and flamingo decorations. Back were the natural settings and relaxed atmosphere. The club entered a halcyon period of growth.

The Ocean Reef Club in Key Largo, Florida

And yet, over the ensuing decade, an increasing disparity emerged between the two categories of equity membership. A small faction of the charter members became particularly mobilized, publishing a secondary club newsletter as a mouthpiece for their growing dissatisfaction. Compounding the problems, an impeding economic slowdown curtailed the club's financials, further eroding the members' *esprit de corps*. Tom Davidson, a longtime member of Ocean Reef and one of the chief architects of the 1993 purchase, recalls, "The recession that followed the 9/11 attacks affected the hospitality industry considerably. Members became more circumspect and judgmental of what was going on rather than just drinking the Kool-Aid and assuming life would always be wonderful." In the midst of these challenges, Spike Yoh became chairman. Having joined the board in 1999, he moved up the leadership ranks and in his fourth year was voted vice chair, meaning he would assume the chairmanship after a transition that typically lasted a year and a half.

Mike Smith, chairman in 2003, remembers asking Spike to become his second in command. "We had just finished a board meeting, and I invited Spike into an empty office across from the board room. I said, 'Spike, I want you to become vice chair and follow me as chairman.' His mouth dropped. He didn't change color, but he got emotional. Usually when something hits Spike, he doesn't react real strongly. But he reacted strongly to that." As to why he thought Spike would make a good board chair, Mike offers, "He could be a contrarian. He might not really be a contrarian, but he could speak like one. If we were all lined up on an issue, he'd be the guy over there shooting holes in things. He made us better think through some of the matters we were deciding. He made us a better board." Unfortunately, Mike encountered health issues shortly after their conversation so—just like at Haverford—Spike became chairman sooner than normal. Mike believed his successor was up to the task. "Spike was ready. He might not have felt like he was ready, but he was ready to be chairman."

Spike took over in April of 2004. Ironically, it was not Spike's contrarianism, but his consensus building that was most in demand. According to Mike, "It was a deeply divided board. Spike saw that there was already enough contrarians, so he sort of came over and sat beside me, if you will, because he knew we had to pull together. He saw the divisiveness, and he wasn't going to be a part of it." These dynamics show how Spike could be a chameleon—consensus builder or devil's advocate—depending on what the circumstances warranted.

Tony Medaglia, another board member, also remembers Spike moving into the position. "He was smart, he was articulate, and he was fair minded and independent. He did what he thought was right." My interview with Tony and his wife Catherine was one of the most enjoyable moments of this biography experience. Tony is a retired lawyer from Boston with a huge personality and a thick New England accent. When I arrived at their house one spring afternoon, Tony, whom I had not met, was bent over at a forty-five-degree angle with one hand on his lower back when he greeted me at the door. I asked how he was doing and he fired back, "I'm doing awful! I put my back out and I can barely move!" I have had my fair share of back pain, so I empathized. Tony unboxed a large bottle of Johnnie Walker Green Scotch that his son had just sent him, announcing that he was going to have a glass "for his back pain." He asked if I wanted to join him. Um . . . yeah. Over the course of the interview, as we worked our way through healthy four-finger pours, Tony's back bothered him less and we had a great discussion.

On the community dynamics at the time, Tony reflects:

> Running the Ocean Reef Club was not an easy task. You've got a lot of bright, articulate people. Most were nice, and some were tough, but nobody arrived here on a subway, if you know what I mean. The members are generally wealthy and well-connected. You had to be on your toes, as many members were very outspoken. But Spike listened to people

and realized how much of an issue the dual-tiered membership
had become. He decided that we should get rid of it and have
one class of equity membership.

And so the stage was set for Spike and the board to tackle this divisive issue.
As a patron member himself, he and Mary had the potential of losing some
of their own patron benefits, but being the "Our Way" guy that he is, Spike
soldiered forth.

In addition to using his strong listening and communications skills, Spike's
down-to-earth style would be on display as well. Rich Miller, a fellow board
member and Spike's eventual successor as chairman, recalls meeting Spike
in the late 1990s:

> It was shortly after his retirement from D&Z. We ended up
> talking at a cocktail party, feeling each other out a bit. Spike
> said to me, "Tell me about your business." I said, "I was
> in the wood products business. I sold it recently." Nobody
> really talked about their revenues with private companies,
> so I proudly said, "We have about 350 employees. It's a fun
> business." I then said, "How about your business, Spike?" He
> says only that, "I had a design-build construct business up
> in Philadelphia." So I said, "Oh, tell me a little bit about it.
> How many employees did you have?" He said, "We are now
> approaching twenty thousand." I said, "What?" He laughed.
> Spike's just got a way about him. Not too many people could
> get away with that. He's unique. He is really unique.

The two fast friends later placed a bet on an NCAA Basketball Tournament
game between Spike's second-seeded Duke Blue Devils and Rich's fifteenth-
seeded Lehigh Mountain Hawks. "Despite being such underdogs, I bet Spike
ten bucks 'straight up' that Lehigh would win. Sure enough, they pulled off

the upset, and the next morning I got this envelope at my front door with ten crumpled-up one-dollar bills. I've kept them ever since." And he has; Rich showed them to me during our interview.

Mike Smith also appreciated Spike's easygoing style, particularly for how it contrasts with the more flamboyant nature of some of the members. "Ocean Reef is a whole bunch of alpha dogs with a lot of money. I never once, ever, was with Spike when he inferred anything about his wealth." When a wine auctioneer came to Ocean Reef and wondered how many members were "sprayers of fire hydrants," indicating their penchant for prattling on about how great they were, Mike said, "I always think about that, because Spike was never a sprayer of fire hydrants." Finally, Mike said, "I'm a wise-cracker. I'm always saying something crazy. But with Spike, before I even got it out of my mouth, he would be there with a retort that was ten yards down the road."

Tom Davidson, one of the leaders of the club purchase in the early 1990s, is a retired Canadian businessman and longtime friend and YPO colleague of Spike's. Given Spike's conclusion that the dual-tiered membership structure should be eliminated, the two men were on opposite sides of the ensuing debate. Despite their friendship—and their wives' and children's friendships—this would not be the first time their relationship generated a bit of friction. Tom recalls an incident in the early 1980s when both men served on YPO's executive board. Tom suggested that YPO consider adding Ocean Reef to its list of meeting destinations. Tom and his family had by then become regulars, whereas Spike and Mary had only been there once, a visit during which some of the local "inhabitants" had been a nuisance. Tom recalls:

> Spike had been bothered by mosquitos during his first visit
> so he rained on my parade in a pretty heavy way, telling the
> board that we should not go to Ocean Reef. I knew that his
> insect experience was an anomaly, and we did, in fact, end
> up getting a meeting there. But it may have delayed it a year

or two. So one of my first impressions of Spike was that he
was not a person to be taken lightly. He makes his opinions
known in a vocal and usually demonstrative way.

Spike's bug encounter was in fact an anomaly, much to the pleasure of all of us
Yohs. Tom and Spike again butted heads a few years later after Spike and Mary
ran the large Caribbean cruise for YPO. The success of the event yielded a
surplus for YPO, and Spike and Tom—both in positions of influence—disagreed
over how to utilize the excess funds. Eventually the two professionals worked
through their differences and came to a compromise. This event, however,
further set the stage for what would become their biggest debate, almost twenty
years later, regarding the dual-tiered membership structure at Ocean Reef.

Tom recalls the patron membership issue coming to a head:

Spike and I were probably philosophically on opposite sides
of that spectrum. My feeling was that the patron members
had taken a substantial risk at the time. Everyone forgets the
fact that we had no business. We'd just had a major hurricane
and the place was beat up. We had no management team. It
was a leap of faith to assume we were going to be able to
just break even.

Alan Goldstein, another principal player in the early 1990s club purchase, was
similarly opposed to Spike on this matter. My interview with Alan involved the
most extravagant setting of all of my conversations, namely a yacht anchored
off the island of St. Lucia. Unfortunately, it was Alan, not I, who was on the
yacht; I spoke to him via satellite from my stateside home office. He recounts:

When Spike became chairman, it was the only time when
we ever had any real problems within the community in
terms of governance. Spike believed it would be better to
have only one level of membership. He was probably more

liberal minded and more accommodative than some other chairman would have been. He handled it as well as could be, given his perspective. But as you can guess, it wasn't necessarily my perspective.

Wait a minute. Spike, liberal minded? That's a first! Apparently he truly *could* morph his style to accomplish a major task.

Regarding the polarity of the membership, Rich Miller recalls how Spike "accepted one of the key dissenters as a member of the board. That was his philosophy, let the debate take place right there. It provided for some really hot board conversations. We spent so damn much time on it." As Spike had done time and again, he faced the issue head-on and made sure that everyone's views were heard.

Spike (far left) and his fellow Ocean Reef board chairs

Paul Astbury, the club president at the time, joins Joe Healy at Haverford and Nan Keohane at Duke in commending Chairman Spike's unambiguous communications style and debate facilitation. In his charming British accent, Paul says:

> I enjoyed Spike for his directness. There was never any misunderstanding about what he wanted to achieve. He was certainly not shy about confronting issues, which I found very refreshing. He worked hard at redefining the board by creating an openness and a respect for others' views, which created warmth among the board members. A lot of that was done outside the boardroom, mostly at breakfasts. Spike was famous for breakfasts.

Paul describes how Spike's inclusive approach also encompassed the membership at large:

> There had been really poor communications around the whole issue of patron memberships. It became rather unpleasant. Spike sought to increase the level of trust that members had in the board and to lead with openness and dialogue. He asked the board members to reserve their Thursday afternoons to meet with any members who were unhappy or had something to discuss. That gave a forum for the members, particularly those who were a little difficult, so they now couldn't say, "Well, I never got to meet with the board or put my thoughts forward." Spike spent an incredible amount of time, and he had incredible patience with difficult and opinionated members. That style, along with his directness with other board members, really set the whole process in motion.

Paul and I discussed the rarity of this leadership duality. Spike was simultaneously direct and patient. Someone who can be blunt might not be the most patient person. But at the helm of Ocean Reef, as in many other situations, Spike could be both, just as he could be both a contrarian and a consensus-builder.

After many months of breakfast debates, backroom discussions, and letter-writing campaigns, the membership issue came to a head in early 2005. Rich Miller says:

> Everything culminated with a meeting of all the patrons. They held it in the Cultural Center and it was packed. People were sitting in the aisles. I remember having to sit on the steps. Spike was on stage alone, fielding questions. Some people mocked him and his position. They denigrated him. It was a tremendous embarrassment for Ocean Reef. But Spike handled it so well. He kept his cool. I don't know how he did that.

Rich's wife Margo recalls that "Spike stayed very calm. He never raised his voice. He's a very good listener, and he just has this ability to get people on his side. He makes so much sense that it's hard to argue with him." Spike's ability to remain composed, as we learned from his prior leadership roles, was partially due to his demeanor and quick thinking, but also due to preparation. He had conducted more conversations, read more documents, and contemplated more deeply all of the issues at stake, than anyone else in the room.

After an hour or so of fiery debate, Rich recalls how the main dissenters "had run out of questions. Spike had answered everything that could have been asked." In order to pass such a monumental change, the bylaws required that 90% of both patrons and charters vote affirmatively. Not surprisingly, the charter members approved the change. Much to people's surprise, the patrons did as well. Tony Medaglia says, "The patrons voted overwhelmingly to give up their patron memberships and take what was still a pretty handsome financial deal. Spike stood tall against his fellow patrons and brought peace to the valley." Tony's wife Catherine remembers the vote's aftermath. "When Spike resolved the membership deal, no one pointed at him and said he ruined our patron status or that he took away this or that. He saw something that was wrong, and he had the guts to correct it. Everyone respected him for doing that." The year was 2005, and the club could now move on from this unprecedented debate. Since then, Ocean Reef has attained even greater levels of growth, success, and beauty.

The inevitable test of time proved Spike and the board of directors correct in their push to eliminate the two-tiered structure. Even Tom Davidson, one of the system's architects, concedes:

> Spike, rightly so, was reacting as any good leader and politician does. He is not afraid of putting the cat amongst the pigeons and stirring things up. Maybe his is not always the most pleasant way for people involved in the process, but it achieves a result that is embraced by all sides, which is what the end game is. In the final analysis, he and I and others ended up linking arms and staring both sides down to come up with an arrangement that the patron group could live with.

Alan Goldstein seconded Tom. "Time proved Spike right. Everybody got used to it. I must say that there's never been a time since then when there's been any kind of movement to overturn or change the structure." Spike credits Tom and Alan not only for their original vision to buy the club, but also for their support of the membership tier overhaul. "Without their understanding and support, it would not have happened."

Tony shares a concluding vignette to the membership issue: "Every year, there's a dinner for the present and past boards. When Spike arrived at the dinner shortly after the vote, all the former patrons booed him. But it was totally a joke, and everyone immediately laughed." Clearly they understood what had taken place, and Spike helped ensure that there was indeed "peace in the valley."

While overseeing the elimination of the two-tiered membership structure was Spike's greatest accomplishment as board chair of Ocean Reef, he also presided over the creation and implementation of strategic plans and various capital projects. Finally, Paul remembers how Spike's constant communications focus was at odds with his at-best remedial computer skills:

> Spike loved to be kept up to date, so I would send him four or five emails a day when he was chairman. He always responded by printing out the email, writing his comments on the piece of paper, and then faxing it back to me. By the time he finished his chairmanship, I had this huge file of all his hard copies. Going over some of it later, it was certainly the most amusing reading.

Many people will attest to receiving facsimile copies of printed-out emails emblazoned with Spike's chicken-scratch commentary. Mike Yoh chuckles about how Dad used to refer to his keyboard as "the typewriter." In Spike's defense, over the past few years, he has in fact located and learned to use the "reply" button on his email program, and he now types (almost all of) his responses.

• • • •

In January 2006, Spike ended his tenure on the board at Ocean Reef. He was nearing the end of a run of volunteer leadership efforts that spanned four decades. He was still, however, fulfilling one final "chairmanteer" role, this time with the Boy Scouts. About an hour away from Ocean Reef, farther into the Florida Keys, sits the Boy Scout's Florida Sea Base, a "high adventure" camp where troops from around the country go to sail, scuba dive, fish, and camp. It is an impressive facility, regarded as one of the most desirable Scout retreats. During his board tenure at Ocean Reef, Spike had agreed to be chairman of Sea Base's Advisory Committee. "It was close to home, it was something I loved, and I knew I could make a difference." Spike ended up chairing Sea Base for almost ten years, helping to grow the size and caliber of the oversight committee, to elevate the exposure and reputation of the facility on a national level, and most importantly, to increase its fund-raising capabilities. After Spike's resignation as chairman of Sea Base in 2013, my brother Mike began serving on the oversight committee, paying homage to his Eagle Scout accomplishment, his love of the Keys, and his respect for Dad.

Spike's volunteer leadership efforts, driven by his personal passions and his deep experience as a business executive, advanced the missions of many important institutions—from youth and business organizations to independent schools and higher education to family living communities. His ability to influence and to impart management doctrine, as well as his skill at building consensus and momentum, left an indelible mark wherever he went. And—as always—Spike notes how important it is to remember one's role when leading an organization. "Always be humble. Your success and praise from your constituents will last only as long as a gin and tonic." Along with his family life and his professional career, volunteer leadership was the final leg of Spike Yoh's sturdy three-legged stool, on which thousands of people have rested, grown, and flourished.

Chapter 9

Family Value

He that raises a large family does, indeed, while he lives to observe them, stand a broader mark for sorrow; but then he stands a broader mark for pleasure too.
—*Benjamin Franklin*

Back in the mid-1980s, while Spike's business continued to grow and his volunteer efforts started to expand, he and Mary entered their second quarter-century of marriage and saw their nest become more and more empty. Once Jeff left for college in 1984, I—as the baby of the family—had a five-year stretch as the only child living at home. This experience was unique in our family and proved impactful in terms of the adult I would become. Children born into families that own successful businesses or otherwise have economic means are sometimes crudely referred to as "lucky sperm." While all of Spike and Mary's children qualify for this label, my diabolic older siblings took the expression one step further, dubbing me "favorite lucky sperm," or "FLS" for short. As usually happens with the baby of the family, my parents—particularly my dad—had softened by the time I came through my teenage years, and I received more positive reinforcement than my siblings. While the trend line is not linear, Spike and Mary instilled in each of us progressively greater amounts of self-esteem, culminating with "FLS."

251

During my five years of sibling-less-ness, which coincided with Spike having more flexibility in his work and travel schedules, I spent a lot of individual time with Spike and Mary. In earlier years, dinners were raucous affairs, with five kids shouldering and nosing their way into the family trough, simultaneously competing for airtime and trying to escape the madness of the kitchen table. But later, I had my parents' undivided attention at mealtime. Prior to sitting down for dinner, I remember the strong, three-part aroma of Spike's post-work reentry to home: Antonio & Cleopatra cigar smoke from a day of puffing away at the office, blended with the Dewar's White Label Scotch and Planters dry-roasted peanuts that served as the starter's pistol for his evening routine. I remember long conversations both during and after dinners, talking about the game I had just played, a trip the family was planning, or the latest heartbreaking loss of one our professional sports teams.

As important as any detail, the number of dishes I had to do was virtually nonexistent compared to the piles of plates, glasses, and pans that used to make up a ceramic castle on the kitchen counter in my younger years. Mom had advanced her cooking skills as well, introducing us to new international cuisine to which she and Spike had been exposed on their many YPO trips around the world. Her wok-cooked cashew chicken with snow peas and water chestnuts were particularly tasty. We also frequented nice restaurants and took many memorable trips to New York to see Broadway shows. I played four sports in high school, and one or both parents attended almost every competition.

Spike's softening also enabled me to take advantage of him as any teenager might. When my oldest brother Hal would go out on the weekends in his later high school years, he had a curfew of midnight. Because Spike liked to keep things simple, he would set his alarm clock for twelve a.m. If Hal turned the alarm off before it rang and Spike woke normally in the morning, all was well. But if instead the alarm sounded, Hal was grounded, no questions asked, no excuses considered. Fast-forward a decade. I, too, had a midnight curfew, though I remember a few nights calling home around eleven thirty or eleven forty-five and giving what was, in hindsight, some lame excuse about car trouble or something similar. Mom and Dad would usually be in a deep sleep, so they would say "okay" and hang up. I suppose it helped that the phone was on Mom's side of the bed. I can't blame my siblings for being upset about this erosion of discipline.

Bill and Spike during my "only child" years

Being an "only child" for five years also instilled in me an inclination to do things my own way. I even hung a poster in my room of two roosters staring at each other, one with a typical rooster's comb, the other with a hair comb. The poster's caption read, "Dare to be different." This independence influenced my college application process, almost to the dismay of Spike. I was a strong student at Haverford, and at the start of senior year, my preference was to apply early to Princeton and play football. While I later learned that Spike was quietly disappointed that I might break the Duke streak, he may have taken solace in the fact that his favorite uncle and my middle namesake, Courtlandt Schenck, had attended. However, fate intervened, namely in the form of weather. Early in my senior year, I visited Princeton and stayed with two student-athletes who had graduated from Haverford the year before. Despite my visit occurring in September, the weather was cold and rainy, a prematurely raw fall day in the Mid-Atlantic Region. These conditions were juxtaposed to a visit to Duke the prior spring when the weather had been absolutely perfect. On my return from Princeton, I sat on the kitchen counter debriefing my parents. Much to their—and possibly my—surprise, I announced that I wanted to apply early to Duke and try to walk on to the lacrosse team. I can still recall both of their faces lighting up and their simultaneously saying, "Really?" Given Spike's earlier confession about scheduling New England college visits in the winter, I'm sure he enjoyed learning that weather had helped fulfill his hope of having another Blue Devil in the family. Despite my rebel inclinations, I came around to the family norm and would soon be on my way to Durham.

• • • •

While I was at home playing sports and (occasionally) breaking curfew, my siblings were finishing their studies and entering the workforce. Each of us took a different path after college, but all eventually ended our early-adulthood journeys in Philadelphia working for Day & Zimmermann.

Hal graduated from Duke in 1983 and soon after put his mechanical engineering degree to work at Westinghouse. It is common practice for owners of family businesses to work outside of the company early in their careers; today it is a requirement for Yoh family members to do so. However, Hal's career decision after college was driven by instinct and experience. "I was tired of people telling me I was going to be running the business someday. I didn't need that. I wanted to do something on my own." Much like Spike twenty-five years before, Hal wanted to blaze his own trail. Among Hal's engineering duties with Westinghouse—at stints in Pittsburgh, Baltimore, and Raleigh—were designing residential electric meters and programming punch presses. Early on he realized that his broad exposure to business during his

D&Z summers inclined him to want to do more than just practice engineering. "The work had an engineering bent to it, but nothing about how to market out there and how to sell out there. I knew I wanted to do more."

Hal had met his wife Sharon at Duke. She was from Dallas and graduated in just three years with a degree in English and psychology. After their marriage in Sharon's hometown in 1984, Sharon moved into Hal's apartment in Raleigh. After one year of marriage and two years into his career at Westinghouse, Hal came to two important conclusions. First, he had gotten his professional sea legs under him and decided that he was in fact interested in joining Day & Zimmermann. Second, he and Sharon were ready to start a family and they did not want to do so in Raleigh. During a family vacation, Hal said to Spike, "I'm ready to come back. I'd like to join D&Z." In the early days of 1986, Hal and Sharon moved to the Philadelphia area, and Hal joined the engineering and construction division, progressing through a series of roles in project management, sales, and business unit leadership. As mentioned, he also briefly oversaw Day Products, the company's foray into the plastic recycling business. Today Hal is in his nineteenth year as our chairman and CEO.

Mike's path into the business was more straightforward, although his landing point was not where he expected. He earned his civil engineering degree from Duke in 1985 and was planning on joining D&Z's architecture company, the Vitetta Group, where he had spent a few school summers. Spike and Gene D'Ambrosio, however, had other plans. As Mike recalls, "Dad and General D. ganged up on me, saying how they contractually needed a civil engineer at the Kansas plant [a 13,000+ acre site with a series of manufacturing and administrative buildings dotting the landscape]. I didn't want to go to freakin' Kansas!" But Mike remembers how Spike convinced his second-born to "'just go out and listen and see what's going on.' I agreed to go as long as I was only there until they found somebody else." Mike's first exposure to Kansas life was far from ideal. "I got there in August, and one day in September I'm sitting on the top floor of this matchstick building looking out at a tornado that had just touched down nearby. I picked up the phone and called Dad. I held the phone to the window and shouted, 'You hear that noise?'" Fortunately, the tornado missed the building. More importantly, Mike was not challenged by his initial work assignment but was soon transferred to a more engaging role at the plant. From there, as Mike says, "The rest is history." Today, he is in his thirty-second year in D&Z's munitions business. He has worked at every one of the company's munitions facilities, all of which are in decidedly rural parts of the country. Additionally, during one four-year stretch, he spent a total of twenty-four months living in India overseeing the installation of an ammunition production line. Though he spent most nights under insect netting, he still contracted malaria. Mike also spent a combined six months in Taiwan. He met his first wife during his second stint in Kansas. He has been the president of the munitions business, reporting directly to Hal, since 2008.

Mary and Spike with Karen during her twenty-first birthday celebration

Karen graduated from Duke in 1987 with a dual degree in psychology and sociology, just like Mary had twenty-eight years earlier. With diploma in hand, Karen entered into a hybrid role at the company; she was a Day & Zimmermann employee but worked as a contractor for DuPont performing various marketing and human resources duties. Additional symmetry came from the fact that Mary had spent two college summers working at DuPont. After her contract assignment, Karen's career progressed through a series of roles, culminating with overseeing D&Z's chartable efforts and running the company's travel agency, Barclay Travel. Yes, Spike owned a travel agency. In addition to being an extreme example of the Spike's diversification strategy, Barclay Travel also showed his practical side. Because so many of our employees traveled for business, he thought it made sense to own a travel agency. Despite there being few synergies between D&Z's core businesses and a travel agency, the venture served the company well and enabled Karen to succeed as the leader of a business. She left Day & Zimmermann in 2005, selling her ownership stake. She then went on to support a number of charities and children-related organizations, including Children's Hospital of Philadelphia.

Jeff's college years led to a degree in mechanical engineering (and many more shirts that said "Duke" on them), while his summers were spent working for the Yoh Company. Much like his decision to attend Duke, Jeff's post-college direction was clear. "I was going to the Yoh Company. It was sort of what I'd been brought up to do. It was the business that Dad came out of and it had that entrepreneurial drive, a very people-oriented business." Jeff is quite the people person, always gregarious and social. He is also very entrepreneurial, just like Spike. For him, the Yoh Company and the staffing industry were a perfect fit. Jeff's early years at Yoh involved stints in St. Louis, Seattle, and Winston-Salem. I personally enjoyed his years in North Carolina, when I was at Duke and he was getting his MBA on the weekends at Fuqua, Duke's business school. He also married his wife Suzanne, whom he had met in

Seattle, during that time. Eventually Jeff became an executive at Yoh and moved his young family to the Philadelphia area.

However, seeds of entrepreneurialism grew in Jeff, creating a desire to blaze his own trail, something he first mentioned to Spike and Mary in 1998. "I wanted to go do something on my own, and Dad didn't want me to go do something on my own. The conversation kind of sucked." Jeff tells how Spike evoked a revered Yoh family role model to make his point. "Dad talked about Coach K's 'five fingers' analogy and how clenched together they make a strong fist but separated they are weak and vulnerable. The five of us were meant to do that. I got some 'tough love' guilt for sure." Reacting to his own troubled business dealings with his father, Spike's objective had always been to build a company that was large enough and diverse enough so that all five of his kids would have their own space, while still remaining united as an ownership group. In Jeff's case, Spike's tough love did the trick—for now—and rather than leave D&Z, Jeff and his young family satisfied their need to strike out on their own by relocating to Charlotte. "Obviously the move down South was the first step. And it might have been the more difficult step for Mom and Dad to accept because I no longer lived near everyone else." Despite the change in geography, Jeff's entrepreneurial itch didn't go away, and he decided to leave the company in 2003—two years before Karen. I remember standing in my bedroom one evening talking to him on the phone about the dynamics between him and the rest of us, his relationship with Larry Suwak—his boss and mentor—and everything that was at stake. Eventually, Jeff said, "You know what? I think it's probably best if I leave." I don't know if that was the first time he had said those words out loud, but the seriousness of his intention struck me; one of us was leaving the business. With his mind made up, Jeff "flew right to Florida to see Mom and Dad. I made it clear that I was not leaving the family but just wanted to do something on my own." Given that he had brought up the possibility of leaving five years earlier and had relocated, Jeff notes that his parents' reaction was much different this time. "I remember them basically saying, 'Well, you've talked about this for a long time. I guess it's what's going to happen.'" After D&Z, Jeff embarked on his own career, eventually becoming the majority owner of Jenkins Restoration, a refurbishment business that rebuilds homes and commercial properties after floods and fires have destroyed them. His post–D&Z success demonstrates just how entrepreneurial he was—and still is.

When Karen announced her intention to leave two years later, we had all been through the process and the cycle of emotions. We knew by then that not all of us were fulfilled by being so professionally and financially tethered to each other. I learned that children—at any age—require a balance of control and support. Spike struggled with this duality and with the departure of two of his children from the business that he had passed on to us just a few years earlier.

As my time at Duke wound down, with a degree in political science and Spanish, my rebellious side compelled me neither to work with nor live near my family. I set my sights on management consulting and San Francisco, both of which had little to do with Day & Zimmermann and the Yoh family. However, a series of knee injuries starting in high school led to two more surgeries in my first year after college, during which I lived at home and worked at D&Z, continuing in the corporate development role I had held the prior summer. Once my knee healed, I moved to San Francisco with Barbara's middle child, my cousin Jill. I had secured a job at CSC Index, a management consulting company, where I started in 1994. I spent two years there, six months of which were consumed by weekly commutes to Minneapolis. During one of these trips, Hal happened to be in the Twin Cities on business and we had dinner. He had recently been named president of Day & Zimmermann and talked about some of the exciting happenings back in Philadelphia. I'm not sure if his comments were meant as a recruiting pitch, but they got me thinking more seriously about rejoining D&Z. I remember he ordered a bottle of William Hill wine, so maybe he was trying to sell me? I also had a girlfriend in Philadelphia whom I had been dating long distance. That woman was Kelly Green, now my wife of twenty years. In 1996, I moved back to Philadelphia and restarted my Day & Zimmermann career. I spent the next twenty years at the company in various business unit and corporate roles. For fifteen of those years, I worked directly for Hal. I transitioned out of most of these efforts at the end of 2015 to research and write this biography.

• • • •

Family has always been Spike and Mary's greatest priority. They worked diligently to create a closely aligned family unit, which is why the introduction of daughters-in-law to Spike's world was such a profound series of events. As each of his sons married—Karen never did—Spike's family both expanded and divided. The expansion meant bigger gatherings, more Yohs out in the community, and eventually many grandchildren. But each new in-law brought her own set of family values and practices, some of which tested the Yoh family structures and routines over which Spike had presided since the 1960s. The individual and collective growing pains that ensued have both challenged Spike and helped him grow as a person.

Sharon and Hal started dating during their freshman year at Duke. Sharon, in her native Lone Star State accent, has clear recollections of her first Yoh family immersion:

> Y'all were all together, and y'all picked me up in the Yoh van.
> We drove to the Angus Barn for dinner. I come from a family
> who's reserved and quiet and keeps things low key. So my
> biggest impression was, "Wow, here I am from Texas, and
> you think everything's bigger in Texas. But this is really what
> 'bigger' is." Honestly, I had never seen so many larger-than-life,

> loud people in one van. Once we got to the Angus Barn, I
> have literally never seen a group eat more onion rings. But
> for me, it was great. It was an all-out college pig fest.

She also recalls how well she and Spike seemed to connect. "He definitely feels more comfortable with people when they share things in common with him. Maybe it was the fact that I went to Duke and Hal had met me there. I never felt anything but that he thought I was okay." Like many people, Spike relishes familiarity, and their shared college experience ingratiated Sharon to him from the jump.

Suzanne's first exchange with Spike serves as a strong counterpoint to Sharon's. "When I first met him, one of the things he asked me was where I went to school. I told him the University of Washington. He came right back with, 'Don't worry, dear. Maybe you can get a degree from Duke as well.'" This was one time when Spike's Duke zealotry clearly trumped his decorum. However, anyone who knows Suzanne knows that such a comment would not derail her. She fired back, "I'm really fine with my degree. And I even went to public school. And I'm okay." After she and Jeff were engaged, Suzanne was told—*warned* may be the operative term—about Spike and the Yoh family. "My family had mutual friends. I heard people say things like, 'You're going to marry him? You know you're marrying the whole family, right? Are you okay with that?'" But Suzanne is strong minded and was capable of dealing with these dynamics. The fact was, however, Spike was controlling and had become accustomed to having things go his way within his family and without. Jeff and Suzanne's wedding in 1993 tested this, as Suzanne explains:

> Ever since I was a little girl, I wanted to have my wedding
> reception at a certain hotel in Seattle. It was only available in
> early May and the end of August, and we didn't want to wait
> until August because we were dating long distance and flying
> across the country almost every week. But the May weekend

coincided with the Kentucky Derby, and Spike and Mary had seats in the Breeder's Box. They really wanted to go the race and sort of made a stink about it. I was bewildered more than anything else. I didn't understand how you could compare a horse race that lasts two minutes to your son's wedding. We got married in May anyway, and of course Jeff's parents were there. But we heard about that one for a long time.

Suzanne and Spike have a great relationship today, but their early encounters showed Spike's initial challenges accommodating new members into his brood.

My wife Kelly's first impression of Spike made a similar but less drastic impression. In 1994, shortly before I moved to San Francisco, she and I went on just our third date, when I subjected her to an evening with my entire family (at a summer concert featuring Billy Joel and Elton John). Afterward, we continued the festivities at my parents' house, where I was living at the time, and Kelly spent the night (in a separate room, thank you very much). She remembers the next morning vividly. "When Bill was getting ready to drive me home, Dad looked up from his breakfast and said, 'It was nice to meet you. Have a good rest of the summer.' He was basically like 'You won't be back.'" Spike had no reason not to like Kelly, but his definitive tone caught her off guard. Little did he know that he would end up seeing her virtually every day for the rest of that summer.

Kelly's first visit to Ocean Reef a few months later was an example of the clashing of family customs that occurred, in this case the Yoh family "cocktail hour." "The thing that stands out to me," she says, "was that we were having cocktail hour before going to dinner. I remember being like, 'What? We're all together all day and later we're all having dinner together. Why are we also all getting dressed up and having cocktail hour in between?' That was not something my family ever did." Our wedding in 1997 also demonstrated the challenges of melding family backgrounds. Kelly is Catholic, and we were to be married in the chapel of her alma mater, Villanova University, where her uncle Frank was a priest and the former chair of the Religious Studies Department. Given that my family was Episcopalian and could not take communion in a Catholic church, Kelly and I had a private Communion Mass with her uncle the day before the wedding. We then had what I'm sure is one of the few communion-less Catholic weddings in the Villanova Chapel's history.

Spike with his daughter and daughters-in-law

Around the time I met Kelly, Mike met his future wife, Gayle, the two introduced by Sharon and a mutual friend. Like each of her sisters-in-law, Gayle has early impressions of Spike and the Yoh family that proved memorable as well. We were all on a family vacation at Skytop Lodge in the Pocono Mountains, the same place where Spike and his father had had their fish-catching competition a half-century earlier. The trip was just two weeks before Gayle and Mike's wedding in the summer of 1998. Skytop is an old, traditional resort hotel, where dinner in the main dining room involves white linens, fine china, and coat-and-tie attire. Unfazed by the formality of the evening, my family decided to play one of our more unique, and quite frankly, obnoxious games. "Spoons," not to be confused with the card game by the same name, requires participants to line up two spoons end-to-end so that the bottom end of one spoon abuts the base of a water glass and the bottom end of the second spoon nests underneath the working end of the first spoon. On this night, as on many nights when spoons is played, the water glasses in the main dining room at Skytop were stemmed crystal. Once the spoons are in place, the player slams his or her fist down onto the working end of the outer spoon, which sends the inner spoon twirling into the air, the objective being to land it in the water glass. The game is quite loud and can be messy. I know what you're thinking . . . and yes, this is not the most sophisticated way to behave in a nice restaurant. In Spike's defense, spoons was often started by Mary, belying the innocent, ladylike demeanor she typically exuded. After taking her turn, she would often accessorize herself by placing the concave side of one of the spoons on her nose, proudly dangling it for all to see.

Regardless of who started the game on this night, things got loud quickly. Gayle, two weeks before her official union with the family, was understandably mortified. "I burst into tears and went running into the ladies room. I remember Kelly and Sharon and Karen all coming after me and me going, 'Oh my god, what am I getting into? What kind of family is this?'" None of us, perhaps particularly Spike and Mary—the elder statesmen of the group—anticipated the impression our boorish antics would have on our soon-to-be family member. We did what we did, largely following the attitude of our patriarch. While still not one to condone loud antics in public, Gayle has been married to Mike for nineteen years and today goes with the Yoh family flow as well as anyone. Helping offset the above prenuptial stunt, Mike and Gayle's wedding ceremony took place at Gayle's place of worship, All Saints Episcopal Church in Wynnewood, the same church from so many of Spike's own family's life events. It can be a very small world indeed.

During the early years of his sons' marriages, Spike's long shadow continued at times to impact his daughters-in-law. Sharon recalls:

> The first real fight Hal and I had was over how we spent
> the holidays. Hal thought we should spend every Christmas
> with his family because Christmas was so important to his
> father. I'm sure [Spike's attitude] was a reaction to his own
> childhood, that his family would always be his family. No one
> would break away. Everyone new would just add to his fold.

Sharon and Hal were the first ones to experience this pressure around holidays and other major gatherings. However, Spike and Mary soon established a practice, which was mostly successful for a number of years, of asking each of their kids and their families to alternate major holidays between their house and their in-laws'.

Though some first impressions of Spike were mixed, subsequent interactions with his sons and their wives showed his generosity and his desire to support his kids' marriages. In 1986, when Hal and Sharon were deciding to move to Philadelphia, Spike and Mary helped them look for houses and paid for a plane ticket for Sharon to fly into town at the last minute to see the house that she and Hal ended up purchasing. Mom and Dad provided both Mike and Jeff with loans to facilitate their moves back to Philadelphia, and they assisted Kelly and me in furnishing our first home. They also advised Karen in the selection of each of the five different apartments and houses in which she lived on the Main Line. Spike helped his kids move home and get settled. He wanted us all nearby. These were largely win-win outcomes.

The arrival of grandchildren provided Spike with another new set of dynamics. Again, the outcomes were mixed, although more positive than not. For example, when Mike and Gayle had triplets, born at twenty-nine weeks, early even for multiples, they weighed one pound, two pounds, and two pounds, respectively. Each of them spent between one and three months in a neonatal intensive care unit before coming home. Gayle and Mike lived about thirty minutes from the hospital, while Spike and Mary's Haverford home was less than ten minutes away. "They opened up their house while the triplets were at Lankenau," Gayle says. "We basically moved in to be closer to them. They let us convert their largest bedroom into a nursery and got us two cribs and a bassinet." As the triplets came home one by one, accompanied by loud heart monitors and around-the-clock nurses, Spike and Mary provided crucial support. Fittingly, many years later, Mike and Gayle bought that home when our parents decided to downsize.

Mike and Gayle have an older son as well, Ryan, whom Mike adopted during his first marriage. Given how much older Ryan is than the triplets, I always enjoy telling people that my brother has (at this time) a thirty-five-year-old son and sixteen-year-old triplets! Among Ryan's many memories of his times with Spike, one stands out:

> I was eight or nine years old and Granddad was driving me to the Shore in the Yoh van [Don't you love how no one ever calls it just "the van"?]. I had a new cassette tape from MC Hammer that included the song "U Can't Touch This." I had only ever listened to that song and maybe one other. When we got in the van, Granddad saw that I had the tape and said, "Throw it in the cassette deck. Let's listen to it." I said, "Granddad, you're not going to want to listen to this music." But he insisted, and we listened to it for the whole trip, the entire album. Even at my young age, I remember thinking that he must be convinced that my generation is lost. But he didn't say a word about it. We listened to MC Hammer for almost two hours.

Spike Yoh indulging his grandson in lyrics such as "My-my-my-my music makes me so hard" and "A super dope homeboy from Oaktown" again shows how adaptable he could be. He saw an opportunity to connect with Ryan and did so, etching a fond memory in his oldest grandchild's mind. Ryan and his wife Ashley have provided the family with the first two members of our next generation, making Spike a great-grandfather as well.

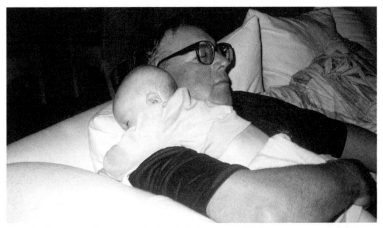

Spike modeling good behavior for one of his granddaughters

Spike and Mary often babysat Jeff and Suzanne's young children, even when Jeff and Suzanne lived in North Carolina and would travel out of town for several days. Spike dutifully drove the kids to school, did the grocery shopping (a task he reveres!), and performed many of the bedtime rites for his grandkids.

Kelly's pregnancies and the births of our children provided a mixed collection of Spike experiences. During all three of her pregnancies, Kelly had hyperemesis, which is a fancy way of saying that she threw up all day, every day, for seven to eight months—with each child (right now you mothers reading this are wondering why she went through that three times). She remembers Spike's attitude not being particularly compassionate. "I felt like he was not supportive through my being sick and not feeling well much of the time." I recall Dad somewhat blaming me for "allowing" Kelly to be sick like that, an accusation that I rejected and for which I scolded him. Like he always did with Mary, I put up a united front with my wife. Offsetting this, Kelly notes how sweet Spike was when each of our children was born:

He was there when every baby arrived, even with the third one when Mary happened to be sick and couldn't visit. They still flew in from Florida. And then he came again the next day as well, by himself. He brought me a Coke and a bagel, because he knew those things made me feel better. It is a great memory that I have, him sitting by my bed at the hospital, just the two of us. He made that extra stop before he got on the plane back to Florida.

Though his knee-jerk comments or overbearing demeanor could dampen a mood, Spike was typically compassionate and supportive, ultimately winning over family members who experienced the entire Spike spectrum.

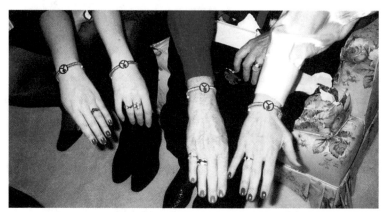

One year's installment of "Spike's Secret"

One special trait that each of Spike's daughters-in-law have come to relish is his sentimentality, the same sappiness that revealed itself long before in the proposal poem he wrote for Mary in 1958. This sweet side of Spike was particularly evident at Christmastime. He has always loved Christmas and has always loved to shower the women in his life with jewelry. Some years the jewelry would be lavish and sometimes it would be symbolic, but it was always well thought out. One year, he delivered the gems in red and gold

Victoria's Secret bags, only he crossed out "Victoria's" and wrote in "Spike's." The women still chuckle about that today. The bracelets and necklaces held special meaning, but everyone knew that for Spike, Christmas was about more than presents. As Kelly points out, "He loves Christmas like nobody. It's not about the gifts. It's about the season and the whole thing around it. He's always been a very thoughtful person, way back to the days of 'Spike's Secret,' carrying around those bags of jewelry for us."

While Spike's four sons all married and provided him with a total of fourteen grandchildren, Karen never married and never had kids. Entering adulthood, Jeff knew her as well as anybody, given that they were only one year apart in school. During the three years they overlapped at Duke, the two had dinner every Sunday as well as went out together other times each week. Jeff recollects:

> She was still living the life that she had planned at that point.
> She wanted to have kids and wanted to be a mom. But she
> didn't get married right after school, so she became this
> domineering businesswoman. I think at the end of the day,
> though, she just wanted to be a mom, to be loved, and to love
> somebody. It's sad that that never happened.

Even without kids of her own, Karen was a great aunt, even creating a special "Disney" room in her home, where the walls were covered with exact replicas of all the princesses and characters that make the Magic Kingdom so magical. Jeff recalls, "My kids still have such fond memories of sleeping over at Aunt Karen's and all the positive love that she would give them . . . as well as all the candy."

Despite not finding a soul mate, Karen had a large, close group of friends as a young adult. Some of them had attended Duke, while others carried over from high school or came into her life after college. All of us—Spike, Mary, each of Karen's brothers and sisters-in-law—knew how important her friends were to her. I remember in January 1996 when I was living in San Francisco, there was a record snowstorm in Philadelphia. Schools and many businesses were closed for days. I recall how Karen and her group of friends sort of adopted Kelly. She was teaching kindergarten and told me how she trudged through the snow with her arts-and-crafts supplies to the neighborhood bar where Karen's group was holed up. They helped her cut out the shapes for her next lesson. Sharon recalls Karen coming to her aid as well. "One time Hal was traveling and I was sick as a dog with a 102-degree fever. The one person who bailed me out was Karen. She took a day off from work and came over to change my sheets and bring me Cheerios in bed." Karen was devoted, fun-loving, and thoughtful. Everyone knew that. Unfortunately, as each of her brothers married and had children, she remained alone, destined for isolation.

● ● ● ●

During the 1990s, Spike and Mary began conducting family meetings, wherein their children and daughters-in-law would join them in multihour, organized discussions about the family. We had actually started these gathering less formally years earlier, but without any regularity. By now Spike and Mary had been influenced by their experiences in YPO, where they learned the benefits of routinely gathering for structured discussions, particularly when a family business was involved. Agenda items ranged from formal discussions, such as developing a family vision statement and family values, to mundane topics like travel plans and holiday logistics.

These latter categories introduced a somewhat common, yet Yoh-meaningful term of importance: "command performances." Like most families, when we children were young, Spike and Mary—with a heavy influence by Spike— decided what trips we would take, where we would have holiday meals, and the like. A family muscle memory developed, and we would all innately fall in line with whatever planning had taken place. As the family grew older and larger, however, this practice became challenged by geographic separation, work obligations, and in-laws' own holiday and family travel plans. As a result, Spike and Mary started labeling certain events "command performances," imposing a strong, subconscious pressure on the five of us to attend. Over time, we came to believe that virtually all of Spike and Mary's events—or at least more than we felt appropriate—were being labeled as "command." This dynamic served as another challenge to Spike's integration of daughters-in-law. In hindsight, I believe that the major contributing factor to the "command performance" concept was that Spike and Mary simply wanted to spend as much time as possible with their children and grandchildren. Kelly and I experience the same thing today when final exams or sports commitments require us to leave a child behind when attending a wedding or other important gathering. Spike and Mary can't be faulted for their wish to be with their kids, but their tactics to achieve that objective felt heavy-handed at times.

The impact of these command performances were by no means all negative. Without insistence that everyone be together—regardless of the inevitable stress that comes with that—large families may not gather that often. Much as parenting is not always about being popular, being a family leader is not always about acquiescing to every subfamily's desires. Some authority needs to be invoked if the broader clan is to come together with any regularity. My nephew Ryan has a good understanding of this dynamic:

> Granddad has always been big on traditions. The Ollie Reunions were always such a big thing. And Christmas morning with him and Grandmom was always great. We'd wake up, then go hang out on their bed, and then take pictures on the stairs. After that, we would open stockings, have breakfast, and then finally dive into our presents. It was a routine that never wavered. These traditions were so important to him. And they were effective at ensuring the family got together on a regular basis. I miss doing that like we used to.

At one time or another, each of us kids has butted heads with our parents over family trips they had planned despite knowing that one of us might have had a conflict. But the benefits of togetherness go a long way toward justifying (some of) the means Spike used to achieve it.

As for the more formal activities in our family meetings, we would have set agendas and would rotate the role of facilitator. We developed guidelines, basic courtesies like "Do not interrupt" and "Keep to the agenda" but also the term "Code 99," which was something you could say to convey that you were becoming uncomfortable with the discussion and wanted it to cease, no questions asked. We learned about this term from another YPO family. While not employed often, "Code 99" provided the attendees with an escape hatch if they felt their comfort ship start to sink below the water line.

Perhaps most importantly, we developed a list of family values. I recall how collaboratively we worked, culminating in the finalization of the list during a family meeting at the Radnor Hotel in the early 1990s. The values on which we landed we were respect, support, communication, integrity, and growth. Each one had a definition that we collectively wrote. As you can see, there was clear overlap between Spike's priorities at Day & Zimmermann and those within the family. In full candor, I don't know that anyone in the family appreciated generating a list of family values as much as Spike did.

Many years later, however, each of us would see that we were not as supportive of or communicative with each other as our values suggested we should be.

• • • •

During the 1980s and 1990s, we continued to have infrequent but routine interactions with Spike's sister Barbara's family, the Judas. Most notably, we spent every Christmas together, alternating which family would host. A fun tradition that emerged was the visiting family gathering on the hosts' front porch, ringing the doorbell and singing "We Wish You a Merry Christmas" as the host family swung the door open. Later in the evening, Mary and Barbara would sit together at the piano and play Christmas carols while the rest of us sang from sheet music that made an annual emergence from its year-round hibernation in the piano bench. I always thought my mom and aunt did a great job providing the musical accompaniment to our, ahem, *broad* range of singing voices. What I learned more recently was how little either Mary or Barbara actually played. As Barbara confessed, "I only played the piano once a year, and it was with you all." Their talent certainly fooled me.

In the fall of 1991, Barbara's husband Al passed away after an October parents' weekend visiting their youngest daughter Elizabeth at Duke. He had been secretly suffering from bone marrow cancer for more than two years prior to succumbing to the illness. I was one year ahead of Elizabeth at Duke and we had become close, often commenting how she was the little sister and I was the big brother that each never had. Unfortunately, I was studying abroad in Spain when Uncle Al died. I still remember my parents calling to tell me the news, then how I called Elizabeth from a street corner pay phone using a prepaid phone card—which was state-of-the-art at the time. It was a dark, blustery evening in Madrid. The conversation was difficult, and I felt removed and isolated. I still feel bad today that I couldn't have been there for her in person.

Spike, though, was a strong support for Barbara. Although he was on a business trip while Al was in the hospital, Barbara remembers his reassurance. "He said, 'I will come if you need me. This is the number of where I will be. Call me.'" When Al passed, "Baby Sis" recalls how big brother didn't hesitate.

> Spike came right away. He was wonderful. He brought a woman from the office who helped with the obituary and the newspaper announcements. We were doing the business part of what had to get done. And he had us all to the golf club for dinner in a private room. All of that was invaluable.

Interactions with the Judas were not the only times Spike spent with his extended family. You may recall that he was close with the Schenck cousins, who moved to Chicago when he was a boy. Although they largely lost contact in adulthood, other than the occasional wedding or family event, Spike's cousin Joan came to the Philadelphia area for a summer program in the late 1980s. "I wrote to Spike and said, 'I'm coming to Bryn Mawr. I'll be there for the summer and would love to see you.'" It had been more than two decades since the cousins had been together, yet Joan remembers Spike's warm reception. "He was so happy to see me and to bring me to the house. I was welcomed into the family. It was amazing. He had me over for a cookout and then took me to the Shore for the Fourth of July. It meant a lot to me." Joan and Spike have since remained in more regular contact. "I admire him tremendously," she says. "He did not have a good start in life with all that stuff that went on. He raised a wonderful family with Mary, who also had childhood trauma. He has made bricks out of straw. It is to be admired."

• • • •

When Spike retired from Day & Zimmermann in 1998, he and Mary embarked on the next phase of their relationship. He reflects:

> We had a lot of lunches together. But moving to Florida also
> gave us a period of time when we both were very busy socially
> and had our own individual lives. It gave us a better under-
> standing of each other. She had always been so supportive
> of everything I did. Then she became very active at Ocean
> Reef, and I therefore tried to support her in everything she
> did. We were a great team.

Spike and Mary had first discovered Ocean Reef when they "won" a long weekend there at a fund-raiser at Karen's school in the early 1980s. They enjoyed it and soon started bringing all of us along for vacations. In 1984, they became members and bought their first home at the club. According to Spike, "We saw a great future for ourselves there. I knew I didn't want to work forever, and Ocean Reef really seemed to fit us. It also had a strong YPO contingent."

Mary and Spike, beaming in early retirement

While my brothers and I all love Ocean Reef, I distinctly recall a time when its existence–quite honestly—ticked me off. The true Yoh that she was, Karen loved to throw parties. Every December, she would host a large holiday open house for her friends, family, and coworkers. Her home would be lavishly decorated, with copious amounts of delicious food in every room and holiday music blaring throughout. They were wonderful affairs. At one such event a few years after Spike had retired, I was standing near my mom and overheard someone ask her about their holiday plans. She said, "We'll be up here in Philadelphia for another week or so, then we're going home to Ocean Reef for the holidays themselves." *Home*? Did she just call Ocean Reef "home"? As a proud Philadelphian, I felt dismay upon hearing my own mother call somewhere else "home." But after a brief period of quiet simmer, I realized that Mom's comment showed that Mary and Spike had become true snowbirds. Time was marching on, and I came to accept that my parents no longer considered my hometown to be their hometown.

In retirement, Spike and Mary continued an activity in which they had partnered a few times before—building houses. Their first project was the Shore house in Avalon in the late 1960s. Later, they designed and built the Haverford house where Mike and Gayle stayed when their triplets were in the hospital. Over the years they replaced then renovated the Avalon house, as well as did major expansions on two homes in Ocean Reef. Spike says, "I loved laying out houses and all of the architecture. I loved making changes to the designs as we went and working with Mary on decorating and picking out furniture. I thoroughly enjoyed that and it took a great deal of time." While these projects generously fed Spike's engineering mindset and fastidious attention to detail, Mary at times seemed slightly begrudging, a compliant partner who occasionally voiced to her children her displeasure at these involved and disruptive projects. But as with many aspects of their marriage, they worked closely together; she knew how important this involvement was to Spike. And with every project, it was ultimately her style and her touch that made each house into a home.

● ● ● ●

By raising their children and sending them out into the world—a world that was close by, both geographically and professionally, Spike and Mary mostly achieved their early-marriage desire to build an intimate, cohesive family, standing in stark contrast to the difficult or dysfunctional experiences each of them had as children. They adjusted to their empty nest by keeping busy volunteer and social schedules and by developing a new cadence with one another. As daughters-in-law and grandchildren entered the fold, Spike got the really big family he had hoped for a half-century earlier. He struggled at times accepting his kids' families' rightful claims for independence, but each daughter-in-law also experienced the warmth and generosity of the Yoh family patriarch. I'm not sure there is such a thing as the perfect balance between nuclear and extended family, and we Yohs continue to work on that to this day.

Most importantly—and unfortunately—Spike and Mary's relationship with Karen would slowly but surely diminish during these early retirement years. None of us was living by our family values of support and communication. Karen drifted away from us, as well as from many of her close friends. These developments made what would happen a few years later all the more tragic.

Chapter 10

Loss

From the outside looking in, you can never understand.
From the inside looking out, you can never explain.
                                          —Unknown

As Spike's volunteer activities wound down in the middle of the new mil-
lennium's first decade, he entered his second phase of retirement, one that
brought a more traditional routine for Mary and him. Largely gone were the
board gatherings and committee-related trips to Duke, as were the seemingly
constant string of Ocean Reef meetings and working breakfasts. He still served
in a few emeritus and adjunct roles for both institutions and periodically
sharpened his chairmanteer saw through his ongoing leadership role at Sea
Base farther down the Florida Keys.

But now was time for Mary. Their snowbird migratory pattern was well
established, with a move to Florida each October and a return to Pennsylvania
and New Jersey each May. Spike took to waiting on Mary hand and foot. He
would bring her breakfast in bed—scrambled eggs, English muffin, skim
milk, and coffee with one Splenda and a splash of skim—virtually every day,
as well as various items that she needed or had misplaced over the course of
the day. Each of my brothers and I have friends who still mimic the humorous
summoning that our mom would utter from rooms or floors away, "Spiiiiike!

Can you please bring me my calendar . . . my reading glasses . . . my . . . !"
Ever the dutiful husband, Spike would snap into Sherpa mode and bring Mary
whatever necessity or frivolity she requested. He assumed almost all shopping
duties, something he had previously done and secretly enjoyed. Spike even
handled most of the cooking and dishwashing for the two of them.

There were two reasons why Spike became such a househusband. First,
the domestic pendulum had swung toward Mary for decades during their
child-rearing years while he built his business. He loved her and wanted to
pay her back. Second, time and health were taking their tolls on Mary. As
the person who shouldered the bulk of the home upkeep, meal preparation,
and child taxi duties—we did typically have domestic help, but she was still
caring for five kids, three houses, and an oft-traveling husband with whom
she planned and attended many events, both local and remote—Mary was
run down. I would always tell people that it wasn't that my mom was old, but
rather that she had too many "city miles" and not enough "highway miles"
under the hood.

As for her health, during their later retirement, Mary had started to become
increasingly ill after eating certain meals, particularly at restaurants. After
consulting a number of local and not-so-local medical experts, they determined
that she had developed celiac disease. Today this severe gluten allergy is
well understood, but over a decade ago, that was not the case. Mary's health,
and at times her dignity, suffered as a result. I can think of few things more
disconcerting than having a constant fear of losing control of your bowels in
a public setting. So gluten free became a way of life for Mary. Consummate
problem solvers, Spike and Mary tried everything, including finding all sorts of
food purveyors and websites that supplied gluten-free options. Mary established
her own cottage industry, sharing various food alternatives with others.
Catherine Medaglia credits her as the driving force behind the introduction
of gluten-free dining at Ocean Reef. Margo Miller felt the same way. "I

remember Mary talking to me about it because I thought maybe I had it too. She gave me a basket of sample foods and she told me where to order them. That's the kind of thing she would do."

As my parents became increasingly thoughtful about health, they adopted pedometers. The idea of wearing a device that would track the number of steps you take on a daily basis was fairly novel a decade ago. But Mom and Dad were encouraged to do so by a trainer who was giving them private aqua aerobics lessons—I'll pause while you process the visual of Spike in swim trunks holding floaty weights and bouncing around his pool to the beat of techno music—in order to remain active and to build cardiac health. Anyone who spent any time with them during this era will attest to why there was no surprise that frenetic, always-moving, "retiree" Spike would routinely clock a step count vastly exceeding Mary's. The man never sat still. At one point, Hal suggested that Mom put her pedometer on the dog, thinking that could be a way for her to keep up with her husband's activity level.

• • • •

During retirement, Spike continued to enjoy the male bonding that had always been important to him. From his early years at all-boys Haverford, to his fraternity days at Duke, to his successful business career with his D&Z dream team, to his foundational and lifelong affiliation with the Ollie Brothers, Spike has always loved spending time with the fellas. Simply heading out for a round of golf with one of his sons and our friends was the kind of male connection that Spike cherished. Through example, he passed on to my brothers and me this primordial need to spend time with other Y chromosomes.

For Spike, however, the women in his life have always been important as well. As a child, he had defended and cared for his mother and his sister. Since his late college years, there was no person with whom he spent more time or loved more deeply than his wife. Finally, he had worked on building strong relationships with his daughters-in-law and routinely emphasized the value and importance of women in any of the organizations in which he worked. This balanced consideration between genders made it all the more difficult for Spike when our family's relationship with Karen began to erode.

Karen, Spike and Mary at an Ocean Reef celebration

As she aged, Karen experienced more and more difficulty entering into or maintaining loving relationships. Perhaps the psychology field would say that she had "intimacy issues"? Regardless, I believe her troubles germinated early in life, even if they didn't manifest themselves then. Spike's first female role model, his own mother, was someone with whom he did not spend a great amount of time nor build a deep, loving relationship, and Harold offered little in the way of how a father might successfully parent a daughter. Furthermore, Mary was raised by a single mother who worked full time, causing Mary to figure out much about life on her own. Spike's and Mary's formative experiences may have impacted their ability to aid Karen in becoming a comfortable, empowered girl or growing into a confident woman capable of being vulnerable with others. Spike says, "I think it was very difficult growing up with four brothers and a father who was probably, in her mind, boy oriented. Yet I felt like I always sheltered her and gave more time to her than I did to anybody else." Spike also wonders if the mother-daughter dynamics at home may have exacerbated Karen's childhood predetermination. "Because they were the only females in a male-dominated family, the two of them were close. Mary and Karen could be very complementary and supportive of each other. But there was also friction, maybe typical mother-daughter stuff, 'You can't do this. You can't wear that dress.' Some of the things just seemed so silly, but maybe there was more to it than I saw." Whether there was or not, time would show that something—or some things—from Karen's upbringing had planted seeds that sprouted unwell in adulthood.

As I mentioned earlier, Jeff surmises that when Karen graduated from college, she had an image of a life centered on marriage and children. Then as the years passed and all her siblings married and had children while she did not, Karen's singleness stood out even more. Her self-confidence waned and she started to slowly pull away from the family. Perhaps exacerbating the declining opinion she had of herself, Karen—along with many members of our family, myself depressingly included—struggled with her weight through most of her adult life. Given society's gender double standard on this topic, being overweight was probably more of an issue for Karen than for the rest of us. I'm sure this didn't help her ability or willingness to open up to a would-be mate.

Karen's boyfriends were few and far between. She met some nice guys along the way, for sure, but none with whom she seemed destined for matrimony. I do recall one boyfriend who spent Thanksgiving with us one year. He was a successful investment banker with a warm smile and gregarious personality. What was memorable about this holiday, however, was that a family argument broke out about Mike and his impending marriage to his first wife—leave it to holidays to bring out raw emotion—and Karen's boyfriend assumed the role of referee. I can still see the poor man's red face as he tried to mediate. Despite this voluntary immersion into our family dynamics, his relationship with Karen—like all the others—did not last. One final contributor to Karen's lack of serious relationships was our family's practice of employing sarcasm, which we did when talking about some of her boyfriends. I'm sure these comments served as another deterrent to her dating, and even more importantly, to bringing suitors around the family.

Even though she never had that one "soul mate" relationship, Karen did thrive in many of her relationships, often as the life of the party—which is saying something in our family. She usually made a big entrance, with her bright clothing, flowing red hair, and flamboyant jewelry, and then she held court, her loud voice and infectious laugh drawing eyes and ears to wherever she was. She was compassionate as well, particularly to the people who worked for her at D&Z and her household help. She could be loving to her brothers, her sisters-in-law, and—almost constantly—her nieces and nephews. She joined my family for Thanksgiving in 2005, only a week after our third child was born (Spike, Mary, and our siblings' families were all in different parts of the country). Given the domestic chaos of two young children and a newborn, neither Kelly nor I was going to cook, so we ordered takeout from Merion. Karen lived near the club and picked up the food on her way over. We had a great time together, a night filled with laughter.

A few weeks later, Karen also joined us for a special evening with Mom and Dad, who had started a tradition some years earlier that I cherish to this day. While they spent Christmas and New Year's at Ocean Reef, joined by whichever sons' families could join them, they would precede the holidays with a weeklong trip to Pennsylvania in mid-December. (During one of these trips was when mom uttered her infamous "*home* to Ocean Reef" comment.) During this week up north, Spike and Mary would spend one evening at each of their sons' homes. Being the dedicated gift-giver that he is, Spike would lead the charge in delivering incredible amounts of presents for each of the grandchildren, carrying them in large, sleigh-worthy red felt sacks, replete with shaggy white trim and ornate gold pull-string ropes. Unlike the chaos of earlier Christmases when *all* of their grandchildren would open *all* of their presents at once, Spike and Mary could now sit with each family on these individual nights and watch each of their grandchildren open every one of his or her presents. Given that they were in their late sixties and seventies, this string of back-to-back-to-back Christmas celebrations was taxing, but they always came and we always had a wonderful time. Just recently one of my children commented on how much they enjoyed their "second Christmases" with Grammie and Granddad. Spike the widower continues the tradition to this day.

Understandably, Karen did not want to be by herself for an individual Mom-and-Dad Christmas, so this particular year she joined ours. It was a great evening, made all the more special because Aunt Karen was there and because of a sweet gesture she made the next day. At our house, Karen had worn a big, bright flower barrette over her ear, its vibrancy remarkable against her long auburn hair. Our daughter was captivated by it. She must have mentioned something to Aunt Karen, because the following day Aunt Karen showed up again at our house to present her niece a barrette of her own. It was in the shape of a bright white lily with a pretty purple accent piece.

The following summer, Spike and Mary took many of us—including Karen—on a vacation to Bermuda, one of those "command performances" scheduled even though one son's family was unable to attend. The trip included a great hotel, fun outings and dinners, and lots of quality time across generations and cousin groups. The long weekend had gotten off to an odd start, however, when my family arrived at Karen's house to pick her up on the way to the airport. As I've mentioned, Spike imprinted in his children a strong commitment to punctuality; being late was simply not permitted for a Yoh. Yet when we arrived, Karen was far from ready, taking about thirty more minutes to finish packing. When she finally joined us in the car, she was beyond frazzled. Any of us can relate to the stress of traveling, particularly if Spike was awaiting you. Karen may also have suffered from not having had the buffer and aid of a spouse or the distraction of excited children. Her gradual withdrawal from the family continued, so the stress of impending around-the-clock immersion seemed evident.

Fortunately, once we arrived in Bermuda, Aunt Karen was in her element, surrounded by nieces and nephews. Every one of them enjoyed her or his Aunt Karen time, and we parents were happy to provide the occasional reprogramming necessary after these spoiling interactions. One evening, however, when my brothers and I were going down to the hotel bar for a nightcap, I recall our wanting to be just "the boys." We didn't tell Karen. Her center-of-attention demeanor was usually enjoyable, but as she got older, she became less able to turn it off and be mellow. Because it was late in the evening and we knew she would be full throttle, we didn't have the collective energy to speed along behind her. Today I don't feel guilt about this decision, but rather a recollection of how strained our relationships with her were becoming. It just seemed easier, or less stressful, not to invite her.

This trip took place in 2006, one year after Karen—at the age of forty-one—had decided to leave Day & Zimmermann. Given that ownership of the company transitioned from Spike to us at the end of 1998, we five children had spent a lot of time working together as an ownership group. Even prior to Jeff's cashing out in 2003, a dynamic had started to evolve with Karen, one that grew worse in the final year or two of her being an owner. It seemed that for stretches of time, one or more of us brothers would be in her metaphorical penalty box for something we had done or said, while the other one or two would be in her good graces. There seemed to be no pattern to what act or exchange would draw the penalty. In hindsight, her attitude and actions seemed to be more about her growing isolation from us, at times almost appearing as paranoia that people were out to get her. A consultant with whom we worked regularly on myriad family business topics had a doctoral degree in psychology. He described Karen's attitude with a vulgar yet appropriate phrase: "F— you. Don't leave me." Unfortunately, this strong wording described the dynamic quite well at times.

Karen's professional look in the early 2000's

When Karen sold her stock in 2005, she became further isolated, both from family and from what had been such a strong and diverse network of friends. Spike remembers, "When she put her hands on some money through the stock sale, she got a little different in her value system. It gave her an independence, which was fine, but also a feeling that she could do anything she wanted regardless of how it impacted her or others. Both her health and her weight got worse as well." An indication of her evolving behavior was that routine chores like bill paying and house straightening were falling by the wayside. One day, Hal, Mike, and I left one of our shareholder meetings to drive to her home to help her. We stayed for an hour or so—probably not making much of a dent—but we wanted her to know that we cared and that no job (opening mail, putting dishes away, wiping out sinks) was too small. Spike and Mary were often even more engaged in trying to help. As Spike recalls:

> There was a period of time before she passed when four or
> five times a week, I would spend an hour or more on the
> phone with her. Mary would be with me as well. Then one
> time I came up from Florida. I told her I was coming up just
> for her and she said "fine." But when I got there, she wouldn't
> see me. It was really difficult. I don't understand the whole
> experience of that time period. She was my only daughter.
> Where did I fail? What could I have done differently? And
> I felt hurt in the process as well.

A man not accustomed to uncertainty, Spike remains unsure to this day. Mike offers another perspective. "Mom and Dad had a view of who Karen should be, and Karen's view of who she should be was very different. It was a weird thing. I never could put a finger on it. Karen was going to do Karen's thing and, 'to hell with Mom and Dad.' It was sad. Just really sad."

Compounding Karen's relationship difficulties, she had become addicted to painkillers. In the past several years, she had undergone a series of medical procedures, including several to combat endometriosis and other abnormalities of the reproductive system. After the surgeries, she would acquire prescriptions from two independent doctors and would use three different pharmacies. Today, the perils of opioid addiction are far better known and publicized than a decade ago. But Karen was hooked, and I'm not sure what anyone could have done about it. We discussed trying to force her into a treatment facility, but we knew that because she was an adult, she could release herself. Despite her overuse of prescription drugs, Karen could still be fantastic to be around—present and coherent and full of energy. The difficulty lay in not knowing when she would be the fun, smack-talking Karen or when she would be the dazed and confused version of herself.

The combination of her addiction and her isolation from family and friends left Karen in a dark place. At one point, she hinted that she might move away from the Main Line to live near a married couple with whom she still maintained a close relationship. Even though we all believed that these particular "friends" had Karen's best interests at heart, time proved that they did not. Karen had money from her stock sale, and we later learned that they had remained close with her—while many others had not—largely to promote their own financial interests. Ugh. At least she never moved.

In early June of 2007, we had what would be our last family meeting. Karen had already declared that she was not going to attend for fear that we might stage an intervention. While this was not our intention, my wife Kelly also boycotted, believing that we were not appropriately addressing this major family issue. Of course we did discuss Karen at length when we gathered, but no one knew what more we could do. We felt helpless. For a family that prided itself on togetherness, we were deeply divided, one of our own holed up in her own home and in her own world.

On Saturday, June 23, Kelly and I moved our family to Avalon for the summer into our vacation home a block away from my parents. This was the second year I planned to commute to Philadelphia each week for work. Kelly and our young children stayed at the Shore, just as I had done several times as a boy. It was already a difficult time for us, as Kelly's uncle Frank—the priest who had married us and with whom Kelly had previously become close during her years as an undergrad and grad student at Villanova—had passed away the week before. For his entire adult life, Uncle Frank had been a sun worshiper. He would spend much of his summers at the Shore, sunning himself for hours on end. I can only imagine what his students thought when they bumped into Father Eigo in a bathing suit. But the years of sun caught up with him, skin cancer first taking its toll, followed by colon cancer and a stroke, which ultimately led to his passing. Kelly had a special relationship with him, as did I. Our emotional tanks were therefore pretty empty when we arrived in Avalon. Kelly recalls telling herself that weekend, "You're done crying. There are no tears left."

After moving the family in, I had to fly that Sunday to San Francisco for a trade association board meeting in Half Moon Bay. Mike and Gayle were on vacation with their kids in Ireland. Jeff and Suzanne were at home in Charlotte, Hal and Sharon in Pennsylvania, and Spike and Mary in Avalon, a block away from Kelly and our kids.

On Monday morning, June 25, I awoke early in California and went to the hotel fitness center. I always smile at how crowded West Coast gyms can be at four and five o'clock in the morning with all the East Coasters not adjusted to the time change. When I got back to my hotel room around six, I had three missed calls from Hal. Something was not right. I called. He told me Karen was dead.

About an hour earlier, he had been boarding a plane when he received a call from a builder who was doing some work at Karen's house. The builder had realized that Karen was in her bedroom and not answering his knock. He knew Hal and called him on his cell phone. Hal immediately left the airport to make the angst-filled drive to her house. He forced her bedroom door open and found her lying in bed. Karen had passed away in her sleep.

After his unimaginable discovery, Hal first called his father, just as Spike had done when he found his mother in the bathtub forty-two years earlier. Spike says, "Hal called us in Avalon. I remember just thinking, 'Oh dear God.' Mary and I were in the car in five minutes." Hal then had the heart-wrenching task of calling each of his brothers. Jeff booked the next flight from Charlotte, as did I from San Francisco. Mike, Gayle, and their children couldn't get home from Ireland until the following afternoon. On his family's flight over the Atlantic, Mike remembers one of his young triplets asking if they could fly higher. When he asked her why, she said, "I want to be closer to Aunt Karen in heaven." In Charlotte, Jeff recalls feeling stunned. "I just felt sadness. Utter helplessness." After I spoke with Hal, I called Kelly, who was still emotionally reeling from her uncle's passing just ten days earlier. After delivering the frying-pan-to-the-face news to her, I called my parents and asked them to stop by our house to give Kelly a hug before they left the Shore.

The ensuing hours and days were a blur of conversations, faces, hugs, and tears. My parents' home became the family headquarters, their foyer a revolving door admitting person after person who came by not knowing what to say but offering a cheerful story or a comforting shoulder. We provided our visitors with a meal and almost all of them dutifully ate it, though many were probably not hungry. Flexing our entertainment muscles was subconscious catharsis for the family.

At Karen's funeral in our childhood church, the Church of the Redeemer in Bryn Mawr, the congregation overflowed into the aisles and the rear antechamber. Hal and Jeff each read from Scripture, and Mike and I delivered remarks on behalf of the family. I will forever remember the two of us the day before the service working in my parents' living room. We were sitting opposite each other on matching sofas, with our feet perched on the coffee table and our computers in our laps, engaged in the surreal "dueling pianos" exercise of writing our sister's eulogy. Fittingly, while we did not collaborate on our remarks, they were strikingly similar.

My comments thanked everyone for their support, then I said, "Like all of you, I have not yet begun to try to make sense about everything that has happened. I hope with time and with the continued support and love of everyone in Karen's life, some sense will come of it all. For now, I know she is with God and she is at peace, and that has given me the strength to get to where we are." Later, I said, "I think Karen loved having me as her baby brother. I was her first babysitting assignment, probably her first dirty diaper, and likely—and regrettably for me—her first human doll for makeup application. She brought me to school for show 'n tell and even nicknamed me Wilhelmina." I went on to talk about how much she valued relationships, and about the energy, passion, and fun she brought to everything—and everyone—in her life. Toward the end, I said, "We all know about the laughter . . . and the giggling. And about more laughter . . . and more giggling. That was truly Karen at her best. We are all so fortunate to have been around her and her infectious ways."

A number of weeks passed before we found out how Karen died. Because she was alone when it happened—called an "unattended death"—an autopsy had to be performed (talk about a requirement we wish we didn't have to learn). I was the one initially to receive the findings from the medical examiner in mid-July, via phone while sitting on the beach, of all places. The official cause of death was "multiple drug intoxication—accidental." While she had a number of prescription and over-the-counter drugs in her system, all were within normal dosage levels except for Benadryl; its level was above normal, but still significantly below what was considered a lethal dose. Most interestingly, no opioids or other painkillers were identified in the report. It was determined that a few of the substances in her system contained various forms of neurological suppressants, and their combination literally shut down her nervous system.

Karen's passing showed me how differently people grieve, including close family members. I recall how stoic Spike was through the service, even when he led the family procession to the gravesite, carrying Karen's ashes in his arms. I remember that his head was bowed and his shoulders shaking ever so slightly under his black suit jacket. He handled the urn like the precious, delicate object it was. One of Spike's YPO forum-mates recalls, "I saw him carrying that little urn, this big guy, with Mary beside him. It was the saddest thing I had ever seen in my life. That image is seared in my mind." Several others from his forum retain the same image.

In the ensuing weeks, Spike responded to his grief—as did many of us Yohs, yet counter to what other people might do under similar strain—by eating a little more and drinking a little more. Mostly, however, I remember a new kind of temper from him, which our family came to call his "flash anger" because it would rear its head quickly and without warning. He had always had a temper, but in the past we could usually see the tempest organizing itself. Not now. His grandchildren were even the victims of a few of his outbursts, which was most unusual. We sought professional counseling as a family, but ultimately only the passage of time led to his emotional calming.

In his retirement, with the softening that comes with age and without the stresses of raising a family and running a business, Spike's arguments with Mary—recall the spats they had when we children were young—had subsided. However, after Karen's passing, the two entered a less healthy phase. As Mike recalls, "I knew Mom and Dad still fought some, but they fought more than normal. Dad had trouble figuring how to deal with everything, which made both of their frustration levels grow." According to Hal, "Mom would be one way, and Dad would be on the other side of the house in another way. Sometimes we would try to bring them together, but they would just be in their own place. Neither one would talk about it." I suppose much of this was generational, as life has shown me that people around my parents' age are less likely to express deep emotions, especially difficult ones. A YPO forum-mate says, "I think Spike kept his emotions to himself. Spike was the kind of guy that kept grief inside. He always seemed to keep bad things in." Not only was he keeping his darker thoughts to himself, but we see Spike's resilience and forged-by-life optimism dictate his emotional expression. Another YPO'er recalls, "Losing Karen was a huge jolt, and I think it forever changed him. It was sudden. It was not expected. It was baffling to him. I can't imagine what it's like to be in that situation. Spike was different after that."

Thankfully, the tension between Spike and Mary slowly receded, like an outgoing tide after a full moon, and they sought to get back to a normal routine. Their visible lack of acknowledgment that Karen was gone was both troubling and understandable. We wished they would share their feelings more, but it was not surprising given their innate stoicism, especially Spike's. One notable exception to his guarded demeanor was Karen's forty-third birthday, which fell two months to the day after she died. He had prepared a poem that he read before a dinner we held to mark the day. The poem was beautiful and also candid. Spike expressed his sadness and remorse through his most comfortable medium—writing down his thoughts then sharing them as a speech. Mary was also mostly quiet about the loss of her daughter. I assume the pain of losing her father so young, coupled with the stiff-upper-lip, glass-is-half-full philosophy of her husband had conditioned her to bottle up rather than pour out. Only toward the very end of her life would she confide in her nurse about her sorrow over Karen's passing.

Despite the circumstances surrounding her final years, Karen will always be remembered for her huge, fun-loving personality and her passion for making everyone feel welcomed and important—traits she inherited from our parents. Late in life, circumstances converged such that she wandered from these strengths. But her family and friends know who she was when she was at her best. When I think of her—which happens every day—it's her passion for life, her keen wit, and her dedication to those she loved that I strive to recall.

• • • •

As the date of Karen's passing drifted farther behind them, Spike and Mary became more ingrained in the social fabric of Ocean Reef, forging close bonds with many friends there. Tony Medaglia recalls how strong their marriage was. "Mary and Spike had a magical relationship. They respected each other, and they doted on each other." Tony's wife Catherine seconds her husband's recollection:

> We became very close with them. One time, we went on a cruise together and our rooms were side by side. We would stay up late just talking. The beauty of their relationship is that they supported one another and listened to what the other one had to say. They had such mutual respect and mutual love. It was a joy to be with them.

Mike Smith says, "The unique thing about them was loyalty. They had a fierce sense of loyalty to each other. Obviously, they loved each other immensely." Alan Goldstein agrees. "You rarely saw Spike without Mary. They were inseparable. Mary and his children were his life."

The Yoh family at Ryan and Ashley's wedding in 2011

As they always had done, Spike and Mary continued to open their home for family and friends. The pinnacle of their party throwing was an annual New Year's Day bash called "The Reef Bowl," a name paying homage to the college football bowl games played every year on January 1. The origin of this family spectacle was Mom cooking huge pancake breakfasts on New Year's morning for us children and some of our friends when we were young adults. Soon, "some" friends turned into "many," and "cooking breakfast" turned into "everyone hanging out for hours." Always event planners in search of an event, Spike and Mary were soon hosting a day-long open house with over three hundred friends, all of whom were encouraged to bring visiting relatives and guests. The invitation was designed to mimic a ticket to a sporting event, the day replete with food stations throughout the house and around the pool and televisions broadcasting games all over. "Everybody looked forward to the Reef Bowl," says Mike Smith. "The food was wonderful, and Spike and Mary were wonderful. They had a whole house full of people, and you would have thought there would have been some stress. But I never saw Mary or Spike looking stressed. Even when we were newbies, they welcomed us and then later came back to check on us. They were very thoughtful." Margo Miller recalls how they decorated not just for the Reef Bowl, but for the holidays as well. "I loved how warm it was with all of their decorations and their Santa Clauses. They loved to open their door for all of their friends and their families. 'Family and friends' just says so much about Spike and Mary."

In addition to their friends, Spike and Mary forged close bonds with the people who worked for them at Ocean Reef. Just as they had with Jean Bright when we were children, they treated the folks in their employ like family. Ronda Perkins starting working for Spike and Mary, or "Mr. and Mrs. Yoh" as she has always called them, in 1997. She would clean and straighten their home, handle much of the laundry duties, and eventually serve as occasional dog sitter and errand runner. She recalls how things were from the start. "I started working with them and they welcomed me with open arms and treated me great." Spike had not yet retired and he still had his Duke chairmanship in North Carolina to come, so he was gone from Ocean Reef somewhat regularly in Ronda's initial years. As a result, she really connected with Mary early on. She recalls how "it was like we were fast friends. We instantly liked each other. She had in her nature what I would call a giving soul. When it came to things that she wanted done or wanted done differently than I had done them, she never had a harsh word for me." As her son, I often overlooked what a strong homemaker my mother was. Ronda was quick to point out, "She took pride in her houses. I was always impressed how she could run three households in three different states. Obviously Mr. Yoh helped in his ways, but she wanted to make sure that all the homes ran well, that they were clean, and that everything was in order. She wanted to make sure that when guests arrived, everything was just right." Ronda and my mom had a special relationship for sure.

As for "Mr. Yoh," the thing that initially and forever drew Ronda to him was their mutual love of the holiday season, as she relates in her laid-back Florida Keys cadence:

> Mr. Yoh has always loved Christmastime, and I'm totally on board with that. He'll bring out crate after crate of decorations and holiday knickknacks, and I will find someplace to put them. When he goes shopping and sees a decoration he wants, he gets this tickled look on his face. I still love that after all these years Christmas continues to excite him so much.

Ronda understood that Mary was not always thrilled with Spike's habit of adding more accessories while never purging any old ones. "He would tell me, 'I've got to sneak this into the house so Mary doesn't see it.' When she would eventually notice the new item on display, I'd just say, 'Mrs. Yoh, this is not an argument you're going to win. You know I'm always going to side with him on this.'"

An example of Spike's—and Ronda's—love of
Christmas decorations

In addition to the lifelong elf that he is, Ronda also saw what a planner Spike could be. "If he's going to be attached to something, it's going to be done right. I see it when he plans his YPO forum or when he's planning a trip for the Ollie Brothers. Every detail is well thought out, and it always seems to turn out great. Even if it's a family meal, it's planned well in advance." Anyone who has visited him at Ocean Reef knows how Spike loves to hand-draw a calendar grid for the duration of your visit. He derives such satisfaction from filling in the little daily boxes with tee times and dinner reservations. It is a form of organization that gives him calm. For some, who consider vacation a time *not* to have everything planned with this level of precision, Spike's calendars have the opposite effect. This conflict of styles has produced a few verbal dust-ups over the years.

When Chairmanteer Spike finally started to slow down, Ronda recalls Mary's insistence being part of the catalyst. "Eventually I would hear Mrs. Yoh say, 'Spike, you're just going to have to pick and choose. You're going to have to pare down the amount of things that you're involved in.' I think for her it all seemed like a lot of work and a lot of travel, but for him it was a source of energy." Finally, with tears in her eyes, Ronda corroborates what so many others have observed about Spike and Mary's relationship. "The two of them worked like a well-oiled machine. You could tell that they loved each other dearly. They spoke their minds and stood strong on their opinions, but they'd always come to an agreement. I was always amazed by that." Ronda knew who Spike and Mary were for sure, and she really connected with Mom. That's a big reason why the role she played when Mom got sick and passed away years later was so meaningful.

Another person who worked for Spike and Mary and who also came to be like family was Steve Soto. Steve co-owns a residential construction business in Miami and in the early 2000s had just started doing work at Ocean Reef. His first job there was a small remodeling project for Spike's long-time YPO colleague and one-time mosquitos-at-Ocean-Reef adversary, Tom Davidson. Tom provided the key reference that compelled Spike to take a chance on the new builder. In his fast-talking Cuban-American accent, Steve relates meeting Spike after the career-changing phone call:

> I didn't know what to expect. How do you visualize a guy named "Spike Yoh"? I was maybe expecting some Japanese rap artist with a gold chain around his neck. But then I saw Spike, wearing a plaid shirt, coral-colored shorts, a bright

white belt, white socks, and sandals. He was the total opposite
of what I expected. He was a pastel palette.

Steve now joins Jack Winters, Sterly Wilder, and me as commentators on
Spike's unique wardrobe decisions.

Given the large scope of work Steve would be performing, he experienced
Spike's business side loud and clear.

> He was very strict and very strong. He said, "These are the
> rules, this is the way it's going to be, and this is how you're
> gonna do it. And let me tell you guys something. I have a
> deadline. I want to be in my new home next Christmas. I
> expect my schedule to be met." We of course said okay, as it
> was very important for us to do this home right. Spike made
> it very clear that he could make us or break us at Ocean Reef,
> which scared the living hell out of me, quite honestly.

Steve also observed Spike's passions for control and detail. One such instance
involved the design of the outdoor kitchen area. "Being an engineer at heart,
Spike got down on his hands and knees with a pencil and measuring tape
and sketched out the barbecue area. He wanted to see exactly what it was
going to look like." Steve dedicated himself full time to Spike and Mary's
home, driven by the opportunity the project presented. As the house neared
completion, Steve recalls a particularly memorable phone call.

> Near the end of the job, I called Spike and said, "Mr. Yoh,
> we have a problem." He goes, "Yeah? What's the problem?" I
> said, "Well, I don't think I'm going to be done for Christmas."
> Before I could say another thing, oh man, did he let me have
> it! I couldn't get a word in to stop him. When I could finally
> break in, I said, "Mr. Yoh, please, can I say something? I'm
> not going to be ready for Christmas because I'm going to be

ready for Thanksgiving. Would you like to spend Thanksgiving
in your home?" There was this eerie silence on the phone.
I didn't know what was going to happen next. He then said,
"Excuse me?" I said, "Your home is almost finished. If you
want to spend Thanksgiving in your home, it will be ready."

Because Steve had exceeded expectations, Spike was true to his word and
provided glowing references. Steve's company is now one of the largest new
home constructors at Ocean Reef.

As they had with so many others, Spike and Mary developed a relationship
with Steve that transcended "work." Steve began calling Spike by his first
name, and he joined them for dinner on many occasions before making the
hour-long drive home to Miami. The first of these dinners provided perhaps
the most touching exchange between Steve and my parents, as Steve explains:

When we finished the project, one of the most incredible
things happened. For the first time, Spike and Mary asked
me to stay for dinner. We had a great meal and talked about
a lot of things like life and kids and family. But I was also
there to pick up the final check. After dinner, they walked
me to my car. When we got to the car, Spike took out the
check and handed it to me. I looked at it and sort of chuckled.
Not sure of what had happened, Mary thought that maybe he
held back a lot of money. She said, "What's wrong, Steve?
Did Spike not pay you what he owes you?" I said, "No, Mary.
Nothing is wrong. But he does still owe me money." And she
said, "How much?"

At this point in telling me the story, Steve's voice hitches and his eyes well up.

I said, "He held back one dollar." Spike then looked at me
and said, "I'm always going to owe you a dollar . . . because

I never want you to leave me." It was such a sweet gesture.
It showed that there was a totally different side to this man,
a very vulnerable and very soft side that I had never seen. I
had only known the hardcore Spike Yoh in business. Even
though it was kind of silly, that gesture went a long way with
me. It developed into the relationship that he and I have today.

• • • •

Over time, Mary's celiac disease and accumulative "city miles" led to other,
more serious cardiac and pulmonary issues. Now in their mid-seventies, she
and Spike spent much of the early 2010s flying all over the Eastern United
States seeing various specialists as well as experimenting with new diet
regimens and medicine combinations. The good news and the bad news
was that Mom had access to a host of medical experts, from primary care
physicians to cardiologists, pulmonologists, and dieticians. Unfortunately,
while these professionals provided great diagnoses and advice, the input she
received was often not coordinated. At times, an expert in South Florida
would provide guidance that conflicted with someone in New Jersey or in
Pennsylvania or at Duke. This whole endeavor would serve as Spike's full-
time vocation, eventually at the expense of his own health, which he started
ignoring more and more. In addition to prior hip and prostate issues, he had
by now been diagnosed with rheumatoid arthritis and type 2 diabetes, both
of which he managed with oral medication—and only partially with lifestyle
adjustments. As Mary's condition worsened, though, he came to rely solely
on the medications. A time bomb started to tick inside of him, the effects of
which wouldn't manifest until a few years later. Ronda recalls:

> Mr. Yoh was very attentive. He always wanted to find what
> he thought was the best care for her. Duke always seemed to
> be an option, but as travel became more difficult, they started

developing relationships with doctors in Miami. He became
convinced that they had the best healthcare he could get and
he didn't have to put Mrs. Yoh on a plane or be away from
Ocean Reef. It also kept him busy, which he needed.

Throughout these years, Spike's unwavering optimism remained intact, sometimes to a fault. As Mike Smith recalls, "I hated to watch him when he was going through the issues with Mary's health. But he was always so supportive and hopeful, and he always saw the bright side." Of course, "always seeing the bright side" has downside as well. When I joined them for a few doctors' appointments, we might hear three or four scary prognoses, along with maybe one or two positive things. Afterward, Spike would excitedly tell people, "Listen to this great piece of news we just got!" I would have to say, "Wait, Dad. I was there. The doctor said a bunch of other things as well. Let's not ignore them." Over time, he got better at hearing *all* the news. The longer we endured Mom's health problems, the more he realized that things were growing serious.

By January of 2015, her health had become a constant roller coaster and her hospital and rehab facility stays were piling up. It was then that the family came together in an unprecedented way. The four brothers and our wives got on a conference call, and—for the first time—combined our data and opinions concerning Mom's situation. Our exchange was candid, constructive, and harmonious. We decided to do several things, among them to canvas our personal networks to ensure that the healthcare she was receiving was top notch (not just convenient), and to begin a family email conversation allowing us to update the others with any new information. I was able to use my YPO network to determine if the health system Mary was principally using, Baptist Health of South Florida, was as good as Spike said it was. Fortunately, our exploratory efforts confirmed she was in great hands.

On this same conference call, we also made another important decision: not to let more than a week go by without at least one of us being with Mom and Dad. Over the ensuing months, every one of us visited them, most doing so multiple times. Jeff and Suzanne were particularly heroic in their efforts, spending many weeks away from home. For Jeff, the most notable memory was an extraordinary role reversal that occurred during one of Mom's more serious hospital stints. "That was my first experience of having to feed my own mother. It was simply bizarre." Our visits allowed us to contribute a second or third set of ears to what the doctors were saying while also spending valuable one-on-one time with Spike when Mary was in the hospital. It was during this time period that I uncovered Spike's willingness to talk about his past. Little did I know that six months later I would commit to changing my career to author his story.

Mary toasting to life

Spike and Mary's many friends at Ocean Reef were aware of Mary's declining health. Of those difficult months in early 2015, Catherine Medaglia says, "When Mary became ill, Spike acted like he had always acted. He was so supportive and very much by her side through it all." Catherine's husband Tony agrees. "It was sad to see Mary become unwell, but Spike couldn't have been more attentive. He was so devoted." Steve Soto says, "When Mary started to fall ill, his whole life turned to taking care of her. It was crystal clear. It was all for her, whatever she needed. That's love." As important as anyone's contributions during this time, Steve connected the family with one of his closest childhood friends, Tomas Villanueva, who was the senior medical administrator at Baptist Health. The number of times that Tom (via Steve) guided Mary's care were innumerous and invaluable.

When Mary was at home, Spike began hiring nurses to support her and administer medications. On one Friday in mid-February, the scheduled nurse called out sick and a last-minute replacement was provided. Emi Gonzalez showed up for an overnight shift, having never met Mary or Spike. Emi says, "We got along right away. But I was only going to be there for that one shift." Then fate intervened, as Emi relates, "Sunday morning the phone rang, and they asked me to work again. One of the assigned nurses was not working out. So I came back. I worked for them ever since." On why she and Mary clicked right away, Emi contends that "we both love family and friends. We always had that in common. In everything we talked about, I learned from her and she learned from me. Mary always had a very positive outlook. No matter how ill she was, she always looked on the bright side, never the negative side." Sounds like someone else we know, huh?

When asked about her first impression of Spike, Emi says:

> Mr. Yoh can be a tough cookie, but always very nice about it. Everything needed to be by the rules and by the book. He's very independent, but he always made sure that everybody around him was taken care of. As far as Mary was concerned, she was his number-one priority. He would do anything for

her. But he really didn't take too much care of himself in
the process.

Even in their early months together, Emi forged a bond with Mary that went
far beyond a typical nurse-patient relationship. "She and I shared a lot of happy
and sad moments in our lives. One of the things that really stuck out was Karen.
There was a lot of guilt there. She missed her so much." Emi is a professional,
and her respect for Mary compels her to keep their discussions private, which
I respect. Emi does say, "She really missed her daughter, especially because
she was ill. One of the things she said was that she always used to think that
when either she or Mr. Yoh got sick later in life, she thought that Karen would
be the one to take care of them." Finally, eight years after Karen passed away,
Mom found the right person with whom to share her deepest feelings about
losing her only daughter.

As winter became spring, Mom's health continued to tick up and down,
with alternating periods of hospitalization and time at home. However, when
Spike and Mary prepared to make their annual migration north in late spring,
her condition improved considerably. In fact, Ronda and Emi, who had by
now become close given their shared affinity for Mary, commemorated her
positive state. Mary had become very thin and few of her clothes fit. On one
warm Key Largo afternoon, as Spike and Mary were riding past the boutique
stores in Ocean Reef's "Fishing Village," Spike suddenly pulled over, parked
their golf cart, and walked Mary into each of these high-end retailers, selecting
outfit after outfit and piling them high on the cashiers' counters. The clothing
options were coming so fast and furious that Mary opted to bring them home
rather than try them on. When the happy couple returned home, unexpectedly
encumbered with large quantities of designer bags and plastic-draped hangers,
Ronda and Emi instantly adapted, culling Mary from Spike and leading her
into her dressing room. What ensued was a poolside runway fashion show
featuring just one model, Mary Milus "Candarenie" Yoh. Ronda and Emi

captured a series of special photographs of her striking stately poses and beaming at the camera. Everyone soon took to referring to her as Ronda and Emi's life-sized Barbie doll.

In early June, a day or two after the fashion show, Mary and Spike relocated from Ocean Reef to Avalon, along with Emi, Ronda, and Duchess—their four-legged companion whom I mentioned in the beginning of the book. The next ten days were wonderful, highlighted by Mary and Spike's spontaneous slow dance in their Shore house kitchen on Father's Day, both of them smiling and gazing into each other's eyes while Frank Sinatra crooned from the ceiling speakers.

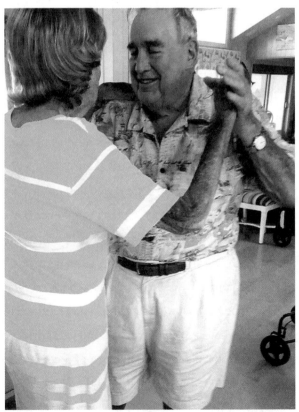

Mary and Spike, more than half a century of love

Right after Father's Day, the same group returned to Ocean Reef for a minor scheduled procedure for Spike. With the benefit of hindsight, Emi reflects upon what ended up being Mary's final visit to Avalon. "She was very excited to be there. She enjoyed the whole trip. I think it was her way of saying good-bye to the Shore. That's what gave me satisfaction, I guess, that she was able to spend those final days there so happy." Soon after returning to Florida, Mom's roller coaster took a deep plunge. One night she became incredibly disoriented and was taken to the hospital by ambulance. Ever the optimist, Spike continued with his upbeat outlook. Emi says, "He was very much in denial. He always thought in his heart that she would beat the illnesses, so he made plans for a lot of things. He even booked an overnight stay at the W Hotel in South Beach for their upcoming anniversary." After she was admitted to Baptist, family members flooded into town. Jeff and Suzanne purchased one-way plane tickets. On Friday, June 19, Mike and I were at work at Day & Zimmermann when Mom's condition deteriorated even further. We headed to the airport and spent most of the weekend in ICU where Mom was largely nonresponsive. That Saturday, June 20, was Spike and Mary's fifty-sixth wedding anniversary. Needless to say, they did not go to the W. But just as he had always done, Spike brought her flowers, presents, and a card. With Mary unable to speak, his words of affection went largely unacknowledged, which was a painful sight for us to witness.

As difficult as that moment was, Mary bounced back on Sunday and was moved out of ICU to another floor. Monday, Mike and I returned to the hospital before flying home. Mom was sitting up in bed and was fairly alert. We were relieved and so happy to have a good semblance of a conversation with her. Emi, who was by now tethered to Mary around the clock, was there as well. Neither Mike nor I knew that this would be the last two-way conversation we would ever have with our mother.

The ensuing days brought another nosedive in Mom's condition. Jeff remembers being at Ocean Reef when his cell phone rang in the predawn hours. He and Spike had returned from the hospital late the night before for a few hours of sleep while Emi kept watch. "Emi called me in tears, saying that the nurses think it's time for a DNR. I didn't know what to do, so I called each of my brothers. None of us had a firm opinion except that if the medical staff was thinking this way, then things must be really serious." After calling Emi back, Jeff and she decided that he should be the one to discuss the grim reality with Spike, given that he could do so face-to-face.

A "Do Not Resuscitate" directive instructs medical professionals not to go to extraordinary measures to keep a patient alive, including not performing chest compression should the person's heart stop. Through an odd set of circumstances, I had been the one to authorize the DNR for Kelly's uncle Frank back in 2007. Signing the document filled me with a sense of guilt and unwanted divine power, which was only partially offset by the insistence of the attending healthcare professionals that it was the humane thing to do.

Jeff says, "Dad's first reaction was anger. 'Why didn't the doctor call me? Why haven't I heard from Emi?' I tried to calm him down, telling him how upset Emi was." Jeff then recalls Dad's whole demeanor changing:

> I remember his look. The optimism that had always been there just disappeared. He looked up at me and said, "Jeff, what would you do?" I said, "Well, I don't know. I don't know about any of this. But if Emi and the doctors are saying it's time, then it's time. You look at Mom, and she's not well." Dad then said he wanted to go to the hospital. We were on the road in minutes.

Fortunately, as those who know Jeff are aware, he takes an incredibly fast shower.

On the forty-five-minute early morning drive to the hospital, Jeff again called each of his brothers to let us know what was happening. Hal and I were at the Shore, and Mike was at his home in Pennsylvania. I recall over the next few hours the surreal combination of processing what was happening with my mother while securing urgent travel arrangements. The weather was horrendous, with heavy rain and high winds—the kind of wretched summer storm for which our part of the country is known. Far from an ideal day to fly.

Jeff remembers that once Spike and he arrived at the hospital, things went from really bad to even worse. "All her doctors were in her room when we arrived. We weren't there five minutes and the advice went from 'sign the DNR' to 'you need to line up hospice.'" Spike recalls, "I can remember them saying 'hospice.' Once I heard that, I thought, I can't believe this. This is the end. I wasn't thinking about the future. I was only thinking about her. I just wanted to make sure that everything was as good as it could be for her." Earlier in her career, Emi had herself been a hospice nurse. Hospice providers, who I consider nothing less than God's angels in nurses' clothes, are responsible for keeping terminally ill patients comfortable with pain medication, while also guiding family members through the excruciating ordeal of watching their loved one's life end. Long before Mary got to such critical condition, Emi had made it clear that she never again wanted to play such a difficult and emotionally draining role. Nonetheless, upon hearing the direction from the doctors, Spike called on Emi. According to Jeff, "They told us Mom might have a few days, but possibly less. Everything was happing so quickly. Dad looked at Emi and said, 'You're going to be that nurse for Mary.' Emi started quietly weeping." Shortly afterward, Mom was discharged. Jeff and Dad led her ambulance *home* to Ocean Reef.

Meanwhile, Mike and I had resorted to hiring a private plane to Florida in such lousy weather. Hal and Sharon were unable to come because Sharon had a medical procedure scheduled in a few days and they could not risk exposure to Mary's infections, which included MRSA. This was a very difficult decision. Fortunately, they had the warm memories and images of Mom's final Avalon visit to preserve in their minds. Eventually, Mike, Gayle, and I secured a plane, and after an aborted attempt to meet at one airport, we rendezvoused in Atlantic City. Despite the weather map on board being entirely "dark green" with the icon representing our small aircraft right in the middle, we managed to clear Mid-Atlantic airspace and make our way to South Florida. Even with sheets of rain and high turbulence on our ascent, I was emboldened by a couple of stiff bourbons and by the comfort that God would not possibly take us now, on our way to see Mom.

When we arrived at Ocean Reef late Saturday evening, Mary was in the large bedroom at the end of the house, lying in a hospital bed that had been delivered earlier in the day. Her entourage was assembled, prepared for an around-the-clock vigil—Dad, Jeff and Suzanne, Emi, Ronda, and Steve Soto. After a blur of hugs, I dropped to my knees at Mom's bedside and grabbed her hand. Some words of affection poured out of me, but I don't remember what they were. Mom was not able to talk, but she acknowledged my presence and what I was saying through changes in her breath and by light movements of her head and hand.

Apparently while I was kneeling at the bed, my shorts started to fall down, which I hadn't noticed. I remember Mike grabbing my belt loop and hiking them back up, sparing the group this unsightly view. That gave us a much-needed moment of comic relief. With Karen and now with Mom, I had learned that grief is a fickle emotion and that tears and laughter are close cousins; any of us could pivot from despair to hilarity pretty quickly. My plumber's crack provided just such a moment.

As Saturday night became Sunday morning, we drifted in and out of Mom's room, mumbling beings not knowing what to say or how to act, only sure that we didn't want to stray far. At one point I tried to sleep for an hour or so on the day bed in the room, but needless to say, no one was getting any real rest. A night nurse arrived to relieve Emi, but there was little chance she would leave Mom for any prolonged period.

The next morning something became clear to me. There was a sisterhood in the house. For most of the time Mary was there, Emi, Ronda, Gayle, and Suzanne stayed in the room with her. I don't think any of them ever said anything about it, but Mom's women never left her side, their kindred, feminine spirit providing every bit of energy it could.

In contrast, at one point in the early afternoon, Mike, Jeff, and I went for a brief boat ride to clear our heads. Having spent so many of our childhood summers and vacations near or on the ocean, our family had become accustomed to seeking enjoyment—or in this case solace—on the water. We didn't putter far from the dock, however, in case someone in the house called.

Later that afternoon something surreal but therapeutic took place. Spike gathered his family around the dining room table where he calmly and diplomatically doled out tasks for each of us to perform in the coming days. It was sad knowing that all of these jobs were associated with my mother's impending death, but it was comforting to see Dad back in his element: at the head of the table, delegating work and leading everyone forward, just as he had done for decade upon decade in his business and volunteer careers.

Emi was amazing. She administered pain medication when needed, and she calmly instructed us about what was happening to Mom's body at various points, letting us know what signs she was looking for—like specific color changes in her feet and alternations in her breathing pattern—that would show when Mom's ultimate time was near. Emi said that Mary was unlikely to make it through another night.

Soon it was time for dinner, which Dad had ordered from the club's catering department so none of us had to spend precious time cooking or cleaning up. When dinner was ready, Spike called everyone to the table. Dinnertime is an important ritual for our family, so it seemed fitting that we should gather to break bread. I, however, saw a look in Emi's eye that told me I should stay with Mom. Ronda did the same. Sure enough, shortly after everyone had begun eating, Emi said the words I had been dreading since the morning before when Jeff called me in Avalon: "Bill, it's time." I walked to the dining room and said what Emi had just told me. I'll never forget how quickly and uniformly everyone shot up from their seats in an unrehearsed and unfortunate maneuver of dryland synchronized swimming.

We all gathered around Mom. We called our family at the Shore and laid the speaker phones by Mom's head. There were simultaneous beautiful sunsets at Ocean Reef and in Avalon. It was literally divine. Each of us took turns saying our final good-byes. Spike's words were perfect as he expertly and innately blended his love for his wife and his way of saying just the right thing for those around him. Then, just as Emi had said she would, Mom took her last few breaths and she was at peace. I was holding her arm. It was incredibly sad. But it was incredibly beautiful as well, her surrounded by family, a warm sunset filling the large sliding glass door by her bed, and the unmistakable presence of God when her suffering ended.

Sunset in Avalon, June 28, 2015

After a brief time during which Emi and the coroner attended to some formalities, we again gathered around Mom to say our final—final—good-byes. I held Dad's hand and we all recited Psalm 23, which concludes with, "Surely Your goodness and love will follow me all the days of my life, and I will dwell in the house of the Lord forever."

Goodness. Love. Dwelling with the Lord forever. Nothing could have been more fitting.

Mom passed away on Sunday, June 28, 2015, three days after Karen had passed eight years earlier. Their final moments on earth were in stark contrast. Mom was surrounded by loved ones. Everyone got to say everything they wanted to say. Karen was alone when she died. We didn't get to say anything. No one should die alone.

Mom's funeral was held on July 7 at the Church of the Redeemer. Despite its taking place in the middle of summer, the church was full, many people interrupting their vacations and traveling great distances to pay their respects. As with my sister, I delivered the eulogy. While the remarks were mostly about Mom, I felt compelled to address Dad as well:

> He has been incredible through all of this. While his patented strength and optimism helped fuel Mom through much of the past few years, the person and the man he has been more recently has been even more impressive. Yes, Pop, you have been strong—but not naively so. And yes, you have remained our leader—but in a very inclusive way . . . Of course you haven't been blubbering this whole time, but there have been tears. Tears of sadness, tears of pain, and tears of joy. God knows all of us have had all of those—and will for some time. But mostly, Dad, you have been real. You've been sad and you've laughed. You've been quiet and you've been chatty (boy have you been chatty—and we love it!). You have been

yourself—the person who has loved and been devoted to
Mom for over half a century.

As with Karen, we held a reception at the Merion Golf Club after the
service, which provided a meaningful way to connect with family, friends,
and acquaintances. The event was like a stage-acted slide show covering our
family's entire existence. Incredibly, Spike made a few remarks to those in
attendance. Naturally, he did an amazing job. He showed compassion and
sadness. He was inclusive of everyone. He expressed his love for "My Mary,"
as he had recently started referring to her. I thought I had done a good job
delivering the eulogy, but his speech at Merion was better. One of our friends
said that hearing him speak was like "listening to Reagan."

Following Dad, Jeff addressed everyone at Merion as well. Given his
strong faith, he referenced several passages from the Bible to pay tribute to
Mom. Last, in homage to Mom's aforementioned love of the game "spoons,"
he had the wait staff hand spoons to the attendees so they could attempt to
dangle the spoons from their noses like Mom used to do.

● ● ● ●

In the span of eight years, Spike lost the two most important women in his life.
His relationships with Karen and Mary were different in many ways, as were
the circumstances around each of their passings. In both cases, Spike's eternal
optimism was tested, as was his childhood-inspired resilience. Through both
of these events Spike also reaped the relationship seeds he had sown over the
years. From Haverford to Duke to Day & Zimmermann to YPO to Avalon
to Ocean Reef, Spike's network mobilized itself, his friends and colleagues
supporting the man who never needed supporting. Facing the tragedy of having
to bury his own daughter, Spike encountered few truly empathetic voices but
for a few contemporaries who had also lost a child. While I was not present
for any of those conversations, I'm sure they shared knowing words more

effectively than anyone else could have. With Mom, things were different. Many of Spike's friends had been widowed as well. While the quantity of empathizers was larger in Mom's case, the loss wasn't any easier for Spike.

The months following Mary's death were filled with family time and houseguests, leaving Spike focused on everyone but himself. He continued to ignore—or more accurately, neglect—his own mounting health issues. The many consoling lunches and dinners at restaurants, coupled with daily cocktail hours, helped Spike grieve, but they also contributed to a dangerous imbalance in blood sugar that would soon rear its head. Exacerbated by Spike's unwillingness to let his physical condition compromise what he did or where he traveled, the coming months would bring unprecedented challenges to his health and force enormous alterations to his deeply rooted lifestyle.

Chapter 11

Transitions

But now the days grow short. I'm in the autumn of my years.
—Frank Sinatra, "It Was a Very Good Year"

After Mary's funeral, Spike settled in Avalon for the balance of the summer. The turnstile of visitors and house guests was constant, as were the prolonged stop-by's from his children and grandchildren. On several occasions he used the terms "smothered" and "helicopter kids" to describe how he felt about all the attention. While he somewhat joked, he truly appreciated the energy and love coming his way.

As the summer of 2015 wound down, Spike wanted to move on from the cycle of friends-and-family-are-visiting-because-My-Mary-died, at which point he chose to embark on a therapeutic effort to simplify his life. He sold their home in Pennsylvania, a condominium in Haverford into which they had moved after selling their larger home to Mike and Gayle some years earlier. It was no secret that if it had been up to him, they would have sold their Pennsylvania residence long ago, but Mary wanted a place to stay near her children and grandkids. A true Avalon lover, Spike was comfortable commuting back and forth from the Shore to see family or for doctors' appointments. Furthermore, his practical side understood that even hiring a driver for all of these trips was cheaper than owning a third home in which they spent less than twenty nights per year.

Spike the widower being visited by fellow D&Z retirees and their spouses

In addition to selling the condo, Spike went through the productive and cathartic exercise of organizing old family photographs, albums, and files. He placed them in bins and made piles to give to each of his sons. He and Mary had begun these pile-making and pile-giving practices years earlier, so I had learned not to question, but rather to take them dutifully and sift through their contents later. The fact that many were duplicates of pictures I already had speaks to the close-knit nature of a family who takes many photos at gatherings where all are in attendance. While I don't need each photo in duplicate—or triplicate—such is the ritual between parents and children in our life stages.

With the arrival of Labor Day, the summer season in Avalon came to a close. I can remember years ago when on the day after Labor Day, it seemed that someone had opened a huge barn door at the windward end of the island from which tumbleweeds rolled, replacing bikers and walkers on the thoroughfares.

While there is far more off-season activity in Avalon today than when I was younger, it's still astonishing to see the demographic shift that accompanies the first Tuesday of September.

• • • •

Unfortunately, as Spike simplified and geographically consolidated his life, he could no longer ignore the internal storm that had been building from all of the grieving and socializing. Spike had been diagnosed with type 2 diabetes in 2003, a common disease among older people with weight problems. Over time, the body ceases to process high levels of sugar effectively, and many health complications can result. While the oral medications he had been taking since his diagnosis helped curb the effects, the years of focus on Mary's health spurred a lack of focus on his own. That fall, Spike set out to right his physical health ship, but the voyage would be long and difficult. "I realized then that I actually better start taking care of myself. I was in bad shape and needed to do something." Compounding his diabetes was his rheumatoid arthritis, an inflammatory disorder that principally attacks the joints—in Spike's case, his shoulders, knees, and ankles. As with his diabetes, Spike had largely been able to curb the disease's effects with oral medication. However, the time he spent focused on Mary allowed the RA to wreak more havoc, manifesting in greater joint pain and more difficulty getting around. Most visibly, Spike resorted to using a walker. Given that Spike's walker had wheels on it, he was happy to put his own stamp on the situation, dubbing it his "pusher." There are few signs of aging more prominent than someone with a walker (or pusher). This admission of age and limitation—what he saw as a display of feebleness—took as much of an emotional toll on Spike as it did a physical one.

With health issues mounting, Spike's glass became—for one of the few if not only times in his adult life—half empty. "I had this toe problem. And then my legs got so swollen. I thought, 'Shoot, why worry about my future? I don't need this if it's going be like this for the rest of my life.' I was really

down. I had never felt that negative before. I guess it was my rock bottom."
Then, like a boxer knocked down but not out, Spike grasped for the first
rope. "That's when I decided to ask Emi if she would work for me full time."
Emi accepted the opportunity for constant work, even though it meant a lot
of time away from her mother, children, and grandchildren in South Florida.
Once she was permanently employed by "Mr. Yoh," Emi cleaned out kitchen
cupboards and refrigerators, restocking them with (mostly) healthy options.

Ironically, and perhaps cruelly, as soon as Spike switched his diet to
center on salads, lean poultries, and light seasonings, the diabetes raged out
of control, his blood sugar ranging dramatically and occasionally peaking
as high as 550. His energy levels were subject to expectedly sharp ups and
downs as well. It was scary for our family to see how much Dad's demeanor
and comfort levels fluctuated during the fall. He even resorted to spending
most nights asleep in a recliner due to the throbbing in his legs and difficulty
breathing. It was as if conceding to his body had helped unleash a haymaker
that packed years' worth of neglect in its wallop. Fortunately, Emi was ever
vigilant, and she forced Spike to seek further medical treatment. Insulin shots
were prescribed, and Spike began what may be a rest-of-his-life routine of
testing blood sugar levels and injecting insulin multiple times per day. He
protested and was sometimes noncompliant, but he mostly soldiered on. For
her part, Emi struck the right balance of caring support and dictatorial dogma,
the latter earning her the nickname "Fidela" in ironic tribute to Castro, despot
of her homeland.

Even with his mounting health issues, Spike Yoh was still Spike Yoh. "I
was in a down mood for a bit, but then one day I did a full 180 and said, 'Nope!
I've beaten everything else in my life. I'll beat this, too!'" Resilience restored.
The fact was, Spike had an important list that was not completed, and there
are few things more unsettling to Spike than lists that go uncompleted:

All of a sudden it occurred to me that I had all of these resources available to help me get better. I pulled out my bucket list and said, "Crap, this is what I want to do." I realized that I was only seventy-eight years old and how badly I wanted to live into my eighties and go on all of these trips. Then the phone call came from Jim Hughes about going on that cruise. That was a much-needed turnaround for me.

Spike first started keeping a formal bucket list around 2010. Today, information and materials pertaining to his list fill a whole cabinet shelf in his Ocean Reef home office. Almost the entire list is composed of places he wants to visit, demonstrating his insatiable love of exploring the globe. Until Mary's final days, he had always assumed—perhaps more accurately *hoped*—that they would take the trips together. "That's what we were going to do, travel all over the world together." What is most amazing about his strong desire to travel so much is how many different places he and Mary had *already* visited. A world map hanging in the front hall of their Ocean Reef home marks with push pins each country they saw. Incredibly, there were already almost sixty red-capped pins sprinkled around the color-coded land masses, giving the look of a large two-dimensional, candle-laden sheet cake.

Though he would miss his marital travel companion of fifty-six years, Spike was motivated by the call from Jim Hughes—his longtime Haverford School friend who was portrayed by Leonard Nimoy on TV. Jim, along with another Haverford classmate, was planning a trans-Atlantic cruise from New York to England in October aboard the Queen Mary. As fate would have it, sailing across the Atlantic was an item on Spike's bucket list. Sharpening his little green golf pencil in anticipation of crossing out an item, Spike agreed to join them, and he brought Emi along. Despite the family's concerns about a trip that included eight days at sea where medical support would be limited only to what was available on the ship, Spike had an enjoyable trip—RA and diabetes be damned.

As Spike settled back into Ocean Reef later that fall, it would be time to see "winter" friends he hadn't seen since Mary passed; virtually all of Ocean Reef's inhabitants had left for the season when she died there in June. His return to Florida brought another wave of lunches and dinners with friends, each requiring Spike to summon the physical and emotional strength to repeat the exchanges and discussions he'd had so many times over the summer. Despite continued fluctuations in energy levels, he was able to accommodate many requests to get together, although he was not able to attend some of the group and club-sponsored events that annually ring in the new season. Catherine Medaglia recalls, "We went out to dinner with him. He talked about Mary a lot and in such a loving way. You knew she was gone, but the connection was still so strong." Steve Soto says, "Spike found himself at a point in his life where he probably never expected to be. It was awkward for him, wanting people to stay close to him. He wasn't comfortable being the center of attention. But people really cared about him."

While Spike struggled with his health, various people voiced the old adage—sometimes to me, but more often to Kelly—how when a longtime spouse dies, the other soon follows. A handful of people assumed that Spike's failing was either consciously or subconsciously his way to reunite with Mary. Those of us who know him well, though, understood that nothing could have been further from the truth. Sure, he had his low moments, but other than his brief instance of private doubt in early September, he never hinted at giving up. During one of our interviews, when he was seventy-nine years old, Spike said, "I want to live till I'm eighty-five. That would be a good time to go." Just as I had dutifully accepted the piles of old pictures and knickknacks earlier, I nodded my head. But I also added, "That's great, Dad. But when you're getting near eighty-five, you know we'll all be talking about your living to ninety."

Mike Smith agrees. "It's gonna be a cold day in hell when Spike gives up. The fact that he's not been mobile and that he's had to go through procedures and see one specialist after another would have made most humans give up. But there's no way I see him ever doing that." Everyone close to Spike felt the same way. And he never wavered again.

Earlier in the year, fate gave Spike exactly what he needed: an event to plan. His niece Lisa was getting married and wanted to have the wedding at Ocean Reef. Lisa is one of Spike's half-sister Marianne's two daughters, Marianne being the third child of Harold and his second wife, Mimi. Mimi had passed away when Marianne was just two months old, leaving Marianne to be raised by Harold's third wife, Esther. Unfortunately, Marianne died at forty-one years old after a protracted fight with ALS. Lisa and her younger sister Linda had visited Uncle Spike and Aunt Mary in Avalon every summer as children. I recall many of these visits with both sadness and joy, as each year's installment showed my godmother Aunt Marianne's continuing decline, but also the unyielding commitment her husband Bruce had to her well-being and to summer fun for the girls. Even after Marianne passed and Lisa became an adult, she continued her annual visits to the Shore. It's a tradition that both niece and uncle cherish greatly. Eventually, Spike and Mary also started inviting her to Ocean Reef, and she happily accepted these winter offers as well.

Planning Lisa's wedding was a tremendous opportunity for Spike. He threw himself into the logistics and details of organizing the perfect celebration weekend, from hotel reservations to catering menus to tee times to gift bags (the contents of which he selected personally). Playing wedding planner distracted him from his onerous diabetic routine and subconsciously helped fill the void of never being able to plan his own daughter's wedding. Ronda, who continued her indispensable work for "Mr. Yoh," was in a great position to speak to the importance of the event.

When Lisa's wedding came up, he went into full wedding planning mode. It really cracked me up, because if there's one thing about that man, it's how incredibly organized he is. After all these years, I am still amazed by it. When I think about all of his wedding files and all of his little notes for putting that weekend together, with everything he had going on health-wise, it was really a sight to see.

The wedding took place on October 24, 2015. It was a wonderful and perfectly planned "Spikian" affair, jam-packed with around-the-clock, only-in-Ocean Reef activities, meals, and excursions. Of course the weather was perfect for the ceremony at "The Point" on Buccaneer Island, a small spit of land jutting east into the southern Atlantic surrounded by indigenous coral rocks and plush palm and mangrove trees. Understandably for the bride and her groom, Brian—but unfortunately for us cousins—the attendees were limited to immediate family and close friends.

Spike stealing a kiss at his niece's wedding

Just one month after the wedding, we held a memorial service for Mom at Ocean Reef. This had been Dad's idea all along, knowing that many of their winter friends would not make it to Pennsylvania for the July funeral. Much of the raw sorrow from Mary's death had passed for Spike and he was again in stoic demeanor. But seeing so many of their friends—all gathered in the community where she had passed away—cycled him through another (albeit toned-down) range of emotions. The church service was similar to the one at the Redeemer, and we again held a reception at the local golf club.

That December, Spike joined Hal, Mike, and me for a special lunch event in Philadelphia. Each year we honor those employees in the Philadelphia headquarters who have worked for Day & Zimmermann for thirty or more years—a tradition started by Spike when he was CEO. Other locations, most notably the munitions plants, have similar events, given the long tenure of many of their employees. The event in Philadelphia was held at the Union League (of course), and there were twenty local attendees from the "30+ Club." This was the first time in many years that most of them had seen Spike. While he sported a classic "Florida retired" look—bright pink short-sleeved button-down, light khakis, no blazer—he was also using his walker, was moving slowly due to the rheumatoid arthritis, and had to sit down for most of the socializing. I'm sure his physical degradation was noted by all. The conversation during the ensuing luncheon, however, was far more memorable, particularly for me as we had recently announced to the company that I would be writing Spike's biography. I listened intently to the ensuing discussion when each person shared a story involving Spike from the years their employments overlapped. I took notes and also observed the group's dynamics and body language.

The first of my takeaways was how attuned Spike still was, seventeen years removed from his last D&Z function, to the attendees and the meeting purpose. His remarks were not general D&Z platitudes but rather specific compliments and references intended for an audience of long-tenured coworkers.

Having noticed one attendee sitting well away from him who seemed uneasy with the formalness of the room and the event, Spike made a lighthearted comment to her shortly after we sat down. Her whole demeanor changed: shoulders dropped, eyes lightened, smile appeared. By making this one person comfortable, Spike relaxed the entire room, allowing for more engagement in the ensuing discussion. This awareness of others is one of Spike's most valuable traits, one he continues to exhibit today.

The other notable, and more obvious, takeaway from the lunch was the string of stories about Spike that the 30+'s shared. One person, a retired financial controller, said of an acquisition candidate from the early 1980s, "Based on my analysis in due diligence, I would not have bought the company." Of course Spike bought it anyway, and the company became a key part of the portfolio. That acquisition also brought a few of the 30+ Club members into Day & Zimmermann. Another person recalled the preparations for a large 1987 D&Z "Centennial Celebration" to commemorate the 200th anniversary of the writing of the Constitution. The employee remembers Spike working right alongside the administrative team blowing up balloons, showing how he recognized the value in every employee's contributions. Finally, another attendee humorously recalled a late-night incident from a mid-1980s management conference when—somehow—the attendee set a pumpkin on fire, triggering the conference center's fire alarms and later a scolding reprimand from the manager on duty as the fire engines departed. Fearing Spike's reaction the next morning, the narrator recalled his CEO simply saying, "Don't worry about it." Spike knew what was important and what wasn't, especially when memorable team building was taking place.

• • • •

As the winter months set in, Spike's diabetes continued to cause damage, most notably to his circulation. His vascular system was compromised, his blood not flowing efficiently. This manifested itself most obviously in the large buildup of fluid in his lower legs and feet. In an eerie coincidence, this swelling of the lower extremities was a regular occurrence for Mary during her final year or two of life. As can happen with type 2 diabetics, Spike's lack of blood flow deprived his feet of sufficient oxygen. When any part of the body lacks oxygen, it starts to deteriorate. Unfortunately, this was happening to Spike's toes. Over the ensuing winter months, he would have three on his left foot amputated. He may never swing a golf club again, which is unfortunate given that playing golf with his sons when he is in his eighties is one of the few non-travel items on his bucket list. While these removal procedures were the worst of his health complications, he also went through long periods of low energy and repeatedly had to make the forty-five- to sixty-minute trip back and forth to Baptist Hospital in Miami to see one specialist after another.

Many of my trips to Ocean Reef to interview Spike occurred during this period. I recall how warm he kept the house since his body was not effectively regulating itself, as well as the fact that even while spending the bulk of six different weeks in Florida doing research, I never once needed to apply suntan lotion because my father never felt well enough to venture outside, let alone partake in any outdoor activities.

Two of the more poignant of my twenty formal interviews with Spike were long rap sessions we had on the nights before scheduled medical procedures, one in February and one in March. The first unusual aspect of these episodes was that as I've grown older, I have become very much a morning person, so an extended post-dinner interview would not have been my preference. While neither one of us said anything about the late timing, I suspect that Spike was motivated to cover as many of my questions as he could for fear that something might go wrong the next day at the hospital. It was unsettling, but I appreciate how even when he was preparing for surgery, with its attendant and somewhat ominous anesthesia, he recognized the importance to both of us that he tell as much of his story as possible.

The second and even more memorable facet of these conversations occurred during the March evening. While seated in our now customary interview chairs in their—I mean *his*—master bedroom, Spike suddenly departed from our biography conversation and said, "I'm nervous about tomorrow." His words hung in the humid Florida air for what felt like minutes. I had already noticed he was preoccupied, as he had been the month before. But hearing those words come out of his mouth showed me just how aware he was of the risks he was incurring. He was also telling me, in very plain terms, that he did not want to die anytime soon. I said to him, "I know. But everything is going to go fine." Did I know that? Did I believe that? Did I *really*? I said what needed to be said, but both of our logical minds knew that the next day would bring risks that exceeded what we could control. My bond with my father deepened.

During these months, Emi recalls the serious challenge of convincing Spike that his health needed attention:

> It was very difficult to educate him on how sick he was and on how important compliance was. He thought he was in control of it all and he could manage it. To make matters worse, he was also so emotionally sick dealing with Mary's passing. Eventually, with all of my nagging and with all of his kids' nagging, he realized that there could be a light at the end of the tunnel. He finally started to get better by doing what he was supposed to do.

Emi also confessed that on more than a few occasions, she was worried that doing her job well might mean losing it. "Mr. Yoh and I fight like cats and dogs sometimes. We really do. There were a couple of times when I thought he was going to tell me, 'Pack your bags, get your keys, and leave.' But at the end of the day, we both know exactly why we're arguing." Just as Steve Soto and Spike developed a bond that transcended their working relationship, Emi and Spike connected deeply as well. As she puts it, "Honest to God, it's important for both of us. In the same way I've helped him, he's helped me with my issues, including the passing of my father."

One evening when I was visiting, Emi went out for dinner with some friends. At this time, she was spending most nights at Dad's house because he would often wake in the middle of the night and try to walk around, though he couldn't move well on his own. On that evening, Spike stayed up until Emi got home as if he were waiting for a daughter. When she arrived—I was half asleep in my bedroom across from his—they talked about where she'd been, who she'd seen, and anything else that came up. I couldn't help thinking that Emi was (and still is) filling a parenting emptiness in Spike that has existed since Karen passed away in 2007, as well as a companionship emptiness since Mary's passing less than a year earlier.

Spike and Emi during one of his blood sugar tests

The most unique aspect of Spike and Emi's relationship is tolerance. By now you can imagine that as magnanimous and people oriented as Spike is, he's not a huge fan of people who try to tell him what to do . . . which is a big part of a nurse's role. Just as Spike can be intolerant of those who might threaten his "alpha dog" status, he can also be—for some people—difficult to spend long periods of time with, given his strong opinions on, well, most everything, and his typical desire to have things his way. But these two people—patient and nurse, father figure and daughter figure—make it work. Each matters deeply to the other, and they fill important voids. The only (minor) breach in the professionalism of their relationship resulted from one of their cruises. Spike was using his pusher, causing Emi to remark that he seemed to "scoot" along. Thus she dubbed him "Scooter." She uses "Mr. Yoh" more often than this nickname, but each time she does, it lends a playfulness to their relationship that each of them needs.

Of course, Emi is not the only one who was close with Spike during his difficult first Ocean Reef season as a widower. Steve Soto reflected on Spike's struggles:

> I've seen him at his worst, and it hasn't been easy. But I can tell you, when he's determined to do something, he's going to do it. I wrote him a letter recently telling him how proud I was of him. It was very humbling for me to write that kind of letter to a guy like Spike, but I've seen what he's been through. He has so much left to offer to his friends, his children, his grandchildren, and now his great-grandchildren. I consider myself one of his children as well.

Speaking of Spike's children, each of us observed our father struggle to adapt to his new reality that first year. Mike recalls in particular how Spike worked through one important change. "Working with Emi helped him a lot in wrestling with his drinking. It was good to see him want his health to be better, knowing that drinking was bad for him." In the big scheme of things, Spike cut down his drinking considerably. As a means of comparison, I sometimes joke about a common occurrence in Avalon from my childhood. At exactly twelve p.m. every day, the fire sirens on the island ring, letting the inhabitants know that it's high noon. My joke is that each day at noon my dad would fire up the blender for some sort of frozen fruit daiquiri as well, its whir drowning out the siren. It was only years later when I happened to be at the Shore without Dad that I finally heard the actual siren. While this is an obvious exaggeration, my father did used to enjoy having cocktails on many weekends, starting in the afternoon. As he got older, however, particularly into his mid-to-late seventies, he curbed his drinking. A few years ago we went out to lunch on a Saturday and he ordered an iced tea. When I asked why he went with an alternative beverage, he said, "I can't drink in the afternoon anymore or my nap will be even longer than it already is." I took this as a positive sign that his genetic predisposition to imbibe was not so strong that he couldn't curtail his consumption. More recently, Spike has gotten even better at limiting his intake. He's not where we would like him to be, nor where full compliance with his diabetes regimen suggests, but he's better than he's ever been.

Modifying his food intake has been far easier for him. I already mentioned how Emi made sure that his refrigerators and cupboards were stocked with mostly healthy options. While he still probably consumes too much fat and salt in restaurants (who doesn't?), his diet at home is much better in both quality and quantity. Spike used to eat a lot and all the time. Now his meals are smaller and his snacking is mostly driven by the maintenance of proper blood sugar levels.

During one of my research visits to Ocean Reef, I located and hired a nutritionist to advise Dad and Emi. While the session provided some helpful wisdom, the biggest takeaway for me was a comment Spike made. He was perched in his wood-backed stool at the kitchen counter where he reads his morning papers, eats many of his meals, opens his mail, and watches much

of his *Fox News* and televised sporting events. At one point he looked at the
nutritionist, Emi, and me and said, "Hey look. It's just food. I eat because I have
to eat. Serve me whatever you want and I'll eat it." This statement came from
a man who, for my entire life to that point, ate a lot—from sugary breakfasts
to elaborate hors d'oeuvres to large dinners to nightly desserts. He had made
an important lifestyle pivot. While he still enjoys his Planters peanuts and
Combos pretzel snacks, his diet is far more appropriate for a man of eighty
with severe diabetes.

   While this shift cannot be attributed to diet or lifestyle, another change we
Yohs have seen is the waning of Spike's lifelong proclivity for giving advice,
solicited or not. According to Mike, "He does still give advice. But my whole
family has noticed that when we've been around him more recently, advice
isn't flying around nearly as much as it used to. We are able to just chat more,
and it's really enjoyable." Mike also speaks to how Spike's temper also seems
less in evidence:

> When he gets a little melancholy, there are times when his
> anger comes out. You can tell he's wrestling with it. It can be
> a tough scenario to deal with. Sometimes, our first instinct
> is "Okay, it's time to leave him alone." But then we take a
> deep breath and say, "No, it isn't time to leave. It's time to
> be supportive." A few times it's been sort of ugly, but most
> of the time it works itself out just fine.

Hal picks up on his mellowing with regard to certain comments he makes.
"He's like 99% of the way there. The problem is he's got to disengage his
mouth during that 1% of the time. It can really take the fun out of something."
Mike finishes Hal's point by saying, "It would be great to figure out how to
disengage the connection between his gut and his mouth on certain occasions
and just let him speak from his brain. He knows that often what he says as
knee-jerk comments can be pretty stupid or insensitive."

Spike is not blind to his behavior. "I've always been outspoken, and I have shown prejudice over the years. I know that I haven't always thought my words through as much as I should before I speak. Over time, however, particularly since I retired, I think I've learned to work better at marrying my words to my actions and to my true beliefs." Paul Milus, Mary's brother, comments on this trait in his brother-in-law. "I never saw him treat anyone with anything other than respect. So even if there was a negative tone to his words here or there, there was always a positiveness to his actions." When Mom was really sick and she and Dad were immersed in the healthcare community of South Florida—a modern-day example of the American melting pot—I noticed how indifferent he was to the gender, race, and ethnicity of her care providers.

We sons are not the only family members to observe these various physical and interpersonal shifts in Spike; his daughters-in-law have as well. "He went through a lot of bad stuff in the year after Mary died," says Suzanne. "To be able to be with somebody when they're experiencing those health problems is tough. Did I want to see him in the hospital wearing only a gown? Of course not. Did I want to poke him with insulin all the time? No. But you do all that stuff because it's what you do. I think it drew all of us closer." Suzanne also sees the wider, more positive effects of this trying period:

> He became significantly mellower than he used to be. He was much more interested in hearing what I had to say or what I might think about something than he used to be. We still have our moments, but he now recognizes when he steps out of bounds and he apologizes. My relationship with him is completely different now.

Sharon sees similar changes:

> As he grew calmer and wasn't drinking as much, he became more reflective and more observant of other people. He started

picking up on signals more and fine-tuning his behavior. Being
more empathetic is not something I would have said was his
strong suit in the past. But he arrived at a point where you're
still not going to change his mind, but he actually started
listening better to why you disagreed with him. He started
respecting your right to do that.

Gayle speaks to how Spike's physical care affected their connection. "My
relationship with him evolved to be rather medical. I became tuned in to his
sugar monitoring and his shots, especially when Emi would be off for the
weekend. I would make sure that the sores on his legs were kept clean." She
also observed the same mellowing that her sisters-in-law had seen, particularly
around the holidays. "Christmastime at Ocean Reef is a very hectic time. Spike
still has his little piece of paper that he uses to calendar all of our events. He
definitely wants to know what's going on and doesn't like surprises. So it's still
pretty scheduled, but not nearly as much as it used to be." Kelly reflections
are consistent as well:

I've watched him soften in some ways. I saw him become
more of a caretaker when Mary was sick, and now there's
this whole other side of him. I see how he prioritizes our
kids' basketball games when he's in town. I watch him give
them advice afterwards, and they listen to him, which is
noteworthy for teenagers. When he is away and misses their
games, there's a void. But there is still an angry side to him
as well. That remains a challenge at times.

Suzanne sums up the period after Mary's passing:

That first year would be my fondest memories with him, the
saddest, but also the fondest. When somebody's so vulnerable
and weak, which he often was, you can't help but grow fond

of him. For Jeff and me, it went from being fine spending time with his dad to wanting to spend time with him and really enjoying it.

Spike and his sister Barbara anchoring a holiday gathering with many of their family members

• • • •

Spike has always been a religious person. From his early years attending church and participating in Christmas pageants, to the decades of his and Mary's dragging us kids to church and Sunday school, God and Christianity were always present. However, in his later years, and even more so after Mary died, Spike's commitment to God and his spirituality have strengthened. In many ways, my faith journey has paralleled his. As one of those kids toted along to church each week, religion has been present for my whole life. But from the moment Mom passed away on that sunset-drenched evening in 2015, an awareness of a greater presence and purpose in my life has truly manifested itself.

I've developed an analogy for the spiritual journey, one I shared with Spike during one of our final interviews: If you live in the Philadelphia area as I do, and you decide to take a car ride to Pittsburgh with a friend, you both get in the same car at the same time, and you embark together. You might stop around Lancaster or Harrisburg to refuel and use the bathroom, and you might do so again in the western part of the state. Then you both arrive in Pittsburgh together. On a spiritual journey, however, you and your "traveling companion" (be that a spouse, family member, or friend) can both be on the same trip, but you'll likely never be in the same place at the same time. You might not even be in the same "car." Of course, neither of you knows when you'll arrive at your final "destination," but you can be together and interact and support one other the whole time.

Spike has a weekly men's fellowship meeting that he attends on Thursday mornings at Ocean Reef. My brothers and I have had the good fortune of joining him occasionally. I saw not only how his reflections could still command the respect of a roomful of peers, but how engaged he was by the subject matter and how willingly he discussed the topics after we returned home. Rich Miller, a routine attendee, speaks to the meetings' impact:

> I think Spike's recent experiences have had as much meaning
> to him and his Christian evolution as anything he has ever
> done. It seems like he has been in search for years and years,
> and he's stumbled at times. But he's now finding a comfort
> zone with fellowship. He's so open and so curious, and also
> so expressive about his feelings. Spike can say things that
> other people are only thinking or can't bring themselves to
> say. He has an ability to express himself so beautifully when
> talking about God and religion.

Bob Henley has been the chaplain-in-residence at Ocean Reef since only 2014, but has ingrained himself deeply in that short period. He has also integrated himself in Spike's and our family's lives as well. Bob corroborated Rich's observation. "Part of the contribution that Spike has made is that there is never a question that he's too embarrassed to ask. If it's a question that comes up in his mind, he says it. That's his integrity at work. This frees up the other guys, many of whom might be afraid to ask what might sound like a dumb question. But Spike's not ashamed to put it out there." As do a multitude of other people in Spike's long life, Bob well remembers their first meaningful interaction. "I had just arrived at Ocean Reef and was introducing myself in a fellowship meeting. Spike asked me, 'What are your goals? What do you hope to accomplish?' He went right to the heart of the issue but did so in a very genuine way. His style was very effective." Bob also recalls his first one-on-one interaction with Spike and Mary as a couple, which was in early 2015 when Mary was sick:

> What Spike said one morning at their home revealed the tenderness of his heart. One of the things I asked them was, "What worries you? What concerns do you have?" Spike answered, "Will I have enough resources to take care of Mary the way she needs to be taken care of?" He had tears in his eyes. That was a window into how deeply he cared for her. On my subsequent visits, I saw how vivacious Mary was in spite of her health issues. There's a verse in the Bible that talks about the outward person wasting away while the inward person is renewed day by day. I saw this in Mary, and in the deep respect and deep love that Spike had for her.

When Bob and I met in his office at the quaint Ocean Reef chapel, his cargo shorts and flip-flops belied my notion of expected ministerial garb—but not nearly to the extent that Uncle Frank's bathing suit had. The most profound topic we discussed was how powerfully Spike's childhood manifested itself in his adult life. What was particularly impressive about Bob's perspective was his knowledge of Spike despite having only known him for two years, and only during the seven months each year of the Ocean Reef season. Bob underscores Spike's connection to two critical figures in his life:

> It's important to know how much our fathers on earth shape our view of our Father in heaven. Spike spoke openly in fellowship one week about the poor relationship he had with his dad. But that relationship did not wrongly shape his view of his Father in heaven. I don't know if people realize how huge that is to separate the two. His father was a man for himself, but Spike is a man for others. His life is an example of the power of choice that we have—the morals, the family, and the ecology that we grow up with need not be deterministic. We have the ability to choose to be different. Spike is a powerful example of that.

Rich Miller also recalls Spike's allusion to Harold. "He told us about his relationship with his father and how difficult that whole thing was. I'm amazed at what an impression that left on him and at how it helped make him into everything he became." Reflecting on what Bob and Rich said, I again realize how Spike expressed his intention, in so many facets of his life, to do the opposite of what he had observed his father doing. Spike himself says, "You are not your father or your mother. You may inherit some of their physical looks or actions, but you are yourself and who you strive to become."

In connecting Spike's youth to his adult temperament, Bob further elucidates patterns others have recognized:

> We tend to stuff pain down inside of us. I think there has been a lot of pain inside Spike from his childhood and his relationship with his father. He probably didn't spend much time in his life processing the pain. To me, it has manifested

itself in the drinking and the diabetes and the temper. The
pain is gonna get you, one way or another.

Spike's spiritual journey has also enriched his relationship with the Ollie
Brothers. Much of their relationship, spanning more than sixty years, centered
on reliving Duke fraternity days and lampshades-on-their-heads memories.
But in recent years, including before Mary died, their mutual, ever-present
spirituality and commitment to God has migrated closer to center stage.

The Ollie Brothers' favorite place to convene has always been Cameron
Indoor watching Duke basketball. Their seats are in the first row catty-corner
to Coach K and the Duke bench. They always dress in their formal "Ollie
attire": grey slacks, white button-downs, blue blazers, and Duke ties. Their
conservative attire stands out in the crowd, as a sizeable portion of Duke's
courtside student fans, the "Cameron Crazies," are covered in blue face and
body paint. Over the years, I've had friends from all over the country send
emails and texts to tell me they again saw the Ollies on TV.

The Ollie Brothers in full courtside regalia

After Cameron, though, the Ollies' favorite place to convene these days is not in a bar postgame or at one of their houses, but in a private room off the main dining area at the Washington Duke Hotel. They meet for breakfast and have deep, intimate conversations about all that truly matters to them. Spike has helped re-create something like the life-changing YPO Forum environment from which he has benefitted so greatly. Bill Lee, a.k.a. "Molars," acknowledges the religious focus of the morning gatherings.

> They are always spiritual, usually with a specific religious aspect. A recent topic was how to deal with grown children when their lives are not going the way we hoped they would. "What is our responsibility? What kind of mentors are we to our grandchildren?" We're getting older, and we're now talking about the impact we've had on our children and our grandchildren.

Rob Townsend ("Sunset"), the most forthright about his Christian devotion, says, "Our conversations have become much deeper. In many of them, at least one person has become tearful. You're talking about the loss of a loved one or other real hardships. In the broader Ollie family, we've had five deaths and ten divorces. A lot of people have been through a lot of things." Rob's wife Sally recognizes this shift:

> In the last several years, I have seen all of them, in their own ways, grow in Christ. They don't hide it anymore. They moved toward a spiritual boldness that they had never shared before. And we started sharing it as couples, too. The Ollie Sisters' conversations have become more spiritual as well. We now reflect together on God and our relationship with Him. It's very special to see and to be a part of.

Even Tom Coffman from Duke, who is close with the Ollie Brothers, has noticed:

> They don't just get together and shoot the breeze. It's gone a lot further as they've come to recognize their own mortality. At the end of the day, we all fear death because it's hard to imagine. Yet that's what faith is, the belief that it will be better. The Ollies know that and they share their awareness with each other. It's a very special thing they have, and I've been lucky enough to join in a very small part of it.

Finally, Steve Soto chimes in on the importance of religion in his relationship with Spike. "I think things were meant to be. I think God put me in his life for a reason. And I think He put Spike and Mary in my life for a reason as well."

I'm proud to say that each of Spike's sons cherishes the importance of Christianity. Hal has always been a loyal churchgoer and jubilant volunteer in many of his large church community's activities. Mike serves as the senior warden of his church, All Saints, which has been the setting for several key events in Spike's family history. Jeff and Suzanne, both currently pursuing master's degrees in Christian Ministries, founded what is now a large not-for-profit organization that has packed over twelve million meals (and counting) for underserved communities in Central America and the United States. Again showing my chip-off-the-ol'-block status, a few of my lifelong friends and I have started our own early morning fellowship group. Much like the Ollies, we have commented on how our most enjoyable interactions no longer take place in bars or back patios, but at six thirty every other Friday morning in a quiet room, talking about Jesus and our spiritual journeys. Each of us Yoh children has Spike—and Mary—to thank for planting in us these valuable seeds of faith.

• • • •

Back in January 2011, Spike attended a memoir-writing workshop at Ocean Reef. Given that a fair amount of Ocean Reef's inhabitants are in the later stages of life, many of them think about how best to capture their legacies, the highlights, and lessons learned. Spike was no different. When asked in the workshop why he would produce a memoir, Spike wrote, "I like the idea of putting my thoughts, experiences, and knowledge on paper, but I'm challenged about how to start, how to group my ideas, and how to make it both educational and entertaining. What is relevant? Who are my target readers, and why would they care what I say?" I had no idea when I approached Dad in August of 2015 about writing this biography that he had already been thinking about a similar project. During the years since he attended the workshop, along with his growing shelf-full of bucket list materials, he had started amassing old speeches, letters, prayers, famous quotes, self-reflections, and correspondence. He secured them with a large rubber band and a handwritten label that simply read, "The Book," which he lent to me during one of my research visits to Florida in 2016. He offered that I could sort through its contents and use anything that seemed relevant. Some of the documents were very personal. In total they provided an intimate look into his mind and his heart.

I was also struck by Spike's above concerns: How to start? What is relevant? Why would they care what I say? In response, I devised an exercise that might help him distill this wealth of information into useful advice—without sounding overly preachy. Given his vast experience at the helm of our family and of many organizations, I titled the exercise, "Spike's Leadership Hits and Misses." I asked for overall points of guidance and—at the risk of rivaling my father's penchant for organizing—delineated six individual topics: marriage, fatherhood, business, volunteering, friendship, and religion. For each, I asked him to express his thoughts as three or four successes ("hits" or advice to follow) and one personal shortcoming ("misses" or life lessons to heed). I gave him the exercise in mid-July of 2016, thinking (hoping) it might occupy him for the balance of the summer. Just two weeks later he presented me with three handwritten, single-spaced pages, which I summarize below, along with a few of my observations:

Spike's Leadership Hits and Misses

Overall

- You must love yourself before you can love others
- You need trust to succeed in anything
- Togetherness is much more powerful than individual efforts
- Being a good listener is a powerful asset
- Verbal beliefs do not always lead to visible actions
- Keep everything simple and easy to understand
- Being on time reflects good character

All of these axioms are evident throughout Spike's life. And given the lack of true mentorship early on, he developed and honed virtually all these principles on his own, with influence from his partnership with Mary, his friendships, his business and volunteer careers, and YPO.

Marriage

Hits:

- Communicate, communicate, communicate
- Prioritize happiness, love, and understanding (in that order)
- Give more than you get
- Be dependable, but mix in the unexpected

Miss:

- Not getting Mary better medical help sooner

The phrase "happiness, love, and understanding" represents one of the most amazing events from Spike and Mary's fifty-six years of marriage. Always committed to self-reflection and personal development, Spike suggested an exercise for Mary and him to do one day when they were in their late thirties or early forties. Each of them would privately write down what they considered the top three keys to successful marriage. Spike wrote down, "love, happiness, and understanding." Incredibly, Mary wrote down the exact same three words! The only difference was that she ordered them, "happiness, love, and understanding." After his initial awe and joy at their synchronous view of the world, Spike realized that Mary's order was correct. She believed, and he agreed, that if you don't have happiness, the relationship is not going to last, let alone flourish.

Fatherhood

Hits:

- You are a role model from day one
- Impart common values, but let each child grow individually
- Be personally involved and be there when needed
- Regardless of their age, you'll always be their father

Miss:

- Not being able to help Karen more

Most notable for me here is the common thread between not getting Mary enough help sooner and not being able to help Karen more.

Business

Hits:

- Surround yourself with excellent, loyal people
- Use teamwork and trust to motivate others
- Communicate clearly and follow up for understanding
- Take nothing for granted

Miss:

- Over-diversifying into unrelated businesses

While Spike's business ethos encompassed far more than these few phrases, they do illustrate the breadth of what his focus areas were, including people, delegation, and accountability.

Volunteering

Hits:

- Give back, but be selective so you can make a lasting impact
- Get involved only if you would want to become the chairperson
- Create passion; be innovative and entrepreneurial
- Weed out the deadwood in the organization

Miss:

- Lack of assigning sufficient responsibility for actions

Spike's chairmanteer philosophies come through here, most notably that if you get involved in something, you might as well run it. He also employed the business priorities of being results driven and ensuring there is a strong management team at each of his not-for-profit ventures.

Friendship

Hits:

- Loyalty, trust, and openness are built over time
- Be uncompromising in your values, and always be honest
- Be there when you're needed
- Work hard to keep the ties strong

Miss:

- Not being more outgoing sooner in life

From Haverford to Duke to business, friendship has been part of the bedrock of Spike's life. He invests in his relationships as much as anyone I know.

Religion

Hits:

- Love yourself first to be truly open with God
- Commit to a life of curiosity and wonder
- Recognize that God's reach and power are amazing
- Be accepting and at peace; don't try to dominate

Miss:

- Seeing people abdicate their responsibilities in the name of God

Knowing that someone as powerful and successful as Spike can carry such a humble and subservient attitude shows the power of religious faith. It's also notable that he sees a risk in becoming too religious; he's clear to point out that putting your trust in God does not free you from being accountable to fulfill your roles on earth, which—he, I, and many others will argue—are part of God's plan.

• • • •

The transition to life without Mary was hard for Spike. It tested his resilience and his optimism more than any other phase of adulthood had. For the first time, his physical health presented obstacles to doing what he wanted. While not as visible, his emotional suffering was perhaps more impactful. He no longer had his time-tested and time-trusted sounding board, event co-planner, travel companion, pillow-talk partner, or fashion governor. The consummate extrovert, Spike realized how little he liked being by himself and how lonely he was without Mary. But his work ethic and determination, buoyed by his (mostly) unwavering optimism, powered him through this huge life transition. With "Fidela's" steadfast support and nagging, he worked himself off the "pusher," got himself back into his bed for sleeping, and stabilized his energy levels to again maintain a more active schedule.

The balance of his Ocean Reef stay and ensuing 2016 summer in Avalon were much more predictable and enjoyable. He crossed two more cruises off his bucket list, adding three more push pins to his world map. He got back to a routine of running errands with his sidekick Duchess—whose role became even more important for her master as a widower—attending grandkids' basketball games and eating out with friends without upsetting his blood sugar.

Spike and Duchess running errands

With Mary's passing and his own subsequent health issues, Spike has confronted his mortality more than ever before. He has modified his lifestyle and mellowed quite a bit in his behavior and how he relates to others, most notably his expanded family. Finally, his accelerated spiritual awakening has helped provide him with the peace and confidence to face each day with contentment and hope. He has transitioned to a new phase of life. And he is at peace with it.

Chapter 12

From Here

I've learned that people will forget what you said, people will forget what you did, but people will never forget how you made them feel.
—Maya Angelou

After two years of difficult health issues and exotic bucket list destinations, the summer of 2017 finds Spike doing well, his health the best it has been in many years. Perhaps even female companionship will find its way into his world. He confesses to be particularly lonely at night, after Emi has gone home. Toward the conclusion of our recorded interviews, Spike told me how he and Mary had discussed companionship a few times during her final months of sickness. He reminded me how until that time period, they had assumed he would be the first of them to pass away, and he loathed the image of Mom taking up with a fictitious man he called "Bad Breath." Needless to say, that dude never showed up. Given Mary's failing health, however, they candidly discussed an alternate scenario:

> Mary and I talked about what would happen if she died first. She said, "You'll never survive without someone. You're going to have to find somebody." She knew me and she was right. Since she passed, I have also talked with my YPO forum about it. They were unanimous. They said, "You've

got to get somebody." After this time without Mary, I have realized that it's just the whole idea of having somebody around. It's great having my kids and other relatives visit, but it's just not the same.

As usual, Spike is both practical and somewhat irreverent when talking about the topic. "I realize that I haven't been in the right state of health so far. I've got to get balanced to know what kind of package I'm selling, you know?" Hal concurs. "If he can find someone, it would be good for him. We all know people who have been widowed and do just fine on their own. But Dad is different. He doesn't like to be alone. I really hope he finds someone to fill some of that emptiness. If I could wish one thing for him, it would be that."

Mike has an expanded view about Spike seeking companionship:

He's got friends at Ocean Reef, and he's got a strong network there. I keep telling him, "Dad, go out to lunch. Grab a friend, call somebody." He responds with, "That's just not what I do." So I say, "Well, maybe it's something you should start to do." For example, I've been to fellowship with him a bunch of times. He gets there right before it starts, says a couple quick "hellos" and then leaves right when it ends. He doesn't want to sit around and chitchat. The calendar says it's over, so he's ready to go home and he leaves.

What's notable about Mike's view is the conflict between Spike's uber-efficient cadence, which compels him to leave an event right when it ends, and the opportunities for bonding that less-scripted post-meeting banter could enable.

Spike does need a companion—perhaps someone with life experiences similar to his—with whom he can discuss politics, attend social events, and continue to winnow down his bucket list. February 2, 2017, would have been Mary's eightieth birthday. When I called Dad to check on him, I was saddened to learn that he was spending the evening at home, dining alone. His tone was stoic and upbeat, but I could tell he was lonely. I couldn't help but reflect on the contrast between that night and his own octogenarian entry date just seven weeks earlier, when he was surrounded by family and friends. He threw himself—appropriately—a big Happy Days–themed party at Ocean Reef. We had a gigantic sparkler cake (sorry, no one jumped out of it), and there was music and dancing, including a spot-on Frank Sinatra impersonator that Emi had secretly arranged. All of the staff wore black, long-sleeve shirts with "Happy Days" on the front and "Spike 80" on the back. But the juxtaposition to Mom's eightieth was stark.

Spike and his sons at his "Happy Days" eightieth birthday party in December 2016

• • • •

In addition to jettisoning his walker, Spike has gotten hearing aids and has begun a fairly consistent routine of physical therapy. I've received a few encouraging reports from friends at both Ocean Reef and Avalon about sightings of Spike and Duchess cruising around and running errands together. He's getting back to many of his normal routines and habits, many of which had been on hiatus since even before Mary passed.

Consistent with the rest of his life, Spike's number one priority remains the same:

> My family really means so much to me. I don't want to lose the closeness with my children and their families. All of them have been so good to me since Mary passed. She and I worked so hard to build a strong family. We were both so very proud of what everyone has accomplished and who they have become and are becoming. At Mary's funeral in Bryn Mawr and her memorial service at Ocean Reef, I don't want to say I was showing them off, but it meant so much to me to see how my kids all acted. The family has gotten to be an even stronger part of my life recently.

Spike has hopes and concerns for every one of us—his four sons, his four daughters-in-law, his fifteen grandchildren, and his two great-grandchildren. Though he sees some of us more frequently than others, he is attuned to each of our situations, to our strengths and to our shortcomings. "The key is to see everybody happy and to see them succeed in whatever they do. At the end of the day, the biggest thing you have is your family and who they are and how they act in the world." Spike understands that his legacy will be best embodied by who his children and their families become.

Some portion of Spike's pride in his family comes from the ways in which his children have continued the family legacy at Day & Zimmermann. "To see the business succeed is such an important thing for me. Day & Zimmermann is a part of the family as far as I'm concerned." He is, though, equally bullish on the professional accomplishments of Yohs who chose to leave the business.

"Of course, Jeff went out on his own and he's been a great success, both with his business and with their meal-packing organization. I don't know what Karen would have done, but she could be a good leader, and I think she could have done good things later in life." These many years after Karen's death, Spike reflects upon the loss:

> They say you'll never get over it and you'll never forget, which have been totally true. It's not something that goes away. I think about her almost every day. Something will come back, on one of two sides. One is her happy, smiling side, like when she was organizing a company event, or even younger in her college days. She kept herself so busy and she was so happy. But then I'll think about the last couple of years of her life, and it just gets really crappy and hard to consider.

Again we see that the man who always has a plan—and an answer—and an explanation—remains bewildered about how things turned out for his only daughter. While he may find solace in the happiness and career success of his other children and their children, it seems Karen and his unreconciled relationship with her will never be far from his mind.

Amid his reflections on family and his pride in our business successes, Spike speaks to the importance of limiting the liabilities that success, with its attendant wealth, can bring:

> Maybe Mary and I were kind of cheap with our kids, but we never wanted to spoil anyone with money. We kept money away from them even after we were in the position where we could have given it. With the D&Z stock, we made sure that it was very difficult to sell, even back to the company. We didn't want anyone to come into too much money before they were ready to handle it.

His concerns in this regard have magnified regarding his grandchildren:

> This scares me about the grandkids. I want to make sure that
> they end up with the right values and that they work hard
> and don't get spoiled because of money. The next generation
> has the benefit of wealth, whereas Mary and I and our kids
> sort of grew into it. I hope they don't lose the appreciation
> for hard work and for the value of a dollar. Money that you
> earn is different than money that was given to you. Don't get
> me wrong. I'm happy with what my kids are doing in this
> regard. But the wealth thing does concern me.

The phrase "money that you earn is different than money that was given to you"
is particularly insightful. Spike is specific about his own inheritance—"given"
to him and thus perhaps less worthy—yet he is clear about how he used it to
benefit future generations. "The inheritance my mother left me was in stocks.
I didn't believe in stocks then and I still don't today. So we sold the stock and
built the family Shore house with the proceeds. When my dad died, we took the
money he passed down and started an education fund for our grandchildren."
This fund has been an incredible blessing for my brothers and me. It covers
much of but not all of our children's tuition. It's important for Spike that the
quality of his grandchildren's schooling not be curtailed by affordability, yet
he still wants us parents to have skin in the education game.

Besides himself and his family, Spike is focused on those people who are
particularly close to him, namely Emi, Ronda, and Steve. Beyond this group,
however, his days of actively serving others appear to be behind him. "I'm
mostly in a mode now of not worrying about others beyond my group like I
used to. I'd still like to be helpful if the opportunity presents itself, but I'm
not going to go looking for it." This brings up an important topic that my
siblings and I have discussed recently with each other and with Dad, namely,

what purpose or merit might his life have going forward? Spike reflects on the need for a broader sense of meaning as well:

> I'm working on my plan. A lot has to do with my health and finding out how mobile I can be. I'd love to play golf again with my sons, but I don't know if that's in the cards. I'd like to go on a couple of cruises per year. I'm on the mend and I'm on the way up, not the way down. So I'm excited to be able to live life going forward, but I'd say I'm also searching for a future right now. I've always been one to know where I wanted to go and how I was going to get there. But I'm not there just yet.

Jeff summed up the opinions of many in the family. "Dad needs more than just a bucket list. He seems a little bored and not as engaged as he could be. What's his purpose? He's got his health to deal with, but maybe that's not enough. I mean, how much *Fox News* can one guy watch?" Mike says:

> Yeah, he's certainly on top of his bucket list, but I feel like he needs something "of purpose" to go along with that. Whether or not we can help him or he needs to figure it out on his own, I'm wondering, "What is he going to do beside travel, and who is he going to be for the rest of his life?" But maybe that's a bridge too far.

Jeff then suggests, "He's not in a position to necessarily be the leader of the family anymore, but he could lead through stewardship. Being a steward is a way that he could help look after everyone and help take care of everyone, without really being in charge. That could be a nice way of looking at his role and his purpose."

Spike crossing off another cruise from his bucket list

Spike's daughters-in-law have also reflected on Spike's future and his legacy. Suzanne articulates themes that will not surprise you by now:

> I hope he continues to gain better health, being more active and drinking less. And of course his bucket list is really important to him. But there are some things on it that are going to be extremely difficult for him, no matter how healthy he gets. I hope he is okay with not being able to complete the whole list. Finally, of course, his legacy is all about being a leader. He has such a strong leadership personality in everything he does, including his big emphasis on family.

Gayle's perspective adds dimension to the family's vision:

> I hope he stays active and busy, not just physically, but mentally as well. Even doing little things like Sudoku and jigsaw puzzles—things to keep his mind sharp. And then there are

his pictures. He still loves making his photo albums from all his trips. He's always got a zillion of them, laid out all over tables and his bed. Recently he was up late at night working on an album, and then back at it at the crack of dawn the next day.

On the wall surrounding the "sheet cake" map at Ocean Reef, Spike has dozens of small shelves holding photo albums from trips he and Mary took, and more recently, voyages he made with Emi and some of his children and grandchildren. He's always been a huge picture taker and album maker. Capturing so much of his and our lives in photos, then going through the meticulous engineer's process of organizing them is a way for Spike to document his life experiences. The photographs promote the value of family and demonstrate the importance of understanding and experiencing the world around us. These endeavors give him a great sense of accomplishment and perspective.

Kelly concurs with both Suzanne and Gayle:

I hope he continues to take his health seriously and continues to get stronger. It's upsetting and frustrating to see how much he needs to fix. Just as importantly, my wish for him is to continue to relax more, to mellow out more. I guess it's a side effect of having to sit so much, but it's nice to see him be calmer and more engaging with others. For as long as I've known him, he's always been about "the next thing," his schedule and all of that.

Regarding Spike's legacy, Kelly sums up the family's sentiments:

When I think about his legacy, I think about love. He has so much love for his family, for his friends, and for the people he's around. Hopefully his grandchildren see that. I feel like they do. When they think of Granddad, I hope they know how

much he loves them and how much he wants to be around
them and support them. I hope that's his legacy.

• • • •

Spike's close friends have a lot to say about where Spike is today as well as
their hopes for his future. They raise many of the same themes as we children
do. Rich Miller says this about his close friend: "He's a tough old bird, but
with such a soft heart. That's him. I'm just amazed at how he keeps on going.
He's the Timex watch. He takes a lickin' and keeps on tickin'. He loves family,
he loves the holidays, and he loves celebrating people's birthdays. All of this
is so meaningful given the fractured relationship he had with his own father."
Rich's wife Margo says, "He certainly lives life. People sometimes just go
through the motions, but he is engaged in everything he does. I can't tell you
how much his and Mary's friendship have meant to us. I hope he has many
more years of health and happiness." Tom Davidson sees the same Spike he
has always known, but with an understandable change:

> He has mellowed some, and his knife is a littler duller. But
> that's all part of the aging process. He's still not shy about
> stirring the pot. In our meetings of the past chairmen at Ocean
> Reef, Spike continues to bring a perspective of a situation
> that others don't see. Sometimes it seems totally out of left
> field. But often, the more you think about what he says, the
> more you see quite a bit of relevance. It forces you to adjust
> your own point of view. That remains very helpful.

Alan Goldstein, another past Ocean Reef chairman, lends a slightly more
somber take. "Any time when Spike and I have worked together on projects,
he's always been there with this talents and his support. Always. But when
you see him today, there's a different look in his eyes. You can tell there's a
void with Mary gone."

Steve Soto touched on his customer-turned-friend-and-father-figure's humility. "It's been an amazing journey getting to know Spike. I've learned so much from him. There are a lot of people that have money and obviously Spike is one of them. But of all the affluent people I know and have worked with, I've never met anyone who was more humble and unassuming about their wealth than Spike. Not one. He and Mary have always treated me like family." As I see it, Spike tries to treat everyone he likes the same way, whether he or she is someone who showers before going to the office or someone who showers after their work shift is complete.

• • • •

Given his business and "chairmanteer" successes, along with his current stage in life—retired, widowed, with increasing health and stamina—Spike could be a perfect candidate to mentor and develop up-and-coming leaders. Never having had many positive role models himself—except for a few people like Don Brownlow at Haverford and Bill Shand in Los Angeles—Spike never experienced mentorship in the Socratic fashion. As a result, his time-tested method for giving advice more often entails collecting all the data on a given topic, then getting everybody's points of view, and finally delivering his unequivocal advice about the correct path forward. In biblical terms, he's better at giving someone a fish than teaching them how to fish. With that said, some people thrive in this model, such as Duke's Sterly Wilder, who earlier spoke about how much she learned simply from observing Spike's conduct and how he prioritized his efforts. Similarly, Steve Soto recalls meaningful career advice:

> Spike and I have had many lunches, many dinners, and many
> sit-downs where we have talked about business. Sometimes
> you listen to older folks and you might think that you know
> more than they do and that their advice is antiquated. You're

respectful and you just say, "Yeah, yeah." But, you really think, "Oh boy, this old man is nuts. This doesn't work in today's world." But life has shown me that Spike's advice is generally right on the mark. Whether it's to make sure to meet a person's spouse before hiring them or how best to spend my time and to delegate more after I became a parent, what he has told me has been very valuable.

Ryan Yoh, Spike's oldest grandchild, recalls, "Granddad every once in a while asks me how things are going at work. He always likes to give advice, whether you want it or not. The first time or two I was like, 'He's been retired for a long time. He's out of touch with business today.' But then a few hours or days later, I realized that's not at all the case." Citing a particular piece of wisdom, Ryan says:

One time he said, "Always make sure you go into everything in business knowing as much as you can about the topic, because if you're working with people who don't know you, you need to show them that you have confidence and that you know what you're talking about. The minute someone sees weakness in you, your credibility sinks." That stuck with me, not just as a Yoh working at Day & Zimmermann, but as a professional in any situation.

Mentor . . . advisor . . . fish giver—whichever term best fits Spike's counselor role—he remains in tune to much of how businesses run and to how group dynamics work.

Spike's proclivity for giving advice carries over to his comfort in sharing his opinions about current events. Among his sacred rituals is the perusal, every morning, of *The Wall Street Journal*, *The New York Times*, *USA Today*, and (depending on where he is in his annual migratory pattern) *The Philadelphia*

Inquirer or *The Miami Herald*. He also digests at least an hour of televised news over the course of a day, mostly from his aforementioned favorite, *Fox News*. This voracious appetite for news and opinions—local, national, and global—keeps Spike's mind sharp while equipping him with enough perspective to think through and communicate his opinions about the world around him.

In our final formal interview, I asked him about his views on the country and the world. The conversation took place in the spring of 2016, during Barack Obama's last year in the Oval Office, while the unprecedentedly ugly presidential race between Clinton and Trump was coming into form. Spike shared his concerns for the United States:

> I worry about our country. Ever since the downfall of the Roman Empire, great countries have collapsed because the people are given a lot of things that they think they're entitled to, instead of working for them. I see this today and it worries me. But I thank God for our system of government, with its checks and balances. Even if it's pretty out of whack, I still think we have a good system, and it will help pull us through.

Spike's views about the broader world vary, involving wide geographical realms and an array of issues. His homeland's primacy, however, remains in the forefront.

> The only way the world is going to succeed is if the United States leads it. I'm concerned that some people in power don't want to lead. We don't have to lead *per se* by running the world. What we need are strong moral values and defendable parameters that we set, just like a parent does for a family. You set parameters and allow people to grow within that framework. It's more about democracy on a global level than about being warlike and adversarial.

China could be a big problem for the US, depending on how their expansion continues. The issues between India and Pakistan are something that we need to worry about because they have nuclear weapons. And speaking of nukes, I'm really concerned about North Korea, because that guy is crazy and he now has the ability to do something. I'd wipe that son-of-a-bitch out as soon as I could, with some kind of pretense, whatever it may be.

Iran and what is happening throughout the Middle East are as troubling as anything. The Sunni/Shiite issue, along with all the interpretations of the Quran and Islam—are they for peace or for war—are huge issues. And all the disputes between Israel and Palestine could have large impacts around the world. America really needs to stay engaged in the Middle East. Things are really ugly and really scary there. You need somebody with a big club, and it can only be us. Otherwise it might be Russia, which is a false prophet, or maybe China, which would want things their way. That's the world today. As a nation, we need to get back to strong leadership, both at home and, maybe more importantly, abroad.

I asked Spike if he would ever want to be president. His response was immediate:

Yes I would. But I wouldn't want to go through the whole nonsense of campaigning. Things have gotten so out of hand with how long campaigns are, how much money gets spent, and how negative everything is. But if I could be appointed president, I really think I could make a difference. I've never met a problem that I didn't cherish tackling.

Given his long track record of driving change, building consensus, and getting things done, who knows what President Yoh would be able to accomplish.

• • • •

I thank you for the music and your stories of the road
I thank you for the freedom when it came my time to go
I thank you for the kindness and the times when you got tough
And Papa, I don't think I said I love you near enough
—*Dan Fogelberg*

Having now read this book, you have likely gleaned that I am *really* into music. The soundtrack of my life spans many decades, genres, and artists. More recently, I've started writing my own lyrics and playing the guitar. I have no delusions of future grandeur, but listening to and now creating music fuels my soul in ways that nothing else can. This verse from Dan Fogelberg's "Leader of the Band" has always made me think of my dad. Now that I've completed the task of researching and writing his life story, the words resonate even more deeply.

"I thank you for the music and your stories from the road"

Dad imbued in me a love for music. While his taste and mine overlap with only a few artists like Frank Sinatra and Jimmy Buffett, he has shown that listening to music, and more broadly stimulating all the senses and enjoying life to the fullest, are a great way to live. Just as one can influence mood by putting on the perfect song, attempts at being happy and creating positive experiences for others can be incredibly rewarding. Spike personifies this for our family and for the thousands of people whose lives he has enriched.

Dad has always traveled a lot, both professionally and personally. "Stories from the road" serves as a great metaphor for how he has taught my brothers and me the importance of getting out of the office and traveling to where the action is: in the field and with customers. He's also taught me how gaining a greater understanding of the world allows a deeper understanding of people and a more profound appreciation for the place I live and the life I lead. All of Spike's sons enjoy traveling, and we appreciate the benefits that "the road" provides. It's no secret where the roots of these passions lie.

"I thank you for the freedom when it came my time to go"

As the youngest of his Spike's five children, I enjoyed childhood freedoms that my siblings did not. I appreciate the latitude he gave me and the way that he and my mom raised me to be independent. It may be ironic that I view myself as independent, given that my dad and I share a birth hospital; diplomas from the same high school, college, and graduate school; a company where we both worked for decades; a zip code where we both raised our families; and a vacation town. All of this may seem like I'm mimicking my father's life, and in many ways, I am. But Spike gave me "my time to go" and compelled me to live in different places and experience different cultures, as well as to approach each phase of my journey with an open-mindedness that has helped make me the man that I am—and my brothers are—today.

"I thank you for your kindness and the times when you got tough"

Spike's mother Katharine was kindhearted. His wife Mary was kindhearted. For these reasons, and because of the adult he became, Spike is kind. He asserts that Mary was always a lot more pleasant than he was—and he's right. He can still be abrupt and overly opinionated. But those who have known my father have consensus over what a thoughtful, magnanimous person he is. Dad, though, also got tough. I may have had it easier than my siblings, but I still got spanked on occasion, and I still knew enough not to want to incur Spike's wrath. Discipline is important, particularly as a parent. Children need guidelines, and they thrive when they know their boundaries. My brothers' and my parenting ethos may differ in many ways from our father's, but Spike showed us how to balance kindness and toughness.

"And Papa, I don't think I said I love you near enough"

Spike will never say he grew up in a loving household. He knows that his parents loved him, both in their unique and less obvious ways. But it took meeting the Ollie Brothers, then Mary, for him to recognize mutual, sustaining love. Not until I was an adult did he start routinely saying to my brothers and me that he loved us (even though we knew he did). And not until even more recently did he hug and kiss us hello and good-bye. Today, Spike can be a total sap. He expresses love to his family all the time. He's building a deeper relationship with his sister Barbara, and he's spending more time with his cousins and other people from his past. I'm happy he's doing all of this. I'm happy that he ends almost every one of our phone conversations with, "I love you, big guy."

I, in turn, have become more adept at expressing my love to him. Whether by initiating one of those hugs or saying "I love you" first at the end of one of those phone conversations, or even giving him "tough love" feedback about something he did that was upsetting, my ability to express affection to Dad has grown as I have grown, buttressed by his more recent role modeling of this behavior.

Spike is not perfect. Like all of us, he has his warts. Many of his strengths have their underbellies. But his well-rounded character is what makes him so relatable, so human, and—more recently—so vulnerable.

Spike Yoh is my dad. And I am his son. He loves me. And I love him. I'll take "Our Way" any day.

Acknowledgments

All things have been handed over to me by my Father,
and no one knows the Son except the Father,
and no one knows the Father except the Son,
and anyone to whom the Son chooses to reveal him.
—Matthew 11:27

I came across this passage during the late stages of this project. It was apropos—not because I compare Spike and me to two parts of the Holy Trinity—but for its words, and because it reminded me that the only way I was able to know my father so well was because of the generosity of time and recall that so many people offered throughout this project.

First, to Dad. Taking this journey with you has been life changing. Your partnership, candor, and at times, raw emotion made this book what it is, no doubt. You are the most comfortable person in his own skin that I know.

My family has been so supportive, starting with Kelly and our children, tolerating my bunker mentality while writing and enduring my absence from many weekend events while on a deadline. And also to Kelly, for "the kiss" that started it all. To Hal, Mike, and Jeff, thank you for your timely and thoughtful reviews of the manuscript, and—for Hal and Mike particularly—your professional support as fellow owners of D&Z. To my sisters-in-law, Gayle, Sharon, and Suzanne, and my nephew Ryan, you provided invaluable outsider-turned-insider insights that completed the Yoh family perspective. Aunt Barbara, thank you for the several long interviews you did, for allowing me to lug a scanner into your home and comb through your basement files, and for answering countless follow-up inquiries. Uncle Paul, Cousin Joan, and Linda Bruce, you were more helpful than you know.

To the former and current members of the D&Z family, thank you for your time, for showing me how connected each of you still feels to Spike, and for all that you have done for our family, for our company, and for our country. Mike Adelman, Anthony Bosco, Suzanne Buechner, Jack and Mary Pat Follman, Bob Giorgio, Bill Hamm, Karen Lautzenheiser, Bob and Rosemary Lynch, Emmett McGrath, Mike McMahon, John O'Connor, Mike Parente, Joe Ritzel, Jerry Smith, John and Solveig Stetson, Larry and Joan Suwak, and Floyd and Linda Walters, I'm proud to call each of you a colleague and a friend.

To Spike's myriad chairmanteer and business community partners, you are true men and women "for others." From Duke, Dick Brodhead, Tom Coffman, Earl Dowell, Allison Haltom, Nan Keohane, John Piva, Bob Shepard, Tallman Trask, Kevin White, Sterly Wilder, and Jack Winters. From Ocean Reef, Paul Astbury, Tom Davidson, Alan Goldstein, Bob Henley, Tony and Catherine Medaglia, Rich and Margo Miller, and Mike Smith. From the Philadelphia business community, Walt D'Alessio, Nick DeBenedictis, Jim Lynch, and Charlie Pizzi. And from The Haverford School, Joe Healey.

To Walt Garrison and the other members of Spike's YPO forum over the decades, you are the board of directors for Spike's life. You know how indispensable your counsel and love for Spike have been. Thank you for your time for me as well.

To the Ollie Brothers and Ollie family—including my interviewees: Shirley Copeland, Bud Copeland, Bill Lee, Zook and Caroline Mosrie, and Rob and Sally Townsend—your role in Spike's life is as important as anyone he has ever known. You transcend friendship.

To Spike's close circle of support—Emi Gonzalez, Ronda Perkins, and Steve Soto—you are like family to Spike and us. Thank you for caring about our father like you do.

Having never embarked on a project like this—in late 2015 I literally googled "How to write a biography"—I am grateful to the many advisors and authors who helped me along the way, including Peter Odiorne, Hugh Braithwaite, Doug Brunt, Kelly Corrigan, Peter Laveran, Mary Lucas, Jim Maguire, John Nagl, Jamey Power, Mitzi Perdue, John Razler, and Howard Stoeckel. To the team at Arbor Books, thanks for transforming my text and photos into an end product fitting for the man my dad is. And to my editor and kindred spirit, Kimberly Ford, thank you for your professionalism, your unfiltered feedback, and for helping me just begin to understand what true quality writing looks like.

Last, thanks to my loyal, ever-present companions, George and Gracie. Even though you slept almost the entire time that I wrote, you always listened; you were the "Wilson" to my Tom Hanks from *Castaway.*

The author's officemates during a rare waking moment

Sources

To augment the interviews with Spike (and the personal documents he provided), as well as the interviews with the other people mentioned in the acknowledgments and my own perspective, I used the following sources.

Overall

The Legend of Day & Zimmermann by Jeffrey L. Rodendgen (Write Stuff Enterprises, Inc., 2001).

Cash and Carry-on by John P. Follman, 2007.

Leadership Looks Back, Day & Zimmermann internal publication, 2011.

Sixty Five Years with the Men of Day & Zimmermann, Day & Zimmermann internal publication, 1966.

Most of the family history and genealogy comes from my relatives, in particular Barbara Juda, Linda Bruce, Joan Leavitt, and Paul Milus.

Chapter 1

"Harold Lionel Yoh" biography (partial), author and date unknown.

The Birth Order by Dr. Kevin Leman (Baker Publishing Group, 1985).

www.upenn.edu/about/history.

www.wharton.penn.edu/wharton-history.

Chapter 2

In Bruce Springsteen's quote that opens the chapter (from a 2016 *Vanity Fair* cover story), the word "life" is "it" in the article. I made this change because "it" in the article references "life," which he was talking about at the time.

https://www.thebalance.com/the-great-depression-of-1929-3306033.

"Edward Sails Away to Exile" by Joseph Driscoll, *New York Herald Tribune*, December 12, 1936.

"The Haverford School 75th Anniversary" brochure and history, 1959.

www.robingordon.com/area/haverford-homes-for-sale 7/28/16.

"Donald Brownlow, 82; WWII Vet Taught History with a Bang" by Sally A. Downey, *Philadelphia Inquirer*, January 12, 2006.

https://www.baseball-reference.com/teams/PHI/index.shtml.

http://library.duke.edu/rubenstein/uarchives/history/articles/cameron.

Chapter 3

http://library.duke.edu/rubenstein/uarchives/history/articles/narrative-history.

http://exhibits.library.duke.edu/exhibits/show/desegregation.

Chapter 4

https://www.endicott.edu/about/our-history.

The Common Sense Book of Baby and Child Care by Dr. Benjamin Spock (Duell, Sloan and Pearce, 1946).

Chapter 5

"Yoh Acquires Control of Day & Zimmermann," *Philadelphia Inquirer*, November 7, 1961.

http://www.devonhorseshow.net/about/history/.

Chapter 6
https://www.ypo.org/about-ypo/.

Chapter 7
http://www.nba.com/history/dreamT_moments.html.

http://www.ucsusa.org/nuclear-power/nuclear-power-accidents/history-nuclear-accidents#.Wc1YVmhSyUk.

Chapter 8
https://www.sports-reference.com/cfb/schools/duke/.

https://www.thoughtco.com/college-football-losing-streaks-791475.

On the Reef (The Donning Company Publishers, 2012).

Photographs

All photos are from the Yoh family and Day & Zimmermann except the following: The cover photo and the photos on pages 226 and 232 are courtesy of Duke Photography. The photo on page 33 is courtesy of Jack Ramsey. The photo on page 168 is courtesy of Mark Mosrie. The photo on page 219 is courtesy of The Haverford School. The photo on page 240 is courtesy of Ocean Reef Club. The photos on pages 321 and 351 are courtesy of Linda Walters.